"Building upon the financial technology themes from his previous books, Chris takes you on an intellectual journey as he methodically thinks through where technology will take us, humans, next. He imagines a new, open banking and financial services system tailored for each one of us. He describes how financial inclusion drives innovation, and how it will change financial services as billions of people join the system. I greatly enjoyed this rare and refreshing optimistic vision in which money is implicit, the invisible digital fabric of the internet connecting new platforms and existing companies."

Konstantin Peric,
Deputy Director, Financial Services for the Poor,
Bill & Melinda Gates Foundation

"Chris' latest book is a tour-de-force that provides a broad sweep of the incredible changes that are impacting our industry—open banking, platforms, APIs and machine learning, to name a few. However, it is his articulate postulation that 'few banks are changing, and if they don't change they will not survive' that makes this book a must-read for anyone in the financial services industry. And his thoughts on the very basis of value in our economy, and how this could evolve in the fourth revolution, make this a great read for the rest of us!"

Piyush Gupta,
CEO, DBS

"Skinner presents a compelling vision of the future of financial services expertly set in 10,000 years of historical context."

Jesse McWaters,
Project Lead, Disruptive Innovation in Financial Services,
World Economic Forum

"In *Digital Human*, Chris Skinner challenges our notion of what it will mean to be human and the role that money and finance will play. With this follow-up to *Digital Bank*, Skinner paints a picture of humanity's digital future, and the future is bright. As he describes, with 7.5 billion people connected in real time through mobile technology, increased access and transparency have the potential to finally tear down the walls of financial exclusion."

David Cotney,
Former Massachusetts Commissioner of Banks;
Board Member, Cross River

"Digital revolution creates the fourth age of humanity, where everyone is connected and included. For the very first time, we have a chance to reach and serve a financial transaction to everyone. As one of the world's most followed voices on FinTech, Chris Skinner provides a survival guide for the financial services industry and the opportunities therein."

Dr. Soner Canko,
CEO, BKM

"At the risk of sounding repetitive, *Digital Human* is yet another must-read book from Chris Skinner. Banks, bankers and 'control freak cultures' everywhere take heed: if you don't yet understand how your roles will diminish in the coming years, this book will make it frighteningly clear."

Dan Dickinson,
Chief Digital Officer, Equitable Bank

"Chris has a sharp eye for industry trends and cuts through a lot of noise with actionable insights, while shedding light on the alarming fact that the majority of banks' IT budget goes to maintenance rather than innovation. If the industry dares to follow Chris' proposed solutions—focusing on partnerships, technology outsourcing and increased collaboration—we would see an unleashing of energy and innovation to the benefit of clients and society at large. As he puts it nicely: 'If banks are average in doing 1000 things, are cemented to their past and are not agile enough to update daily and refresh their core regularly, they will be outsmarted by those who can. And those who can will recognise that banks are doing 1000 things mediocrely—and will naturally come together to do 1000 things brilliantly.'"

Kim Fournais,
CEO and Founder, Saxo Bank

"Chris Skinner has the remarkable ability to distil complex issues to their simplest form, which results in a book that can be easily digested. *Digital Human* evolves as a one-on-one conversation, as Chris describes how technology has become the equaliser in our global society. His vast experience evaluating global markets brings a real-life perspective to understanding both the history and future of digital transformation. Chris takes the approach of a fireside chat, speaking to us in a personal way where, no matter what our experience with digital transformation, we can relate to his stories, as well as to his honest passion to inform and educate."

Wayne Brown,
Managing Partner, The Walker Group

"*Digital Human* gives you a view into the future in a bold and imaginative way. Bankers the world over would benefit from Chris' practical clarity about where the evolution of financial services will lead us."

Chris Nichols,
Chief Strategy Officer, CenterState Bank

"Buckle up—Chris Skinner helps the reader peer around the corner by examining the past, present, and future trends leading humanity down a digital path of human revolution. *Digital Human* tackles the challenges of financial inclusion in a digital world struggling to assist with the plague of poverty. The internet of things is omnipresent in Skinner's unique journey, as digital advances are explored in the context of a human revolution and changing financial infrastructure."

Stephen G. Andrews,
Community Bank President

"If you're a traditional banker, reading Chris Skinner's *Digital Human* will feel like a SoulCycle kick-your-butt spin class. It will gut your view on traditional banking and likely freak you out on the long list of things your institution ought to do, including dumping your legacy core system. But you will walk away healthier and it will leave you with a wonderful possibility on how tech can rethink financial services into something that benefits everyone. Skinner has travelled the world and is one of the few that write about FinTech in an informed, funny and no-BS banker kind of way. Not only will you learn where the word 'harlot' originated but you will uncover the direction banks are going—namely, transforming from control freaks into open banks in a world destined to let people share their financial data where and when they want."

Mary Wisniewski,
Deputy Editor, *BankThink*;
Reporter, *American Banker*

"Chris Skinner, wise guide of the FinTech world, takes us on a new journey with his new book *Digital Human*. It gives us a chance to look into the past with the light of the future. For banks and financial players, this book is a perfect bi-directional mirror that will provide a better understanding of a new world. If they would use this mirror with Chris' guidance, they will find a path for their future; otherwise, they will just turn into memories of the past."

Ahmet Usta,
Chief Editor, *FinTech Istanbul*

"In order to be ready for the future, we should understand how the digital transformation has developed. Chris Skinner provides an in-depth look into what has happened and what is happening today. It is time for the financial services industry to reimagine how to offer finance through technology in the new era. *Digital Human* will help you understand digital transformation, make you think about your business and, above all, make you think about what you are going to face in the future."

Özge Çelik,
Senior Vice President, BKM

DIGITAL HUMAN

HUMAN

The fourth revolution of humanity
includes everyone

CHRIS SKINNER

WILEY

THIS BOOK IS DEDICATED TO MY WIFE KAMILA—
THE SWEETEST AND FUNNIEST PERSON I KNOW,
MY BEST FRIEND, AND MUM TO OUR
TWO LITTLE MIRACLES, EDDIE AND FREDDIE.

CONTENTS

CASE STUDY: ANT FINANCIAL

ACKNOWLEDGEMENTS

Books don't just appear but are an amalgam of ideas and inspirations. I've been travelling non-stop since *Digital Bank* was released in 2014, and a lot of the content of *Digital Human* is a reflection of those travels. However, I wouldn't be able to travel so much if my lovely wife Kamila wasn't so tolerant, and that's why this book is dedicated to her.

Then there are the many friends in my network. Too many to reference everyone individually but I would like to pull a few names out.

First of all, the 11:FS team of David Brear, Simon Taylor and Jason Bates. Great guys, great company and our podcast *FinTech Insider* has stormed the charts over the past year thanks to their hard work and dedication. Well done, guys.

Second, the FinTech Mafia, particularly Brett King and Jim Marous. Both gentlemen produce an amazing amount of content, and the quality never wavers.

Third, the people at Ant Financial, specifically Rita Liu and Xinyun Yang who were instrumental in getting the case study completed at the end of this book.

Fourth, the team at Nordic Finance Innovation, which I chair, particularly Iren Tranvag who has created a network across the region in the last two years that is second to none.

Finally, Soner Canko and his team at BKM Turkey, whose country is going through turbulent times but their solid support of my work is gratefully received.

There are many other people I would like to mention, and I could probably fill a few hundred pages of the book. However, there is one other person that I've worked with for too many years who is now reaching retirement, Andy Coppell. Andy and I set up the Financial Services Club in 2004 and he decided to retire in 2017. A great friend and inspiration, Andy will no doubt continue to bounce around the hallways of the City. Great technologists never retire; they just go and code more quietly.

INTRODUCTION

I have always travelled but since *Digital Bank* was published in 2014, I have been travelling non-stop around the world. To show how hectic my schedule can be, there have been several occasions where I've travelled from the United States to Asia via Europe and back in a week. That's crazy, I know, but it has given me some amazing opportunities. Opportunities to learn and expand my horizons and knowledge, the sort of experiences that can only be gained through such travel. I have explored the caves of the Cradle of Humankind in South Africa, Roman remnants of Baalbek in Lebanon in the Fertile Crescent and the West Lake of Hangzhou, China, where I understood 4,000 years of civilisation through food.

Such extensive travel has led me to some fairly surprising conclusions that I'll share here. These conclusions are a mixture of my travel experiences, extensive reading whilst travelling and my own knowledge of financial services and humanity. Money and banking are at the heart of our world. After sex and food, most of us think about money more than anything else. Money is the single thing that controls our lives. It gives us the ability to live life to excess if we have more money than we need or it leads us to misery and depression if we have too little.

Unfortunately, far too many people have too little. One in eight Americans officially lives in poverty, translating into a figure of 43 million people in 2015, whilst one in five British people lives in poverty. Around the globe, almost half of the world's population lives in poverty. That's over three billion people living on less than $2.50[1] a day. Of those, one in three—1.3 billion people—lives in extreme poverty, living on less than $1.25 a day.

When I was growing up, we thought poor people lived in Africa, India and China. In the early to mid-1980s, our media covered terrible famines in Ethiopia and huge campaigns were launched, resulting in the first ever global music event, Live Aid, in 1985. What is intriguing today is that the very markets that were considered the poorest are now getting richer through a mixture of aid and opportunity. This aid is being distributed by the likes of the United Nations (UN) and World Bank, which are working with philanthropic and charitable non-governmental organisations (NGOs) like the Bill & Melinda Gates Foundation and Oxfam.

What I have personally seen, during the last decade, is that technology is playing a major role in making these problems change. Sure, there will always be poverty but a lot of today's poverty is created by the system. If you cannot get access to financial services, you are locked into poverty. The poorest people pay the most for moving money. They often are the most vulnerable, too. This combination of vulnerability and being locked out is the reason why so many people will never escape the poverty trap. But, as I've already said, that is now changing. Today, thanks to the simple mobile telephone, everyone can be connected globally in real time.

Mobile has been the real game changer. It is the driving force behind traditional retail financial institutions becoming a digital bank, and for creating new financial models for new financial technology firms, or FinTech firms as we know them. I discussed a lot about the foundations of the Internet of Value (IoV) created by FinTech and mobile in my last book, *ValueWeb*. In this book, I guess I've moved away a little from purely writing about tech and finance, although this is still core to my writing.

---

1   Unless otherwise stated, the currency used throughout this book is the US dollar (US$).

Yes, people have written about the fourth Industrial Revolution and focused on the latest technologies from robotics to artificial intelligence (AI). That's all in this book too, as no book about our future should overlook these huge ramifications of technology. However, the bigger picture is what I focus on here, and that bigger picture is not that we have a new industrial or technology revolution, but that we actually have a revolution of humanity.

The last great human revolution was the Industrial Revolution. Before that, there was the rise of civilisations during the second human revolution five thousand years ago. And before that, we had the first great revolution of humanity, which was becoming human ourselves. However, no one has written about the revolutions in humanity, or not that I know of. That is why this concept intrigues me so much. The enormous impact of the digital revolution, creating the fourth age of humanity, is that we are *all* connected one-to-one in real time for the very first time.

Now, 7.5 billion people, who were all unconnected a decade ago, are able to connect immediately through the mobile telephone. By connecting through technology, we instantly turn the simple telephone into something far more intelligent—it becomes a trading machine. Therefore, for the first time, we can all transact and trade with each other in real time, one-to-one. This is indeed a transformational revolution, and this is the revolution that I focus on here.

Digital Human takes the ideas of *Digital Bank* and *ValueWeb* and turns them into something wider. The book looks at the implications for humanity, trade and commerce and, the most encouraging thing of all, our future. What is happening through our digitalisation of humanity is that we are eroding boundaries and overcoming exclusion.

Financial exclusion applies to nearly two-thirds of humanity. Financial exclusion creates challenges because it's hard to transact and trade or achieve any real change if you cannot send and receive money. Therefore, the digitalisation of humanity is achieving the inclusion of everyone. For the first time in history, the system—the mobile network systems to be exact—is including everyone. This is the remarkable impact of the mobile network of value and is illustrated really well by Ant Financial, a spin-off from the Chinese internet giant Alibaba. Ant Financial is currently the only company in the world that is trying to build a global financial inclusion programme. The company's mission of inclusivity means that it aims to support two billion users by 2025. This is precisely why I chose to feature Ant Financial as a major case study at the end of this book.

Between Jack Ma, Mark Zuckerberg, Bill Gates and other leaders, who just happen to own nearly all the wealth on this planet,[2] there is a vision of creating financial inclusion and alleviating poverty. Giving everyone the chance to access microloans, microsavings and microinsurance via mobile networks gives everyone a chance to improve their lives. That is the vision and it is starting to take shape.

This digitalisation of our planet is bringing about a major transformation. Everyone on the planet will be included in the network and everyone on the planet will get the chance to talk, trade and transact with everyone else on the planet in real time. Unlike the Industrial Revolution during which only a limited number of humans gained access to wealth and trade, this digital revolution will give everyone a chance.

Welcome to the fourth revolution of humanity and the biggest change our world has seen since the steam pump was patented in the seventeenth century.

---

2   Half of the world's wealth sits with just a few men. At the 2017 World Economic Forum (WEF), Oxfam published a report that showed eight people own the same wealth as the 3.6 billion people who make up the poorest half of the world's population.

THE REVOLUTIONS OF HUMANITY: DIGITAL HUMANS

The history of money is wrapped up in sex, religion and politics, the things we are told not to talk about. Yet these are the themes that rule our lives, and money is at the heart of all three. The origins of money reflect the origins of humans. As you will see, there have been three great revolutions in human history: we first formed communities, next civilisations and then industry. We are currently living through a fourth great revolution in humankind, with a fifth in the not-so-distant future. And each revolution in humankind, in turn, creates a revolution in monetary and value exchange. That is why it is important to reflect on the past to understand the present as well as forecast the future. To put all of this into context, we need to begin at the beginning and talk about the origins of humans.

THE FIRST AGE: THE CREATION OF SHARED BELIEFS

Seven million years ago, the first ancestors of mankind appeared in Africa. Fast-forward seven million years and mankind's existence is being traced by archaeologists in South Africa where they believe they will find several missing links in our history. A history traced back to the first hominid forms. What's a hominid, I hear you say?

Well way back when, scientists believe that the Eurasian and American tectonic plates collided and then settled, creating a massive flat area in Africa, after the Ice Age. This new massive field was flat for hundreds of miles and the apes that inhabited this land suddenly found there were no trees to climb. Instead, just flat land and berries and grasses. This meant that the apes found it hard to thunder over hundreds of miles on their hands and feet, so they started to stand up to make it easier to move over land. This resulted in a change in the wiring of the brain which, over thousands of years, led to the early forms of what is now recognised as human.

The first link to understanding this chain was the discovery of Lucy. Lucy, named after the Beatles' song "Lucy in the Sky with Diamonds", is the first skeleton that could be pieced together to show how these early human forms appeared on the African plains in the post-Ice Age world. The skeleton was found in the early 1970s in Ethiopia by paleoanthropologist Donald Johanson and is an early example of the hominid australopithecine, dating back to about 3.2 million years ago. The skeleton presents a small skull akin to that of most apes, plus evidence of a walking gait that was bipedal and upright, akin to that of humans and other hominids. This combination supports the view of human evolution that bipedalism preceded increase in brain size.

Since Lucy was found, there have been many other astonishing discoveries in what is now called the Cradle of Humankind in South Africa, a UNESCO World Heritage site. It gained this status after the discovery of a near-complete *Australopithecus* skeleton called "Little Foot", dating to more than three million years ago, by Ron Clarke between 1994 and 1997. Why was Little Foot so important? Because it's almost unheard of to find fossilised hominin remains intact. The reason is that the bones are scattered across Earth as soil sank into the ground and remains were distributed amongst the porous caves underneath. An intact skeleton is therefore as likely to be found as a decent record by Jedward.

All in all, the human tree of life that falls into the catch-all of the *Homo* species, of which we are *Homo sapiens*, has several other tributaries including *Homo erectus*, *Homo floresiensis*, *Homo habilis*, *Homo heidelbergensis*, *Homo naledi* and *Homo neanderthalensis*. The question then arises: if there were several forms of human, how come we are the only ones left?

Some of that may have been due to changing times. After all, there aren't any mammoths or sabre-toothed tigers around today, but there are several forms of their ancestors still on Earth. Yet what is interesting in the order of hominids, according to Yuval Noah Harari, author of *Sapiens* and a leading authority on the history of humankind, is that *Homo sapiens* defeated all other forms of hominid because we could work together in groups of hundreds. According to his theory, all other human forms peaked in tribes with a maximum of 150 members, about the maximum size of any ape colony, because with this sized group, too many alpha males existed and the order of the group would fall apart. One part of the group would then follow one alpha male and another part the other.

Homo sapiens developed beyond this because we could talk to each other. We could create a rich landscape of information, not just grunts and signs, and began to build stories. By building stories, we could share beliefs and, by sharing beliefs, hundreds of us could work together in tribes, not just one hundred. This meant that when *Homo sapiens* villages were attacked by other *Homo* forms, we could repel them easily. We could also, in return, attack those human forms and annihilate them. And we did. Neanderthals, who share about 99.5 per cent of our DNA, died out 40,000 years ago and were the last *Homo* variation to survive. After that, it was just us human beings, or *Homo sapiens* if you prefer.

Now why is this important as a background to the five ages of man? Because this was the first age. This was the age of enlightenment. It was the age of Gods. It was an age of worshipping the Moon and the Sun, the Earth and the Seas, the Fire and the Wind. The natural resources of Earth were seen as important symbols while the birds of the sky, the big cats of the earth and the snakes of the below were seen as key symbols for early humankind.

We shared these beliefs and stories and, by doing so, could work together and build civilisations. One of the oldest surviving religions of the world is Hinduism but there were other religions before Hinduism in Jericho, Mesopotamia and Egypt. Then the Sun God and the Moon God were the basic shared beliefs, and these shared beliefs were important because they kept order. We could work together in larger and larger groups because of these shared beliefs.

This is why there is a lot of commonality of Old Testament stories in the Bible with that of the Qur'an. Jews, Christians and Muslims all share beliefs in the stories of Adam and Eve, Moses, Noah and Sodom and Gomorrah, and even some of these beliefs originate from ancient Hindu beliefs of the world.

Shared beliefs is the core thing that brings humans together and binds them. It is what allows us to work together and get on with each other, or not, as the case may be. I will return to this theme as the creation of banking and money is all about a shared belief that these things are important and have value. Without that shared belief, banking, money, governments and religions would have no power. They would be meaningless.

THE SECOND AGE: THE INVENTION OF MONEY

So man became civilised and dominant by being able to work in groups of hundreds. Eventually, as shared beliefs joined us, they joined us together in having leaders. This is a key differential between humans and monkeys. For example, the anthropologist Desmond Morris was asked whether apes believe in God, and he emphatically responded no. Morris, an atheist, wrote a seminal book in the 1960s called *The Naked Ape*, in which he states that humans, unlike apes, "believe in an after-life because part of the reward obtained from our creative works is the feeling that, through them, we will 'live on' after we are dead."

This is part of our shared belief structure that enables us to work together, live together and bond together in our hundreds and thousands. Hence, religion became a key part of mankind's essence of order and structure, and our leaders were those closest to our beliefs: the priests in the temples. As man settled into communities and began to have organised structure however, it led to new issues. Historically, man had been nomadic, searching the lands for food and moving from place to place across the seasons to eat and forage. Suddenly we settled into larger communities and farmed, thanks to the invention of the plough. This meant that far fewer people were engaged in creating produce and food, and could do other things. It meant that the most powerful individuals could gather others around them and become kings or be designated as the leader of shared beliefs, or a priest in common nomenclature.

Eventually, large cities began to emerge. Some claim the oldest-surviving city in the world is Jericho, dating back over 10,000 years. Others point to Eridu, a city formed in ancient Mesopotamia, near Basra in present-day Iraq, 7,500 years ago. Either way, both cities are seriously old. As these cities formed, thousands of people gathered and settled because the city could support complex, civilised life.

Using Eridu as the focal point, the city was formed because it drew together three ancient civilisations: the Samarra culture from the north; the Semitic culture, whose people had historically been nomads with herds of sheep and goats; and the Sumerian culture, the oldest civilisation in the world. It was the Sumerians who brought with them the earliest form of money.

The Sumerians invented money because their system had broken down. It broke down because humankind was settling into larger groups and farming. The farming and settlement structures introduced a revolution in how humankind operated. Before, people had foraged and hunted; now they settled and farmed together.

Farming resulted in abundance in the good years, but when there was drought, no food was stored because there was no way to encourage farmers to store their over-production in the good years to cover the bad years. So there was a need for a new system and the religious leaders of the time—the government if you prefer—responded by inventing money. From the outset, money has been the control mechanism of societies and economies. Countries that have money have respected economies; countries that don't, don't.

So how did the priests make this new belief viable? Sex. There were two gods in ancient Sumer: Baal, the god of war and the elements, and Ishtar, the goddess of fertility. Ishtar made the land and crops fertile, as well as provided pleasure and love.

This was the key to Sumerian culture: creating money so that the men could enjoy pleasure with Ishtar. Men would go to the temple and offer their abundant crops to the priests. The priests would place the crops in store for harder times, insurance against winter when food was short and against crop failure in seasons of blight and drought. In return for their abundance of goods, the priests would give the farmers money. A shared belief in a new form of value: a coin.

What could they do with this coin? Have sex, of course. The Greek historian Herodotus wrote about how this worked:

"Every woman of the land once in her life [had] to sit in the temple of love and have…intercourse with some stranger… the stranger men pass and make their choice…. It matters not what be the sum of money; the woman will never refuse, for that were a sin, the money being by this act made sacred. After their intercourse she has made herself holy in the sight of the goddess and goes away to her home; and thereafter there is no bribe however great that will get her. So then the women that are tall and fair are soon free to depart, but the uncomely have long to wait because they cannot fulfil the law; for some of them remain for three years, or four."

So money was sacred and every woman had to accept that she would prostitute herself for money at least once in her life. This is why Ishtar was also known by other names such as Har and Hora, from which the words "harlot" and "whore" originate. It is why prostitution is the oldest profession in the world, and accountancy the second oldest. Money was created to support religion and governments by developing a new shared belief structure that allowed society to overproduce goods and crops, and still get on with each other even in years of drought.

THE THIRD AGE: THE INDUSTRIAL REVOLUTION

The Industrial Revolution can more or less be aligned with the emergence of steam power. While the steam age created lots of new innovations, the one that transformed the world was the invention of the steam engine. Moving from horse power to steam power allowed ships to steam across oceans, and trains across countries. It led to factories that could be heated and powered. The range of transformational moments that emerged during this time culminated in the late nineteenth-century innovations of electricity and telecommunications. With the move from steam to electricity, there was a shift from heavy-duty machinery to far lighter and easier communication and power structures. This shift from factories to offices ultimately heralded the end of the Industrial Revolution.

The use of money as a means of value exchange, alongside barter, has been commonplace for centuries or, to be more exact, about 4,700 years. During this time, beads, tokens, silver, gold and other commodities were used as money. Perhaps the weirdest money is that of the Yap Islands in the Pacific where stone is still used as currency.

The trouble is that stone, gold and silver are pretty heavy as mediums of exchange and vulnerable to attack and theft. Thus, as the Industrial Revolution powered full steam ahead, a new form of value exchange was needed. There had already been several innovations—the Medici bankers created trade finance and the Chinese had already been using paper money since the seventh century—but none of these went mainstream until the Industrial Revolution demanded it.

To address this need for a new form of value exchange, the governments of the world started to mandate and license banks to enable economic exchange. These banks appeared from the 1600s, and were organised as government-backed entities that could be trusted to store value on behalf of depositors. It is for this reason that banks are the oldest registered companies in most economies. The oldest surviving British financial institution is C. Hoares & Co., created by Richard Hoare in 1672. The oldest British bank of size is Barclays Bank, first listed in 1690. Most UK banks are over 200 years old which is unusual as, according to a survey by the Bank of Korea in 2008, there are only 5,586 companies older than 200 years, and most of these are in Japan.

Banks and insurance companies have survived so long as large entities because they are government instruments of trade. They are backed and licensed by governments to act as financial oil in the economy, and the major innovation that took place was the creation of paper money, backed by government, as the means of exchange.

Paper bank notes and paper cheques were created as part of this new ecosystem in order to make it easier to allow industry to operate. At the time, this must have caused quite a stir. A piece of paper instead of gold as a payment? But it wasn't so outrageous. Perhaps this excerpt from the Committee of Scottish Bankers provides useful insight on why it took off:

The first Scottish bank to issue banknotes was Bank of Scotland. When the bank was founded on 17th July 1695, through an Act of the Scottish Parliament, Scots coinage was in short supply and of uncertain value compared with the English, Dutch, Flemish or French coin, which were preferred by the majority of Scots. The growth of trade was severely hampered by this lack of an adequate currency and the merchants of the day, seeking a more convenient way of settling accounts, were amongst the strongest supporters of an alternative.

Bank of Scotland was granted a monopoly over banking within Scotland for 21 years. Immediately after opening in 1695 the Bank expanded on the coinage system by introducing paper currency.

This idea was first viewed with some suspicion. However, once it became apparent that the Bank of Scotland could honour its "promise to pay", and that the paper was more convenient than coin, acceptance spread rapidly and the circulation of notes increased. As this spread from the merchants to the rest of the population, Scotland became one of the first countries to use a paper currency through choice.

And the cheque book? The UK's Cheque & Clearing Company provides a useful history:

> By the 17th century, bills of exchange were being used for domestic payments as well as international trades. Cheques, a type of bill of exchange, then began to evolve. They were initially known as 'drawn notes' as they enabled a customer to draw on the funds they held on account with their banker and required immediate payment … the Bank of England pioneered the use of printed forms, the first of which were produced in 1717 at Grocers' Hall, London. The customer had to attend the Bank of England in person and obtain a numbered form from the cashier. Once completed, the form had to be authorised by the cashier before being taken to a teller for payment. These forms were printed on 'cheque' paper to prevent fraud. Only customers with a credit balance could get the special paper and the printed forms served as a check that the drawer was a bona fide customer of the Bank of England.

In other words, in the late seventeenth century, three major innovations appeared at the same time: governments giving banks licences to issue bank notes and drawn notes, cheques and the replacement of coins and valued commodities with paper. The banking system then fuelled the Industrial Revolution, not only enabling the easy trading of value exchange through these paper-based systems, but also allowing trade and structure finance through systems that are similar to the ones we still have today.

THE FOURTH AGE: THE NETWORK AGE

The reason for talking about the history of money in depth is to serve as a backdrop to what is happening today. Money originated as a control mechanism for governments of Ancient Sumer to control farmers, based on shared beliefs. It was then structured during the Industrial Revolution into government-backed institutions—namely, banks—that could issue paper notes and cheques that would be as acceptable as gold or coinage, based on these shared beliefs. We share a belief in banks because governments say they can be trusted and governments use the banks as a control mechanism to manage the economy.

So now we come to bitcoin and the internet age, where some of these fundamentals are being challenged by the internet. Let's first take a step back and see how the internet age came about. Some might claim it dates back to Alan Turing, the Enigma machine and the Turing Test, or even further back to the 1930s when the Polish Cipher Bureau were the first to decode German military texts on the Enigma machine. Enigma then led to the invention of modern computing, as British cryptographers created a programmable, electronic, digital computer called Colossus to crack the codes held in the German messages, alongside developments in the United States.

Colossus was designed by engineer Tommy Flowers and was operational at Bletchley Park by February 1944, two years before the American computer ENIAC appeared. ENIAC, short for Electronic Numerical Integrator and Computer, was the first general-purpose electronic computer. It had been designed by the U.S. Military for meteorological purposes and was delivered in 1946.

When ENIAC launched, the media called it "the Giant Brain", with a speed a thousand times faster than any electro mechanical machines of its time. ENIAC weighted over 30 tons, took up 1,800 square feet of space and could process about 385 instructions per second. Compared to an iPhone 6 that can process around 3.5 billion instructions per second, this was rudimentary technology. However, we are talking about seventy years ago, and Moore's Law hadn't kicked in yet.

The key is that Colossus and ENIAC laid the groundwork for all modern computing, with this becoming a boom industry in the 1950s. You may think that surprising when, back in 1943, the then president of IBM, Thomas J. Watson, predicted that there would be a worldwide market for maybe five computers. Bearing in mind the size and weight of these darned machines, you could see why he thought that way but, my, how things have changed today.

However, we are still in the early days of the network revolution and I'm not going to linger over the history of computers here. The reason for talking about ENIAC and Colossus was more to put our current state of change in perspective. We are seventy years into the transformations that computing is giving to our world. Considering it took 330 years from the emergence of steam power to the last steam power patent, this implies that there's a long way to go in our transformation.

The main difference between the fourth age and those that have gone before is the collapse of time and space. Einstein would no doubt have a giggle at this, but it is now a fact that we no longer are separated by time and space as we were before. Distance is collapsing every day, thanks to our global connectivity. We can talk, socialise, communicate and trade globally, in real time for almost free. Today, we have almost unlimited storage and connectivity, thanks to the rapidly diminishing costs of technology. As a result, there are $1 phones out there today, and the cheapest smartphone in the world is currently the Freedom 251, an Android phone with a 4-inch screen that costs just 251 rupees, around $3.75, in India. In other words, what is happening in this revolution is that we can provide a computer far more powerful than anything that's come before and put it in the hands of everyone on the planet so that everyone on the planet is on the network. Once on the network, you have the network effect, which creates exponential possibilities as everyone can now trade, transact, talk and target one-to-one, peer-to-peer (P2P).

This is why I think of the network as the fourth age of humanity, as we went from disparate, nomadic communities in the first age; to settlements, farming and cities in the second; to travel across countries and continents thanks to steam power in the third age; and to a world that is connected globally, one-to-one, today. This is a huge transformation and shows that man is moving from single tribes to communities to connected communities to a single platform—the internet.

The importance of this is that each of these changes has seen a rethinking of how we do commerce, trade and, therefore, finance. Our shared belief system allowed barter to work until abundance undermined bartering, so we created money. Our monetary system was based on coinage, which was unworkable in a rapidly expanding industrial age, so we created banking to issue paper money. Now, we are in the fourth age, and banking is no longer working as it should. Banks are domestic but the network is global. Banks are structured around paper but the network is structured around data. Banks distribute through buildings and humans but the network distributes through software and servers.

This is why so much excitement is hitting mainstream as we are now on the cusp of the change from money and banking to something else. However, as in each previous age, the "something else" doesn't replace what was there before. It's added to it. Money didn't replace bartering; it diminished it. Banking didn't replace money; it diminished it. Something in the network age isn't going to replace banking but it will diminish it.

Let's put diminish into context. Barter is still at the highest levels that it has ever been—about 15 per cent of world trade is in a bartering form—but it is small compared to the monetary flows. Money in its physical form is also trading at the highest levels it has ever seen—cash usage is still rising in most economies—but it is not high compared to the alternative forms of monetary flow digitally and in foreign exchange (FX) markets and exchanges. In other words, the historical systems of value exchange are still huge but they are becoming a smaller percentage of trade compared with the newest structure we have implemented to allow value to flow.

This is why I'm particular excited about what the network age will do, as we connect one-to-one in real time, because it will create massive new flows of trade for markets that were underserved or overlooked. Just look at Africa. African mobile subscribers take to mobile wallets like ducks to water. A quarter of all Africans who have a mobile phone have a mobile wallet, rising to pretty much every citizen in more economically vibrant communities like Kenya, Uganda and Nigeria. This is because these citizens never had access to a network before; they had no value exchange mechanism, except a physical one that was open to fraud and crime. Africa is leapfrogging other markets by delivering mobile financial inclusion almost overnight. The same is true in China, India, Indonesia, the Philippines, Brazil and many other underserved markets. So the first major change in the network effect of financial inclusion is that the billions of people who previously had zero access to digital services are now on the network.

A second big change is the nature of digital currencies, cryptocurrencies, bitcoin and shared ledgers. This is the part that is building the new rails and pipes for the fourth generation of finance, and we are yet to see how this rebuilding works out. Will all the banks be based on an R3 blockchain? Will all clearing and settlement be via Hyperledger? What role will bitcoin play in the new financial ecosystem? We don't know the answers to those questions yet, but what we will see is a new ecosystem that diminishes the role of historical banks. Thus, the challenge for historical banks is whether they can rise to the challenge of the new system.

The fourth age of humanity is a digital networked value structure that is real time, global, connected, digital and near free. It is based on everything being connected, from the more than seven billion humans communicating and trading in real time globally to their billions of machines and devices, which all have intelligence inside. This new structure obviously cannot work on a system built for paper with buildings and humans, and is most likely to be a new layer on top of that old structure.

A new layer of digital inclusion that overcomes the deficiencies of the old structure. A new layer that will see billions of transactions and value transferred at light speed in tiny amounts. In other words, the fourth age is an age where everything can transfer value, immediately and for an amount that starts at a billionth of a dollar if necessary.

This new layer for the fourth age is therefore not like anything that we have seen before and, for what was there before, it will supplement the old system and diminish it. Give it half a century and we will probably look back at banking today as we currently look back at cash and barter. They are old methods of transacting for the previous ages of man and moneykind.

This fourth age is digitalising value. Banks, cash and barter will still be around but will play a much smaller part of the new value ecosystem. They may still be processing volumes greater than ever before but, in context of the total system of value exchange and trade, their role is smaller.

I don't expect banks to disappear, but I do expect a new system to evolve that may include some banks, but will also include new operators that are truly digital. Maybe it will be the Googles, Baidus, Alibabas and Facebooks or maybe it will be the Prospers, Lending Clubs, Zopas and SoFis. We don't know yet but if I were a betting man, I would say it will be a hybrid mix of all, as all evolve to the fourth age of humanity.

The hybrid is one where banks are part of a new value system that incorporates digital currencies, financial inclusion, micropayments and peer-to-peer exchange, precisely because that is what the networked age needs. It needs the ability for everything with a chip inside to transact in real time for near free. We're not there yet but, as I said, this revolution is in its early days. It's just seventy years old. The last revolution took 330 years to play out. Give this one another few decades and then we will know exactly what we built.

THE FIFTH AGE: THE FUTURE

Above, I've talked about the main types of money used by people throughout the revolutions in humankind, namely:

- barter
- coins
- paper
- chips

What could possibly be the fifth? When we are just at the start of the Internet of Things (IoT), and building an Internet of Value (IoV), how can we imagine something beyond this next ten-year cycle?

Well, we can and we must. After all, people are already imagining a future beyond today. People like Elon Musk who see colonising Mars and supersmart high-speed transportation a realisable vision. People like the engineers at Shimizu Corporation, who imagine building city structures in the oceans. People like the guys at NASA, who are launching space probes capable of sending us HD photographs of Pluto when, just a hundred years ago, we only imagined that it existed.

A century ago, Einstein proposed a space-time continuum that a century later has been proven. What will we be discovering, proving and doing a century from now? No one knows, and most who predict usually get it terribly wrong. A century ago, people were predicting lots of ideas but the computer had not been imagined, so the network revolution was unimaginable. A century before this, people believed that the answer to the challenge of clearing horse manure off the streets was to have steam-powered horses, as the idea of the car had not been imagined. So who knows what we will be doing a century from now.

What will the world look like a century from now? Well, there are some clues. We know that we have imagined robots for decades, and robots will surely be pervasive and ubiquitous within the next hundred years as even IBM is demonstrating such things today. A century from now, we know we will be travelling through space, as the Wright Brothers invented air travel a century ago and look at what we can do today. Emirates now offers the world's longest non-stop flight between Auckland and Dubai, lasting 17 hours and 15 minutes. We are already allowing reusable transport vehicles to reach the stars and, a century from now, we will be beyond the stars, I hope.

Probably the largest and most forecastable change is that we will be living for longer. Several scientists believe that most humans will live a century or more, with some even forecasting that a child has already been born who will live for 150 years. Just imagine what that child will see!

The reason why we will live so long is because a little bit of the machine will be inside the human and a little bit of the human inside the machine. The Robocop is already here, with hydraulic prosthetics linked to our brainwaves that are able to create the bionic human. Equally, the Cyborg will be arriving within 35 years, according to one leading futurist. Add to this smorgasbord of life-extending capabilities from nanobots to leaving our persona on the network after we die, and the world becomes a place of magic.

We will have smart cars, smart homes, smart systems and smart lives. Self-driving cars, biotechnologies, smart networking and more will bring all the ideas of *Minority Report* and *Star Trek* to a science that is no longer fiction, but reality. It might even be possible to continually monitor brain activity and alert health experts or the security services before an aggressive attack, such as in Philip K. Dick's dystopian novella *The Minority Report*.

So, in this fifth age of man where man and machine create superhumans, what will the value exchange system be? Well, it won't be money and it probably won't even be transactions of data but, instead, some other structure. Money may no longer be a meaningful system in the fifth age of man. Having digitalised money in the fourth age, it will just become a universal credit and debit system. Digits on the network recording our taking and giving; our living and earning; our work and pleasure.

After robots take over so many jobs, and man colonises space, do we really think man will focus on wealth management and value creation or will we move beyond such things to philanthropic matters? This is the dream of Gene Roddenberry and other space visionaries, and maybe it could come true. After all, when you become a multibillionaire, your wealth becomes meaningless. This is why Bill Gates, Warren Buffett and Mark Zuckerberg focus on philanthropic structures because money and wealth have become meaningless to them.

So could the fifth age of man—the man who lives for centuries in space—be one where we forget about banking, money and wealth, and focus on the good of the planet and mankind in general? If everyone is on the network and everyone has a voice, and the power of the one voice can be as powerful as the many, will we move beyond self-interest?

I have no idea, but it makes for interesting questions around how and what we value when we become superhumans thanks to life-extending and body engineering technologies, when we move beyond Earth to other planets and when we reach a stage where our every physical and mental need can be satisfied by a robot.

THE EVOLUTION OF THE DIGITAL AGE

Alongside the revolutions in humanity, we have also seen evolutions in digitalisation. Digital humanity did not just arrive overnight; it has been emerging over the last seventy years. Many people a decade ago, for example, were talking about web 2.0, the second-generation internet. Having worked with technology throughout my life, I actually think we are in the fourth evolution in technology. Digital 4.0 if you prefer. Therefore, alongside our understanding of humanity living through digital transformation, it is important to understand the origins and emergence of how that digital transformation has developed.

THE BIRTH OF COMPUTING AND DEVELOPMENT OF THE WEB

The origins of the web start with the beginnings of building computers. I'm not going to linger on this too much as hopefully you've seen *The Imitation Game* with Benedict Cumberbatch in the role of Alan Turing solving the Enigma Code during the Second World War (although the Polish claim to have solved the code a decade earlier). Wars often stimulate progress.

Just look at aircraft design and development in the first and second world wars, and how the Second World War brought about the development of computing.

As I mentioned earlier, ENIAC was the world's first general-purpose electronic computer. After building ENIAC at the University of Pennsylvania, J. Presper Eckert and John Mauchly, the inventors, formed EMCC, the first commercial computer company, to build new computer designs for commercial and military applications. The company was initially called the Electronic Control Company, but the name had changed to Eckert–Mauchly Computer Corporation by the time it launched. Eventually, their firm offered the UNIVersal Automatic Computer (UNIVAC), which was the computer system used by NASA in the 1960s to get a man on the Moon. Bearing in mind Moore's Law which states that computer power doubles every year whilst cost halves, those systems were pretty basic. In fact, you have more compute power in your Apple watch today than was carried in the *Apollo* moon shots, which is why we're now saying that the colonisation of Mars is a real possibility.

It was during this period that computer power in private companies began to take off, with a spray of other firms entering the fray. IBM became the biggest of these firms, and *the* company to buy from, having purchased the Series 360 instruction set from an incredible inventor and founder of Wang Lab, Dr An Wang. By the 1980s, the comment was that nobody ever got fired for buying IBM, and the result was that a lot of its competitors— Digital Equipment Corporation (DEC), Wang, International Computers Limited (ICL), Burroughs and Sperry—all fell by the wayside by the end of the decade. A remarkable achievement for a firm whose president originally dismissed computing as limited to a worldwide market of just five systems.

However, IBM did initially dismiss another rising technology as irrelevant—the personal computer (PC) operating system—even though it owned that space as the first commercial PC manufacturer. In fact, a little-known fact is that it was Bill Gates' mother Mary who made Microsoft what it is today.

Mary Gates was one of the first women to serve as a director of a bank, the First Interstate Bank, and was later appointed to the board of the United Way of America. In 1983, she became the first woman to lead it. Her tenure on the national board's executive committee helped her son's company at a crucial time. This is because, in 1980, she discussed her son's company with John Opel, a fellow committee member. Opel was the chairman of IBM, and Mary told him that her son's firm might be able to help the new business IBM was developing. A few weeks later, IBM took a chance by hiring Microsoft to develop an operating system for its first personal computer. The success of the IBM PC gave Microsoft a lift that eventually made it the world's largest software company. Funny how things turn out.

Another giant of technology at the time, who also dismissed the PC, was Ken Olsen, founder of DEC. He believed that "there is no reason anyone would want a computer in their home". This is the same guy who dismissed the operating system Unix as snake oil, even though, back then in the 1980s, he was running one of the largest computer companies. No wonder his firm went by the wayside. Unsurprisingly, Olsen was forced out of DEC in 1992 and the firm was acquired by Compaq in 1998.

Around the same time, several leading figures were playing their part in developing the modern internet, including Ivan Sutherland and Robert Taylor's work on the Advanced Research Projects Agency Network (ARPANET), and Kevin Kelly's work on the Well that led to the founding of *Wired* magazine. However, for me, the standout figure has to be Sir Tim Berners-Lee.

Berners-Lee is viewed by many as the founding father of the modern internet due to his development of the foundations that we use today: HTML, URLs and HTTP.

- **HyperText Markup Language (HTML):** the mark-up (formatting) language for the web
- **Uniform Resource Identifier (URI):** a kind of "address" that

is unique and used to identify each resource on the web, also commonly called a URL
- **Hypertext Transfer Protocol (HTTP):** allows for the retrieval of linked resources from across the web

He proposed these three concepts in an October 1990 research paper at CERN, the European Organization for Nuclear Research, near Geneva, where he had been working since 1980. The 1990 paper was an extension of what many consider the founding paper of today's internet, "Information Management: A Proposal", which had been presented to CERN in March 1989. Believe it or not, his initial proposal was not immediately accepted. In fact, his boss at the time, Mike Sendall, wrote the words "vague but exciting" on the cover. The web was never an official CERN project but Sendall managed to give Berners-Lee time to work on it, and that led to the breakthrough in 1990.

So the first generation of the modern internet was born in 1990, some forty-five years after the birth of computing. Since then, each generation of the internet has lasted about ten years. In the 2000s, there was web 2.0. Now we are developing web 3.0, the Internet of Value. Soon, we will be entering the era of the Internet of Things, web 4.0. Then, in the 2030s, we will be immersed in the Semantic Web, web 5.0.

WEB 1.0: THE NETWORK BEGINS

As mentioned, almost half a century of developments in technology led to the launch of the web as we know it today, following Tim Berners-Lee's paper detailing HTML and URLs. This was in 1990 and, subsequently, the internet morphs almost every decade. This makes our decade, the 2010s, the era of web 3.0 and the building of the Internet of Value which, for those of you who read my last book, I call the "ValueWeb". But let's go back to the 1990s and see what happened then.

The first website was launched by Tim Berners-Lee on 6 August 1991 and was pretty basic, as were most of the early websites. Most of these sites were launched by academic and research firms, and were there to collate information. For instance, *Wired*, Bloomberg and the Internet Movie Database (IMDb) launched websites in 1993, and more soon followed. While these websites mainly provided information, some were more visual than others but none were interactive.

Interactivity didn't really start until pornographers saw the potential of the internet. As with any new technology, sex and pornography are the catalysts that drive early adoption. For example, Event Horizons BBS was grossing more than $3.2 million dollars a year by 1993. Jim Maxey, who ran Event Horizons, employed ten people simply to scan photographs, format them and put them online for download. They didn't do any marketing as such; news simply got around through word of mouse. Consequently, a whole raft of sites launched that led to commerce online.

In other words, the drive of pornography led to online commerce, with the first payments being taken through credit card forms online. The first commercial website that took credit card payments was books.com. The books.com website was owned by Book Stacks Ltd, a U.S. bookshop that had been running a bulletin board in the 1980s and then moved online in 1992, three years before Amazon launched. It was eventually acquired by Barnes & Noble.

Another notable online first took place on 11 August 1994 when the first secure, commercial online payment was taken by American retailer NetMarket. This transaction opened the door to the era of internet commerce. With the launch of Amazon in 1995, as did eBay, other modern standards like Google (1998), PayPal (1999, originally as x.com) and Alibaba (1999) quickly followed. Within just twenty years, by 2014, online retail commerce was worth £100 billion a year in the United Kingdom alone.

This was the decade of web 1.0: the evolution of the first website into thousands of sites delivering everything from infomercials to easy commerce. It was the time of Netscape and AOL, of dial-up lines and modems.

The key features of this first-generation internet were that it was highly controlled and structured. Businesses ran the internet. Websites were offered by business to consumers (B2C), and everything was about B2C and business to business (B2B). Following information services, commerce enabled the web to really take off. The first payment services were just credit card forms, as mentioned, but soon companies realised that form filling was onerous and a barrier to commerce, so firms dedicated solely to payments launched.

PayPal is the American firm we all recognise today as the clear leader in online payments in Europe and the United States (in Russia it's Yandex.Money, and AliPay in China), but this wasn't always the case. This 2001 article on Bloomberg[3] discussed PayPal's potential initial public offering (IPO):

> In an Internet market starved for success stories, PayPal (PAPXX) is one of the few upstarts brimming with potential. Still, the Palo Alto (Calif.) company, which handles payments for buyers and sellers on the sites of auctioneer eBay Inc. (EBAY) and other e-commerce players, left the high-tech world agape when it filed paperwork on Sept. 28 for an $80 million initial public offering … earlier this year, PayPal executives discussed selling to eBay, Citibank (C), and other companies, but no one would approach PayPal's asking price of more than $700 million, according to analysts and investment bankers.

At the time, eBay had its own system called Billpoint which had been developed in partnership with Wells Fargo. Considered PayPal's main rival, Billpoint processed around 25 per cent of all online payments while PayPal processed 65 per cent. eBay then went on to acquire PayPal in 2001. Interesting how times change. Valued at $700 million in 2001, PayPal now has a market capitalisation of near $50 billion. It just goes to show how important the payments system is to online commerce.

---

3   "Can PayPal Pull This Off?" *Bloomberg Businessweek*, 29 October 2001.

Here's a final thought on web 1.0. During this time, banks launched their own online services and, eventually, offered online banking. Most bank websites were initially just brochures, and the first online banking systems began around 1995 with Wells Fargo. I remember these times quite well, as most banks believed they could shut branches and shift all their customers to online banking, but it wasn't that easy. Customers didn't trust banking online and, in many instances, the online banking services were pretty awful too. The sites were just a transition from the branch-based ledger of debits and credits to an online ledger of debits and credits, and it hasn't changed much since.

WEB 2.0: THE SOCIAL NETWORK BEGINS

Following the emergence of e-commerce and a plethora of payments services and commercial websites by the end of the first decade of the internet, not a great deal happened until the internet became social. Blog platforms like WordPress and Typepad emerged in 2003, Facebook launched in 2004 and YouTube came on board a year later. The era of the social web had begun.

In the mid-2000s, I had three key moments that were awakenings around social networks. The first was at a beautiful conference retreat on Lake Como, Italy, in 2006. I was the keynote alongside various banking alumni, and talking as usual about the future of finance. One of the senior management team of the host organisation got up to tell the story of how his chief executive had been blindsided by the appearance of YouTube a year earlier. The morning papers had appeared on his desk with the headline "Google acquires YouTube for $1.65 billion". As he had never heard of this company, he called in his team and asked, "What is YouTube?"

None of them knew. So he typed in www.youtube.com on his PC and the following message came back: "You are firewalled out of this website. Please contact the administrator if this is a problem." It certainly was a problem. This particular CEO ran a firm called McKinsey and suddenly a revolution was bubbling under its feet and he was firewalled out. The company has changed quite a bit since but, hey, that was then and this is now.

The second awakening was while I was running a training programme with a University Corporate Education team for a large global bank. A top futurist talked about the future of the world in the morning, and I talked about the future of banks in the afternoon. This was again back in 2006, and Facebook was just rising.

At this time, I was hungrily joining everything that was social, just out of pure interest. Facebook was a nice website but MySpace was rocking. After all, people were launching music careers in their MySpace profiles. Meantime, Friends Reunited was doing pretty well, too. I therefore included a social network discussion in my presentations, and would recount how bad people were at using these new capabilities. By way of example, I made up a story about how a senior manager at a bank had started using Facebook, and was happily posting details of her life. There was no privacy set on her profile, as people were not aware of privacy as a problem back then. This meant that anybody could see her email and telephone number. They could also see her husband, children, family and friends and where she hung out at the weekend. This led to her being blackmailed into giving criminals access to the bank after they kidnapped her children one Friday afternoon, just before she was due to pick them up from school.

I stopped telling this story in 2009 when my fiction became reality, and the head of a call centre in one big bank lost her life. It was too close to home but, again, it frustrated me that so many people who attended these courses would come up to me at the end and say, "Tell me more about Facebook and Twitter. I would love to use these capabilities but spend the days at work firewalled out and I'm too busy at the weekend doing other things." These people didn't know what was going on in the internet world because they were firewalled out, again.

The third realisation came from blogging. Now I've been blogging every single day since 1 February 2007—over ten years now—and that's why I have a pretty good memory of my life, workwise. I'm always blogging stories about how things are developing and changing. But there was a specific moment that I remember with regard to banking and blogs. It was 2007 and Wells Fargo chose to share their story of becoming social online during a presentation that I was giving. The story focused on the issue that when you did a Google search for "Wells Fargo", the number one search record that came back was a website called WellsFargoSucks.com. Oh dear. This was not the only spark for blogging, but it was one and having an angry customer running an anti-bank website galvanised the bank to launch a blog and engage with customers online.

My UK bank friends listening to this speech were horrified that Wells Fargo launched a blog, as they could not imagine engaging their customers socially online. "Weren't you attacked with a lot of hate?" they asked, prompted by the fact that they had tried an internal social experiment that ended bloodily with employees sharing their gripes more than anything else.

"Sure," said my friend Tim from Wells Fargo, "but we overcame it by engaging in a conversation."

And that is the bottom line here: a conversation. It's just a conversation that has moved from the desk to the desktop to the mobile app. Banks that ignored or were firewalled out of such conversations know they are missing a trick, and it still amazes me how few banks leverage social media well. For example, I just entered "bank blog" on Google and found that start-ups like Starling and Atom appear in the first ten results, but if I enter "Lloyds bank blog" or "Barclays bank blog", there's not much. There's a blog about Lloyds' digital transformation and Barclays wealth management has one, but both sites are very corporate and not particularly social. And as for Twitter? Well, banks have relegated Twitter to a customer service and public relations (PR) programme, and the rest doesn't matter.

It's interesting as the best practices of financial social networking are shown by banks in Turkey, where they provide conversations through Facebook platforms, and in India, where ICICI bank goes an extra mile to use Facebook as its bank platform rather than as a channel. Equally, I still love the story of Fidor Bank using Facebook Likes to determine its interest rates.

Some banks truly understand the compelling power of the social network, and that power is that it is customer created. People create their networks. People create their content. People are living their lives and recording their lives digitally. My decade of blogging and being social is there forever. In fact, if Facebook or Twitter were to delete my digital social history, I would sue them, as that's my life, right there. And my friends? I've never met many of my best friends. They might be psychos for all I know but that is the beauty of the web 2.0 age. We have allowed everyone to connect easily and create content without friction. Now I, like the billions of other people on this planet with a mobile phone, continually update my profile with shares, Likes, updates, video, photos and more.

This is the internet age, and the big change in web 2.0 was the movement from business to consumer. The consumer was put in control. People now created content, and the strong control structures that businesses had locked into web 1.0 were eradicated in web 2.0. Consumers are now media channels with millions of followers. Bloggers, vloggers and podcast radio shows are the new name of the game. People like PewDiePie rise from the minions to become megastars, with millions of subscribers to their premium YouTube channels, only to fall just as fast. But it wasn't just the social network that drove this change. It was the combination of mobile social.

As the nascent industry emerged, so did the smartphone with the launch of Apple's first generation in 2007. Since then, there are more phones than people on this planet and there will be more smartphones than humans by 2021. I'm not going to go into a deep dive of the mobile phenomena—I did that in my last book *ValueWeb*—except to underscore that without it, there would be no social networking as we know it today. 24/7 in your pocket and bag is the transformation, and before the iPhone we mostly used our Nokias and Blackberrys for email and telephone calls. Now we live our lives through our phones. That has been the parallel innovation of web 2.0 which, interestingly, was almost missed by many including Mark Zuckerberg. In

2012, Facebook was so mobile-challenged that it had to warn investors publicly via a Securities and Exchange Commission (SEC) filing about its weakness in the mobile market.

This near oversight was possible to overlook because, until around 2012, it was easy to separate mobile and social; mobile used the telephone carriers' network whilst social was on the internet. Since then, the two have converged thanks to 3G and its successors, 4G and soon 5G. Many firms separated apps from their services, and didn't see the rise of the messenger, the chat room, the photo stream and the like. This is because the leading social media firms of the time focused on online social rather than mobile social.

The camera on the phone is a specific innovation that made a huge difference in adoption, and today's mobile smartphones carry digital cameras that are a hundred times better than the high-end dedicated digital cameras that were available a decade ago. That is why more photos are taken in a day today than the total number printed in the last century. With digital, it's easy to take a hundred photos a day; in old money, that was three Kodak films that would need to be taken to the lab, printed and picked up a week later.

So the web 2.0 age was a combination of factors from mobile smartphones to phones with cameras to the mobile internet, combined with social mobile apps. This naturally led to web 3.0, where customers create their own value network structures. Who needs institutions and governments to do this when we all live lives connected globally with people we've never met?

WEB 3.0: AN INTERNET OF MARKETS

So, what exactly is web 3.0, the third-generation internet? It's not been well defined or described. Many would say it's the Internet of Things, but I disagree. The Internet of Things is emerging but it cannot exist until a bridge between the mobile social network and the Internet of Things has a strong underlying architecture for device-to-device commerce.

I call that the Internet of Value, and it is covered in depth in my book *ValueWeb*. Consequently, I'm not going to go into great depth about the Internet of Value here but, essentially, the Internet of Value discussion went along the lines of building an underlying real-time and near-free value exchange structure based on mobile internet and shared ledgers. I've changed my mind about that since, in terms of how it's positioned in web 3.0 as yes, you need an Internet of Value for the Internet of Things but no, web 3.0 is not about just the Internet of Value. The technologies discussed in *ValueWeb* are important, and included my initial outline of the new business model of the bank based on front-office apps linking through middle-office application program interfaces (APIs) that are fed non-stop by intelligence from back-office analytics engines using artificial intelligence and deep learning.

More recently, I've talked a lot about Open Banking and open marketplaces. Open Banking is based on apps, APIs and analytics, and offers access for everyone in an open marketplace. This is all about moving us from vertically integrated control structures to a marketplace of plug-and-play processes that are delivered through platforms. Platforms where taxi firms own no taxis, hotel chains have no rooms and media companies produce no content. The taxis, rooms and content are created by those who play in your marketplace as you have become their preferred digital platform. It is the people who need lifts that connect to the taxi drivers registered on Uber. It is the people who need accommodation that connect to the people offering rooms through Airbnb. It is the individuals who create and share content on social media through Facebook and more.

These marketplaces are the digital platforms for the sharing economy and many of us have struggled to find a good banking example. We have struggled because there isn't one yet but Open Banking will get us to move there. In fact, the nearest we get to an Open Bank today is Ant Financial, which is one of several reasons why it is the in-depth case study at the end of this book.

In an open marketplace, everyone can play. Banks therefore are moving from proprietary structures that they control to open platforms where everyone can play in their marketplace. That is a massive cultural and structural change, not just the offering of an open API. Banks have the opportunity to be better positioned to be the digital platform that allows open marketplaces to operate. That is because they currently own the customers' accounts and have the size and capital to control the marketplace. It does not mean they will succeed, as there are a lot of FinTech start-ups also focused on building marketplace structures based on apps, APIs and analytics. Such FinTech start-ups include Leveris, Thought Machine, solarisBank, RailsBank, ClearBank and CBW Bank, to name just a few.

For banks to be players in such a marketplace, they will have to open their historically closed systems to offer their APIs for others to use. Equally, it means that they will most likely become a curator and aggregator of other apps, APIs and analytics in order to give their customers the best user experience. This is what Open Banking is all about.

When you have an Open Bank, you can move really fast. You can incorporate any other FinTech into the Open Bank and, just as powerfully, you can connect the Open Bank into any other FinTech. The key to the Open Bank vision is that everything can be connected from the Bank to Business to Consumer structure. In other words, they can plug and play into any FinTech, payments or other player.

In doing so, and combining this with the themes of rearchitecting the bank for open sourcing, I can see one particularly powerful play—the Semantic Bank. The Semantic Bank has been alluded to for a while, and already has some crude illustrations such as the BankAmericard Rewards. Using Cardlytics, Bank of America can push you a reward coupon via its app at the point of relevance, for instance, as you're walking past one of your regular shopping haunts. I'll discuss this in more depth in the chapter titled "The Rise of Robots".

Other powerful capabilities have come into play today, such as using AI to analyse terabytes of data non-stop in real time to better serve customers.

These analytics will then enable the bank to delve deep into the psyche of its clients and use neural networks to proactively predict their needs, provide advisory services and improve support mechanisms.

These support mechanisms will be provided in non-stop real time to my devices, which will tell me what is important and, consequently, the devices can transact and manage what is not important. The delivery of knowledge to my devices will sometimes be via the bank direct, but often through third-party APIs that have plugged into my open-sourced bank. As a result, my financial ecosystem will be greatly personalised at a micro level, and I stop thinking about questions. Who would ever ask "What's my balance?" or say "Must remember to pay that bill", now that my system has taken over all of those tasks for me? All I would really need to know is "You are low on your deposit balance" or "You should save more for that holiday this month", and I'd just say yes or no, depending on my mood and feeling. This means that banking will move from a pull industry—where I have to go and find my information and manage it—to a push industry—where my bank tells my devices what to do.

I love the idea of the Open Bank and a financial ecosystem personalised to my lifestyle and managed for me. The problem we have today is that banks have only just got to the point where they can take a debit and credit statement and plug it into a mobile app. An open-sourced structure proactively pushing service to my IoT ecosystem is going to be a big stretch.

Some banks are proactively moving in this direction though. A good example is BBVA and Santander, both of which have not only been investing in FinTech start-ups but are also moving generally towards partnering and including firms in their marketplace. BBVA has Holvi, Simple and Atom Bank whilst Santander is the leading European bank for investing in start-ups. Santander has made thirteen investments into twelve unique FinTech start-ups, including small business lender Kabbage.

What we are seeing, therefore, is banks curating their marketplaces and choosing the cream of the FinTech crop to offer their customers a better user experience and service. After all, is your average Joe or Mary going to test a thousand start-up products and find the cream of the FinTech crop? Probably not, which is the real opportunity here for the collaborative Open Bank. After all, the collaborative Open Bank recognises that it controls nothing, can only build some decent functionality and needs lots of other players to play on its platform if it is going to be able to offer choice to its customers. So, an Open Bank offers its customers this choice but also offers to aggregate such services on the customers' behalf. After all, when faced with a thousand different P2P services, which one do I choose? Why choose at all? Let the Open Bank do it for you.

That's the beauty of a marketplace. Do you choose the Facebook content you read or the Uber taxi driver you want, or let Airbnb, Facebook or Uber do if for you? It depends how much time and interest you have. The same applies with banking.

The Business Model of an Open Bank

So what is the business model of an Open Bank? What exactly does it look like? This is probably the most important question tackled in this book, and the diagrams that follow are ones that I will refer to often, so please take note.

I've been working on this model for a while, and the diagram below shows the bank structure based on a back office manufacturing products and services, a middle office processing transactions and payments and a front office retailing intimacy and experiences.

BACK OFFICE
Manufactures products
Focused upon innovation

MIDDLE OFFICE
Processes transactions
Focused upon quality

FRONT OFFICE
Retails experiences
Focused upon intimacy

My assertion is that in the old, industrial era bank, all of this front-, middle- and back-office structure was proprietary and internalised and now has to move to open and externalised. This is because smart devices are where the relationships are developed in the front office. Plug-and-play software across the operations allow anyone to offer code through APIs to improve the middle office link between front and back office, and those APIs and apps are fed through data leverage based on machine learning and artificial intelligence through the cloud.

As a result, the back office is all about analytics, the middle office about APIs and the front office is smart apps for smart devices.

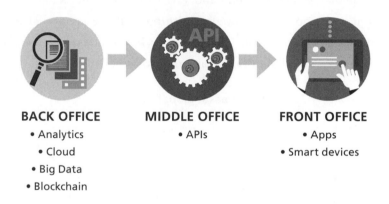

BACK OFFICE
- Analytics
- Cloud
- Big Data
- Blockchain

MIDDLE OFFICE
- APIs

FRONT OFFICE
- Apps
- Smart devices

The banks that can pivot from being monolith, vertically integrated, physically focused structures to microservice, open market, digitally focused structures within the next ten years are the ones that will survive and thrive.

WEB 4.0: THE 2020S AND THE INTERNET OF THINGS

We are already entering the fourth-generation internet, the Internet of Things, but it won't really take off until the 2020s. Sure, we have self-driving Teslas and Nest home appliances, along with Samsung's SmartThings, but none of it is mainstream yet.

This will change though, and it's not just devices on the internet, but a whole raft of technologies from robotics to artificial intelligence to machine learning, combined with IoT, that will make it happen. These technologies are already playing into every aspect of our lives, from street lighting to gene editing, and are transforming our world into a connected smart structure. The idea is that you can place a chip inside anything and make it smart. Smart roads, smart buildings, smart cities, smarter people. In the next decade of the internet, a number of key developments will come into play to start building the Semantic Web, or web 5.0.

In other words, whether we consciously know it or not, we are building a smart planet where everyone and everything will be connected and communicating non-stop. How many things will be connected in this future planet? There are various estimates. For instance, research house IHS Markit estimate 78 billion things communicating by 2025.

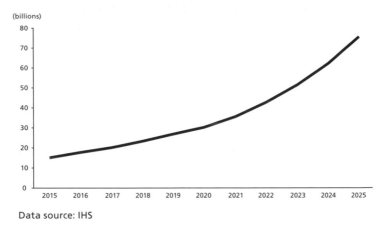

IoT installed base, global market

Data source: IHS

Management consulting firm McKinsey & Co says it will be a multitrillion-dollar market that, after the mobile internet and artificial intelligence, will be the most impactful of all technologies for the next decade.

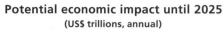

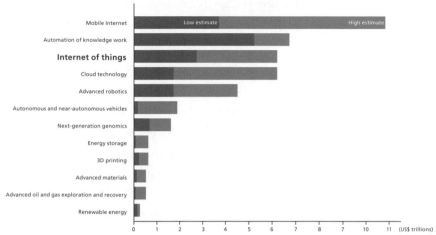

Data source: McKinsey Global Institute analysis

And, if you like that sort of thing, *Forbes* does an annual roundup of what the research firms are thinking about IoT, including headline grabbers like:

- Bain predicts that by 2020 annual revenues could exceed $470 billion for the IoT vendors selling the hardware, software and comprehensive solutions.
- General Electric predicts investment in the Industrial Internet of Things (IoT) is expected to top $60 trillion during the next 15 years.

This is big.

In my own mind, I'm just thinking that I'll have a TV, a car, a fridge, a heating system, a desktop or tablet or both, a mobile, a watch, a health monitor possibly swallowed and inside me, a robot to look after the house, a security system, a dog, children and an automated personal assistant all on the net. That's fifteen things on the net just for me. Then my wife and kids will have a few things, probably at least five each. So, in a typical household in a developed economy, there will be an average of thirty things on the internet.

Bearing in mind we live in a developed economy, there will be smart governments that will roll out a further average five things on the net per person, for instance, security monitors, car sensors on the roads, automated toll systems, tracking services and the like. My household of four people will add another twenty things to the internet, thanks to the government. So, we're looking at a minimum of ten things per person in a developed economy online.

In developing economies and in countries where some of society are excluded or have less inclusion, there will still be a lot of things on the internet supporting them. Definitely a mobile device, but equally government monitoring systems and smarter infrastructure. For the purposes of this book, I am going to be conservative and estimate that two-thirds of Earth's population, which will have risen to eight billion people by 2025, will be using multiple devices on the network. Building on this, we then have the United Nations' aim to increase inclusion by that time—it is one of its sustainable goals—and we could assume that only half the planet will be living in poorer conditions, compared to two-thirds today. That means you have four billion people with an average of five things on the internet monitoring their activities, and four billion with ten things, of which five are for their lifestyle and five are for the government.

That's a minimum of sixty billion things on the internet, and these things are communicating non-stop. The fact that they are communicating means that they have intel inside, and that means they can transact. If sixty billion things are trading and transacting non-stop, 24/7, you're talking trillions of transactions. It wouldn't surprise me if there were billions of things transacting trillions of times a minute in very small amounts, all day long.

What is the financial system that will support that structure of operation and how will it know what things are allowed to transact with which?

You can find the detailed answer in *ValueWeb*. However, this does raise two crucial questions. First, how are machines authorised to trade on behalf of humans? Second, when do the machines need to be kept in check? For example, if my fridge orders twelve bottles of white wine when it usually orders six, is that a mistake? Should it be verified? And how often does the human want to verify what their fridge, or TV, car, house, etc., is doing? Equally, how does the bank know that the fridge, or TV, car, house, etc., belongs to that human, and what they've authorised it to do?

This is something that leads us naturally to a discussion on digital identity ... or does it? To be honest, the more I think about my Internet of Things, the more I think that my things will be wrapped up in a mobile wallet. This is why the Alipay (China), Paytm (India), Vipps (Norway) and Venmo/PayPal (USA) wallets become so key because these wallets can wrap a range of things inside, and aggregate the payments they need to make.

This is the real underlying play by Apple Pay. After all, I have my mobile (iPhone), watch (Apple), TV (Apple TV), car (soon to be a self-driving Apple car) and more. They are all in my Apple account for which they Apple Pay. So what if I were to ask the following question: When you have billions of devices transacting trillions of times a minute in very small amounts, what is the financial system that you'll use to support it?

Stop and think about it. It doesn't have to be blockchain, machine learning, data analytics and cloud—although in the back office, these technologies will create new and dynamic efficiencies. However, if you really want to take away the friction of transacting, then the device aggregators will win, and those device aggregators are already out there doing their thing. By aggregating devices, you can aggregate their transactions and, thereby, allow trillions of transactions amongst billions of devices non-stop, and then bill monthly.

It's such a great yet unrecognised idea that when we do wake up to what these guys are doing, we're going to go wow, just wow.

WEB 5.0: WELCOME TO SAMANTHA

Take this line from the 2013 film *Her*, "It's not just an operating system, it's a consciousness." The film is about Theodore, played by Joaquin Phoenix. Theodore is a lonely writer who gets to trial OS1, the world's first artificially intelligent operating system. OS1 tailors itself to the individual's habits and needs, and is almost alive, as represented by the personality of its voice, Samantha, played by Scarlett Johansson. From IMDb:

> Theodore quickly finds himself drawn in with Samantha, the voice behind his OS1. As they start spending time together they grow closer and closer and eventually find themselves in love. Having fallen in love with his OS, Theodore finds himself dealing with feelings of both great joy and doubt. As an OS, Samantha has powerful intelligence that she uses to help Theodore in ways others hadn't, but how does she help him deal with his inner conflict of being in love with an OS?

Sound silly? Not really. Samantha is likely to appear some time in the next decade and, by the 2030s, will be superintelligent. There are actually three levels of artificial intelligence:

- **Artificial narrow intelligence (ANI):** AI that specialises in one area, such as an AI that can beat the world chess champion in chess, but that's the only thing it does
- **Artificial general intelligence (AGI):** AI that reaches and then passes the intelligence level of a human, meaning it can "reason, plan, solve problems, think abstractly, comprehend complex ideas, learn quickly and learn from experience". This level beats the Turing Test in which scientists are unable to tell the difference between the machine and the human.
- **Artificial super intelligence (ASI):** AI that achieves a level of intelligence smarter than all of humanity combined, "ranging from just a little smarter ... to one trillion times smarter". This

is the era where the machines run the planet and learn from each other, vis-à-vis Skynet in the *Terminator* films.

Intriguingly, in most science-fiction movies, the future is portrayed as scary and dark, as in *The Terminator* and *Ex Machina,* but it is far more nuanced than that. I often look back at history for examples of the future, and see things like the invention of Coca-Cola to relieve people of the fear of fast cycle change:

1886: Coca-Cola is invented by Colonel John Pemberton, who has been injured in the American civil war and developed an addiction to morphine. He decides to invent a tonic to cure him of his habit and comes up with a coca wine – which uses coca leaves (the basis of cocaine) and kola nuts (a source of caffeine) – to cure him. Eventually, Coca-Cola becomes widely available, sold as a medicine at soda fountains across the US, with Pemberton claiming it could cure ailments including impotence, headaches and dyspepsia.[4]

Back in the late 1800s and early 1900s, the fast movement of technology from railways to manufacturing to the appearance of aeroplanes and moving pictures meant that the Victorians and Edwardians greatly feared what was in store for the future. After all, this was the era of H.G. Wells telling stories of alien invasions in *War of the Worlds* and the chilling story of *The Machine Stops* by E.M. Forster. If you haven't read the latter, I recommend you do. Here's a short synopsis:

In a future world, humans live in isolation below ground due to some form of toxic event poisoning the air of Earth. The Machine is a kind of Skype service by which people conduct their only activity, sharing ideas and knowledge. The two main characters, Vashti and her son

---

4   *See* "128 years of Coca-Cola and its many brand extensions," *Campaign*, June 2014.

Kuno, live on opposite sides of the world. Kuno tells Vashti that he has visited the surface of Earth without permission, and without the life support apparatus that is supposedly required to survive in the toxic air, and he saw other humans living outside the world of the Machine. However, the Machine has recaptured him and he has been threatened with "Homelessness", that is, expulsion from the underground environment and sent to the surface of Earth, meaning death by exposure to the outside air.

As time passes, two things happen. First, the life support apparatus, required to visit the world above ground, is abolished. Second, a kind of religion is established in which the Machine is the object of worship. People forget that humans created the Machine, and treat it as a mystical entity whose needs supersede their own. Those who do not accept the deity of the Machine are threatened with Homelessness. Due to humans giving into the Machine, they worship it without further thought, and without maintenance.

I won't say any more except to reiterate the title in the context of having read the above: what happens if the Machine stops?

You see? Scary is the future, is it not?

And yet, when we look back in hindsight, the past is not scary at all. In fact, it seems primitive. What did we do before we had cars? Who lived a life without a mobile phone? What would we do without the Facebook Machine?

So, when I look ahead to see what the internet will look like in twenty years, I cannot be certain but, what is clear, is that it will be a consciousness. It will be all around us, running everything, and with super intelligence built into robots that look like humans and humans who live with robotics inside them.

Some call this the Semantic Web, and it has been forecast for years. The phrase "Semantic Web" was coined by Tim Berners-Lee back in 2001 in an article published by the *Scientific American*, co-authored with James Hendler and Ora Lassila. They defined it as an internet that "will enable machines to comprehend semantic documents and data, not human speech and writings".

Since then, it has become a bucket used by many to describe the web when it wakes up. When the internet is ubiquitous and conscious. Whatever you want to call it, by the 2030s, it is pretty obvious that we will have a networked planet with devices intelligently trading on that network. Where robots have intelligence as good as or, in many cases, better than humans. Where we are travelling as space tourists and where the most likely skills will be creativity and science rather than trading and retail. We will still need to eat and drink, be entertained and operated on but as so many of these needs will be serviced by machines, we will live lives that are much improved in comparison with those who have lived before. It is far more likely that by this period, we will have automated most menial tasks as well as many of those that currently require cognitive skills, such as brokers and traders.

What will we be doing? Well, I've already tried to answer some of those questions in the opening chapter: repairing robots, creating next-generation systems, curing the world's ills and servicing our spacecraft. It all sounds like science fiction but, as I so often repeat, a lot of science fiction becomes science fact. In fact, the reason why Victorians wrote scary books about a future dystopia is the same reason why we make scary movies about a future dystopia today. Because it sells. It sells because people are frightened of change, and the future is always changing.

THE RISE OF PLATFORMS AND MARKETPLACES

As mentioned, we are currently experiencing the rise of Open Banking and open marketplaces. However, it is the rise of the platform marketplace, illustrated well by this slide, that charts the change in the world's largest companies over the last fifteen years.

Top 5 publicly traded companies by market cap
(Tech companies in bold)

	2001		2006		2011		2016	
#1	GE	$406B	ExxonMobil	$446B	ExxonMobil	$406B	**Apple**	**$582B**
#2	**Microsoft**	**$365B**	GE	$383B	**Apple**	**$376B**	**Alphabet**	**$556B**
#3	ExxonMobil	$272B	Total	$327B	PetroChina	$277B	**Microsoft**	**$452B**
#4	Citigroup	$261B	**Microsoft**	**$293B**	Shell	$237B	**Amazon**	**$364B**
#5	Walmart	$260B	Citigroup	$273B	ICBC	$228B	**Facebook**	**$359B**

Data source: Visual Capitalist

As you can see, companies focused on the internet and providing marketplaces that connect people are now far more valued than their industrial era predecessors. A book that tracks this change well is *Platform Revolution* by Geoffrey G. Parker, Marshall W. Van Alstyne and Sangeet Paul Choudary. I saw Geoffrey Parker present the summary of the book at a recent conference, where this slide was particularly impactful:

FIRM	ESTABLISHED	EMPLOYEES	MKT CAP
BMW	1916	116,000	$53B
UBER	2009	7,000	$60B
MARRIOT	1927	200,000	$17B
AIRBNB	2008	5,000	$21B
WALT DISNEY	1923	185,000	$165B
FACEBOOK	2004	12,691	$315B
KODAK	1888	145,000	$30B (peak)
INSTAGRAM	2010	13	$1B (acquired)

Data source: Geoffrey Parker, September 2016

The statement is clear: monolith firms are industrial age; platform firms are digital age. It also clearly shows the difference in focus. Monolith firms are heavy-lifting physical assets; platform firms provide open markets. This is why the industrial age firms have hundreds of thousands of employees to generate their market capitalisation whilst platform firms have just a few thousand. After all, an open marketplace has thousands of other people doing the work to buy and sell on your platform. In contrast, monolith firms do it all themselves.

This is almost like an aha moment as, when I look at banks, they are monolith firms. Built for the industrial age, they like to control everything internally. They do everything themselves. Banks are A-grade control freaks. The idea of opening up to all and sundry in a marketplace is like an enema to them, but they will have to do this to survive in the digital age. This point really strikes home when you think about today's financial world.

Today's world is one where one PayPal is worth three Deutsche Banks …

PayPal Holdings, Inc. (PYPL)
39.88 -0.30 (0.75%) 7 Oct 21:00

Prev Close	40.18	Day's Range	39.62 – 40.42
Open	40.36	52wk Range	30.52 – 41.75
Bid	39.51 x 100	Volume	6,109,946
Ask	41.15 x 200	Avg Vol (3m)	8,383,970
1y Target Est.	44.26	Market Cap	48.13bn
Beta	N/A	P/E (ttm)	36.25
Next Earnings Date	20-Oct-16	EPS (ttm)	1.10

Deutsche Bank AG (DBK.DE)
12.09 +0.06 (0.46%) 7 Oct 16:35

Prev Close	12.04	Day's Range	11.96 – 12.31
Open	12.11	52wk Range	9.90 – 27.98
Bid	N/A x 555100	Volume	16,415,749
Ask	N/A x 230000	Avg Vol (3m)	14,405,900
1y Target Est.	N/A	Market Cap	16.53bn
Beta	N/A	P/E (ttm)	N/A
Next Earnings Date	N/A	EPS (ttm)	-5.90

Data sources: NasdaqGS; Xetra

… where Ant Financial is one of the largest financial firms in the world (valuation $60 billion) and where Stripe has risen from nowhere to be a challenger. Using Geoffrey Parker's chart, you can see the stark contrast:

Market capitalisations based on figures from 14 October 2016

FIRM	ESTABLISHED	EMPLOYEES	MKT CAP
BARCLAYS BANK	1692	130,000	$30B
PAYPAL	1999	13,000	$48B
DEUTSCHE BANK	1870	101,000	$17B
ANT FINANCIAL	2015	5,000	$60B
STRIPE	2011	400	$9.2B
JPM CHASE	1799	235,000	$245B

Data source: Geoffrey Parker

The only standout bank is the world's most valuable bank, JPMorgan Chase. Its market capitalisation of $245 billion is pretty impressive. But let's set that against Stripe, a seven-year-old company at the time of publication. Stripe was valued at $5 billion in 2015 but has grown up a lot more since then. It has expanded into Asia and gained investment from Sumitomo Mitsui, the largest Japanese credit card provider. Based on that development, its valuation almost doubled within a year to $9.2 billion. After five years, Stripe's staff of 400 was generating $22 million of value per employee. JPMorgan's 219-year history (est. 1799) and 235,000 employees has given it the ability, as the most valuable bank in the world, to generate just over $1 million in value per employee.

Now some cynics will be sitting back and thinking, Chris is quoting wildly overrated unicorn figures to make a point that banking is dead. However, they are wrong. I'm not saying that banking is dead. I'm merely pointing out that something has changed and if banks can't turn into open marketplaces, they will not survive. The above charts make that clear. If any bank CEO is holding back, believing that the heady days of monolith structures still work, they need to see these charts.

BUILDING THE NEW FINANCIAL MARKETPLACE

If we are building a new marketplace for money, who are the new competitors? Are they the upstart FinTech start-ups or are they Google, Amazon and brethren?

The answer is it's both. I wouldn't worry about Google, Amazon and co as much though because they are attacking banks in a very different space to the way in which the FinTech start-ups are. The start-ups are attacking narrow finance and trying to replace core bank functions like credit and payments with new capabilities. The TransferWise and Lending Club business models should worry banks. I'm not so sure about the others. Yes, they're big and cool but what is their space? Processing.

Now consider this quote, which is often cited in meetings and presentations, from TechCrunch:

> Uber, the world's largest taxi company, owns no vehicles. Facebook, the world's most popular media owner, creates no content. Alibaba, the most valuable retailer, has no inventory. And Airbnb, the world's largest accommodation provider, owns no real estate. Something interesting is happening.[5]

---

5   Tom Goodwin, "The Battle Is For The Customer Interface," TechCrunch, 3 March 2015.

Something very interesting is happening. It's called infomediation, and we've seen it coming for years. We just wonder why we aren't doing it for ourselves.

If you take my business model chart, which I mentioned in the previous chapter, the Ubers, Facebooks and Alibabas are all operationally excellent processing houses. They have no product or service themselves and, if you think about it, they have no customer relationship either. They just have a great ability to connect those who need with those who have in real time.

- I need to get from A to B—connect me with someone who has a car to drive me.
- I need to stay overnight in this place—connect me with someone who has a spare bedroom to sleep in.
- I need to share my social life—connect me with all my friends and family who might be interested in it.

The same applies to Amazon and Google.

- I need to buy some stuff—connect me with the lowest cost provider and get it delivered.
- I need to find some stuff—connect with the information I need.

In other words, all of these great new companies are infomediating the content—cars, beds, photos and updates, products and information—with the context—the app in my hand or the page that I'm browsing from wherever I am. Their processing is recognising our context and delivering the content.

If I were to draw a chart for the new world of infomediation that we admire (the Ubers, Airbnbs, Facebooks, Amazons and Googles), it would look like this:

	BACK OFFICE	MIDDLE OFFICE	FRONT OFFICE
PERSONAL TRANSPORT	Vehicles	**Uber**	Uber app, drivers
ACCOMMODATION	Properties	**Airbnb**	Airbnb app, hosts
SOCIAL LIFE	Media	**Facebook**	Facebook app
SEARCH	Web content	**Google**	Google search
COMMERCE	Books, etc.	**Amazon**	Kindle, etc.

This leads me to the following question: what is the processing machine for banking and what is the role of banks around that machine?

It's a great question as, historically, the processing engine for the financial system has been SWIFT, Visa, MasterCard, TARGET2, STEP2, Fedwire, CHIPS, BACS and more. Now this is not going to disappear fast, if at all, but there is a new marketplace structure appearing. Originally, I would have said it was PayPal, as it has removed the friction of paying digitally, but it's not PayPal. PayPal is good but … it hasn't changed anything.

Then it came to me. The reason why we're so excited about the Internet of Value is that the blockchain is our new processing engine. The blockchain can infomediate the financial system to deliver our processing engine for value exchange: I want to exchange value—connect me with the right value tokens and value stores to exchange. The thing is that the blockchain is not the engine. It's the technology. So right now, there's an open ground for something, someone or some firm to own that space.

YOUR CFO IS AN ALGORITHM

What is a CFO? Today, it stands for a chief financial officer. OK, that's what the acronym means but why do we have them? Ah yes, they are there to manage our suppliers and customers, do our billings and receivables, manage our working capital and supply chain, deal with foreign exchange and cash pooling and all that stuff. Admin, in other words. Admin.

Even the word "admin", short for "administration", is pretty contemptible in a world being eaten by software. Why are we doing admin when everything can be automated? This thought occurred to me when talking to some bright young CEOs who manage their whole companies' books through Xero. They call Xero their digital finance officer, or DFO. The DFO is an algorithm presented as an API that automates everything. And there's the bottom line. I don't need a CFO when their function can be automated.

I know some people will say that this is greatly oversimplifying the complexity of the treasury, accounts and CFO role, but is it? If I could put all of my bills of lading, letters of credit, purchase orders and receivables in a shared ledger connected through APIs to intelligent algorithms that can reconcile and recognise everything, is it really so unimaginable that my CFO could become a DFO? Maybe. However, I have dealt with some of the biggest firms in the world that all have hundreds of thousands of suppliers. So yes, it is tough if you scale.

Three decades ago, companies were radically changing their financial processes for efficiency, and we can go further today. We can reduce financial departments to an API and an algorithm. In other words, the CFO becomes an algorithm presented as an API.

The only issue with this is that businesses cannot imagine such an operation. This is, in part, a two-fold dilemma. The first part of the dilemma is to imagine the complete treasury operation moved into a digital ledger. It can be done, but the idea of not having someone accountable for the processes of billings and receivables, payables and invoicing, just seems wrong. This mentality that we need humans to manage these financial processes dates back to the industrial age and remains strong today.

Even if we can overcome our industrial era thinking that humans need to manage financial processes, we have the second issue of mass redundancies. A CFO today in a large company may be sitting on top of a heap of underlings that count into the hundreds or even thousands. Any CFO, when challenged, will justify having so many people by the complexity of the tasks they do. They are necessary.

The reality is that they are not, but the CFO's ego will not allow the CEO and executive leadership team to undermine their empire. It has taken them a long time to get to that position of CFO. Now that they are there, they have an empire. The empire is sizeable and reinforces the stature and power of this role. To even challenge that role's importance and beg the question "Do you really need so many underlings?" will beg defiance.

So, beware when you ask the CFO to automate everything and move it along to a shared ledger. When you challenge their empire, sometimes the empire strikes back.

THE BANKING BAZAAR AND THE BIZARRE BANKER

A growing number of financial marketplaces are appearing: lending marketplaces, credit marketplaces, payments marketplaces and more. Consider a marketplace to be the bazaar. Market stallholders gather to meet with prospective clients, and the digital version of the marketplace is the focal point for many FinTech start-ups because they can create stalls here that become major technology businesses like Stripe and Square. Banks have to think differently. Banks have the regulatory licence to be marketplace owners, enabling them to create the spaces for the new players and start-ups to move into. As a marketplace owner, the bank does not provide all the products and does not run the stalls. It just owns the space where a stallholder offers their goods and services and they can charge the market stallholder a fee to be in their space. It's a good space to be.

Over time, as banks open source their operations to move to a microservice architecture[6], they will recognise that the primary opportunity

---

6   For those of you who are unaware of this system, here's an explanation from Wikipedia: Microservices are a more concrete and modern interpretation of service-oriented architecture (SOA). As in SOA, services in a microservice architecture (MSA) are processes that communicate with each other over a network in order to fulfill a goal. Also, as in SOA, these

today, thanks to their licence, is to create the FinTech marketplaces and own them. Lots of partners sell services in their market to the banks' customers and, equally, banks can sell lots of services to the market stallholders and their customers. It's a win-win situation.

The problem is that very few banks see the world this way today. Most of the banks I meet are locked into internal structures that are proprietary and legacy. They want to keep it that way. They want their customers locked into an end-to-end delivery of mediocre digital services in a monolith structure. They want to lock out any third parties, most of whom are not trusted even if the regulator believes the opposite.

The banks that fall into this unimaginative camp are the ones that will fail. You cannot have a proprietary, vertically integrated player in an open marketplace of platforms linked through APIs in a value exchange ecosystem. What it means is that the banks that offer marketplaces will attract many different players to operate in their space. The banks that try to lock out the third parties and play by themselves will do just that. They will just be playing with themselves. Over time, demand will naturally evolve to open markets based on plug-and-play structures of interoperability. An old legacy proprietary player who does not offer platforms that work in open markets will wither and die.

Right now, there are few players in the open bazaar of financial marketplaces offering a level playing field of platforms and interoperability. I can name only a couple of banks, specifically PrivatBank and Saxo Bank. I can name more new entrant banks that are in this space, such as Fidor TecS and solarisBank. Then there are the FinTech start-ups moving into this

---

services use technology-agnostic protocols. Microservices' architectural style is a first realisation of SOA that has happened after the introduction of DevOps, and this is becoming the standard for building continuously deployed systems. Unlike SOA, microservices services are small and the protocols lightweight. The benefit of distributing different responsibilities of the system into different smaller services is that it enhances the cohesion and decreases the coupling. This makes it much easier to change and add functions and qualities to the system at any time. It also allows the architecture of an individual service to emerge through continuous refactoring, and hence reduces the need for a big up-front design and allows for releasing software early and continuously.

area, such as Thought Machine and Leveris. These are all players who are building technology marketplaces to provide interoperable apps, analytics, APIs and more as platforms for both the bank and third parties who engage in their communities. They are different. They understand the orchestra and how to be a conductor.

Then I visit some of the more traditional institutions, and they huff and they puff and they frown and they sigh and they say, "This is not for us." They have thousands of developers and they want to keep their customers locked in to their legacy ways. Hmm ...

When I go to their management team and explain this idea to them, they throw me out. Their management team are bankers, trained in compliance and audit and risk and accounts. They can see that this idea will wipe out profitable product and revenue streams and give others, namely third parties, the opportunity to steal their customer relationships.

Well, it's their loss. After all, a bank that has zero technology vision, zero understanding of microservice architectures, zero appetite for open sourcing and zero knowledge of platforms and marketplaces has zero future.

BUILD OR BUY OR BUILD AND DIE?

Historically, banks have wanted to control all of their systems internally. Their biggest question has always been whether to build or buy their systems, and often they chose to build them. This is why many banks have larger systems development departments than the biggest software companies in the world.

This will have to change under Open Banking. Banks will have to turn into a collaborative and partnering structure where much of the banks' systems are sourced via APIs with third parties. A collaborative and partnering culture, however, is hard for a bank that has historically been a control freak.

This was well illustrated by a chat I had with a banking buddy who was frustrated with the bank's Payment Services Directive (PSD2) developments.

These developments were required following the implementation of a European law in 2018, which forces the banks to offer their customers' payment details to third parties via APIs. This banker was irritated that it was not going the way he wanted. He had found a nice little FinTech start-up with a great open API capability that could be used by the bank within days. However, the head office retentive told him that they didn't want to work with a third party and would instead have to develop it themselves.

This is the mentality of a lot of banks. They don't trust third parties to develop capabilities because they have always done it themselves. A lot of this is down to the complexity of their systems, they say. That the bank cannot risk third parties getting it wrong, they say. That regulators would not allow the bank to outsource such critical processing capabilities, they say.

I say it's because they are control freaks, stuck in the last century and not able see their way out into an open-sourced world of apps, APIs and analytics. My banking buddy agreed, although I was, of course, pandering to his frustrations.

The way I see it is that this Build or Buy discussion is more like Build and Die. It is already obvious that a thousand FinTech start-ups are focusing on doing one thing really well. Then they develop and code that one thing well to hell and back, and continually update and add capability to remain relevant. In contrast, a bank does a thousand things averagely, much of it fragmented by ageing systems and the limited use of today's technologies or capabilities. Why would I want to work with an organisation that does a thousand things averagely when I can work with a thousand companies doing one thing well?

The answer to that is time. I don't have the time to work with a thousand companies. I want one company to rule them all and, in the ideal world, that one company should be a bank with a bank licence as that then insures my money in a trusted value store. Some banks are waking up to this open marketplace opportunity and they see their future role as a curator of a thousand apps and APIs. Their data is cleansed in an enterprise data architecture, then analysed in the cloud by machines that learn and have intelligence about the data to proactively, predictively and cognitively service that data into their thousand curated apps and APIs. This is my vision of a Semantic Bank.

The reality is somewhat different. Research found that banks believe they are two-thirds along their digitalisation path while the research team felt that they weren't even a quarter of the way through the journey. The difference, as one banker pointed out, is that many banks think their digitalisation path is rolling out a decent mobile app; they don't see the wider picture of changing the organisation.

This was described as Digital 1.0 versus Digital 2.0. 1.0 is the accessorisation of the bank with apps and API, but no core change to the foundation of the bank. 2.0 is the digitalisation of the bank across the whole enterprise, with core change of structure and people. Few banks have started 2.0, but many are well into 1.0.

So how will we know when the bank's digital transformation is complete? My view of the end-game is an open-sourced structure of front-office apps, middle-office APIs and back-office analytics that allow you to select services from a marketplace of thousands of technology companies doing one thing well, curated by the bank to give the best and most differentiated customer experience. This bank will curate components, integrate them through APIs and provide the aggregated customer delivery at the front end.

The issue with most banks is that they think it's all sorted out simply by having an app and a chief digital officer. I meet many chief digital officers in many banks, and there is often more than one of them. There's a chief digital officer for payments and another one for retail and another one for corporate banking and another one for wealth management and another one, and another one, and another one. Banks structured this way are accessorising their products with digital, but not changing the bank or its thinking one iota. This is obvious as the bank is just adding digital to products and functions, but without changing the bank structure at all.

A bank that is truly into their digital journey would never build anything, but would curate everything. There are very few of them out there, but they are starting to appear. Give it five to ten years, and all banks will play that way … or disappear somewhere along the way.

HOW DOES A FINANCIAL CURATOR MAKE MONEY?

Often when I talk about banks having to move from being control freaks in a proprietary operation building everything themselves, to becoming collaborative partners in an open marketplace curating everything, I'm asked, "How do you make money out of curation?"

It's a good question as marketplace curators make money very differently from proprietary product providers. This is why a bank's thinking has to change. I often say that banks in ten years will make zero profit from the products they provide today. Today, retail banks make money from the margin on savings and loans, from cross-selling to deposit account holders and from fees and charges for overdrafts and borrowings. This will disappear in the next decade as traditional revenue streams are squeezed by specialist digital providers of these products and services.

A good example of this squeeze is Zopa. Founded in 2005, Zopa is expanding its footprint into full service banking as it is applying for a full banking licence. Right now, it is the most mature peer-to-peer lender in the world—it was actually the first—and provides a significant amount of UK lending. In February 2016, Zopa blogged:

> Zopa lent £530 million in 2015, and has now lent over £1.2 billion in total. By loan volume we are the largest peer-to-peer lender in the UK and in August 2015 we became the first UK P2P lender to reach the £1 billion lent milestone.[7]

Today, its website states that it has lent more than £2.38 billion to UK consumers. Zopa is doubling its lending year-on-year, and the peer-to-peer

---

7   "Record growth for peer-to-peer lending in 2015," *Zopa* (blog), 1 February 2016, https://blog. zopa.com/2016/02/01/record-growth-for-peer-to-peer-lending-in-2015/.

loans market in the United Kingdom is growing rapidly with cumulative levels of lending at almost £8.5 billion, originating in excess of £1 billion during the first three months of 2017. Considering that unsecured borrowing in the country increased by £23 billion in 2016, peer-to-peer lenders are starting to make major inroads into this traditionally core market for banks, nearing a 20 per cent market share.

If roboadvisors, peer-to-peer lenders and payments-focused start-ups take the margin from all of these traditional core banking areas, how will banks make money? They won't make money from their traditional products. As mentioned, if banks make no money from their current products and services, how will they make money? From curation. However, the core of their curation structure will involve two key components.

First, the bank has millions of customers, billions of capital and centuries of history. By recognising that the bank has this strength of position today and that it may lose this position tomorrow, the bank has to rapidly pivot from being an integrated vertical value chain of tightly coupled proprietary products to an open marketplace platform of loosely coupled partners.

However, if a bank can do this, it becomes the curator of choice for its customers. A customer does not want to select from hundreds of start-up companies that they know nothing about. They want their trusted bank partner to do it for them. After all, the bank has the history and trust to select these partners and, of course, it can charge a premium for curating these partners on behalf of its customers. That's what Amazon does. The tough ask for a bank to change is illustrated well by the Amazon versus WalMart war.

Walmart was also hesitant to let outside sellers list their wares on Walmart.com. This "marketplace" idea generates half of Amazon's unit sales. It also creates a prodigious amount of unseen internal conflict, since Amazon employees have to compete with third-party sellers who are pursuing the same buyers. But the company tolerates and even encourages the tension because choice and price competition are good for customers. WalMart, accustomed to dominating its relationship with brands and showing its entire assortment in its massive stores, was reluctant to foster such competition, and it didn't have the technological chops to support an expansive marketplace. Instead of focusing on increasing online selection, WalMart kept building supercentres—more than 700 from 2010 to 2016 in the U.S. alone. Walmart.com only started adding third-party sellers in 2015, and though it now has more than 40 million products in its marketplace—Toms canvas shoes, Rebecca Minkoff satchels, and other stuff it doesn't sell in stores—the number is small compared with the 350 million or so items available on Amazon.[8]

This is the denial process that many banks are caught up in. They continue to invest in super branches and bells and whistles on their internally built apps instead of encouraging co-creation and curation of pedigree partners. There is a limited time to move into this process, however. As Zopa and its brethren won't want to partner with every bank, the curation and co-creation process to move from a controlled value chain bank to an open financial marketplace platform is limited. This is one critical change to banks and bank culture.

For a bank that gets the co-creation and curation culture, the second component is making money. If no money is made from traditional products and services, as credit and savings and investment moves to the co-creation partners, then a bank has to make money from new capabilities and services. This will be by a strategy of using machine learning about its customers' financial lifestyle and habits to gain a far deeper knowledge of their customers, integrating financial data with contextual and social data.

In this case, a bank has to become a much better advisor and analytical firm, knowing more about its customers' needs by being a cognitively active

---

8   Stone, Brad and Matthew Boyle, "Can Wal-Mart's Expensive New E-Commerce Operation Compete With Amazon?" Bloomberg, 4 May 2017.

partner with the customer, predictively and proactively supporting their needs and recommending partners in context. The fact that the bank could provide incredibly personalised digital advice and support is something customers would pay for; the same applies to its value-adding information services about the customers' financial lifestyle.

I guess I'm describing a radically different beast to today's financial services firms. Tomorrow's big financial firms will offer their own products and services in open competition with third-party products and services on their own platforms to their own customers. They will win customers' business by being the preferred provider through their trust, service and convenience, or will lose business based on price, cost and appropriateness. However, as any marketplace platform firm knows, even when you lose, you win because you have the customers' trust in your platform above all others, thanks to your deep data analytics and knowledge of their needs.

THE FUTURE BUSINESS MODEL IS CLEAR

For many years, I have used *The Discipline of Market Leaders* by Michael Treacy and Fred Wiersema to talk about the business model of banking. According to Treacy and Wiersema, all companies comprise three major components: a manufacturer, a processor and a retailer. The book claims that most companies are only good at one of these things, and few are good at two let alone all three. Apple is probably one of the few that do succeed at all three, but even this company fails on occasion (note recent iOS updates).

Some time ago, my thinking moved along a little bit, in that I realised that banks talk about front, middle and back office. Front, middle and back office are the same as the authors' retailer, processor and manufacturer, but just in a different parlance.

You may recognise the following diagram from an earlier chapter that discussed the business model of Open Banking.

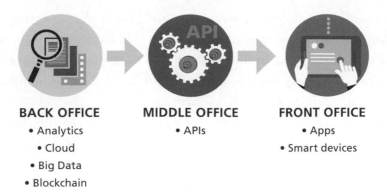

BACK OFFICE
- Analytics
- Cloud
- Big Data
- Blockchain

MIDDLE OFFICE
- APIs

FRONT OFFICE
- Apps
- Smart devices

This outline business model of Open Banking is useful when considering any project. For example, I have been a proponent of business transformation for many years. The method of transforming is to map out the key customer interactions and build the business based around that customer-centricity. This structured view of the customer-focused organisation would then be built around the key principles of people, process and product. Again, I realised recently that the focal point of building a business by defining the people, process and product structures also fits back into the retail, processing and manufacturing view of a company. A company, and a bank in particular, is built based on people, processes and products in the front, middle and back office.

BACK OFFICE
Products

MIDDLE OFFICE
Processes

FRONT OFFICE
People

People sometimes talk about products, platforms and experiences. Again, it's just a different way of referring to the same back, middle and front office. The back office is all about product and service innovations, the middle office is all about the platform infrastructure that connects the back and front office for processing transactions and interactions while the front office is all about customer intimacy and the user experience. No matter how you word it, this is how it works.

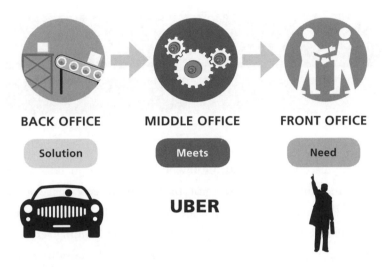

The critical aspect of this dialogue is that the middle office is now where the action is, as it moves from physical to digital. Digital platforms providing open-sourced infrastructure to connect those who need something with those who have something is the way in which P2P works. eBay, Zopa, Prosper, Uber and more are all about connecting front and back office—needs and solutions—in real time. That is the platform revolution we are experiencing and it is seriously changing the game.

THE BURNING PLATFORM

There is a burning platform in all banks, and it's called the legacy system. The following chart illustrates my point perfectly.

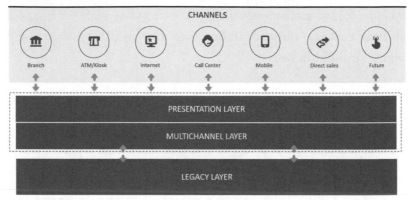

© Chris Skinner

I actually used this chart during my NCR days back in 1997 to sell the concept of the multichannel integrator. Back then, the emergence of internet banking caused an issue so we offered the multichannel integrator to overcome the issue. The issue was that banks offering internet banking services were worried about exposing their legacy core systems to the customer, thus the multichannel integrator was a great way to hide the problem.

In other words, twenty years ago, we knew that the systems we had implemented twenty years earlier were a problem. Twenty years later, it's an even bigger problem. Twenty years later, we are still offering those presentation layers to stick lipstick on that legacy pig.

That's how I know it's a burning platform because, for every year that passes, more fuel is added to the embers that were first ignited with the emergence of internet banking. Mobile banking; digital reach; new open platforms; blockchain, cloud and APIs; machine learning, apps and analytics; and more. All of these open, internet-based technologies have been attacking that proprietary internal legacy, and the longer it goes on, the hotter the problem gets.

Give it another five to ten years, and a bank will be uncompetitive technologically in an open marketplace where all of its competition and the start-ups that are taking the friction out of banking will be offering agile, microservice innovations whilst the legacy bank system will be holding the bank back. I liken it to a slow death through inertia.

Of course, this is avoidable if the bank starts to change today. However, bearing in mind a data rationalisation and core systems upgrade programme takes about five years to complete, this burning issue is getting hotter and hotter every day. There is a bright future for those out there willing to engage but there's also going to be a lot of dead banks for those that do not.

WHAT A LOAD OF COBOLX

I was inspired to think more about the legacy challenge in the legacy economies when I read an article[9] by the inimitable Anna Irrera. She was lamenting the state of U.S. bank systems and how they are hiring retired programmers just to keep the lights on. What really struck me were the charts.

Average age of COBOL developers

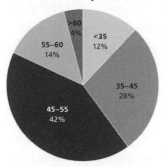

43% of banking systems are built on COBOL

80% of in-person transactions use COBOL

95% of ATM swipes rely on COBOL code

220 billion lines of COBOL are in use today

Data sources: Reuters; TIOBE Index; International Cobol Survey Report; IBM; Microfocus; Celent; Accenture

---

9   Anna Irrera, "Banks scramble to fix old systems as IT 'cowboys' ride into sunset," Reuters, 10 April 2017.

That's real COBOLx.

Financial consulting firm Celent estimates that 75 per cent or more of the $200 billion spent by banks on IT is to maintain legacy systems. The Royal Bank of Scotland (RBS), which paid a record fine to regulators for a big systems outage in 2012, hoped to solve its problems by replacing its core-processing engine at a cost of £750 million. However CEO Ross McEwan conceded three years later that there was still a big job to be done to reduce the number of systems and applications at RBS from *more than 3,000*.

In a related comment, Andrea Orcel, global head of UBS's investment banking division, has said, "The challenge for most banks is that they are not technologists … As technology continues to evolve at a fast pace, becoming ever more critical to their business, they are having to navigate a space that is both highly complex, and does not play to their core competencies." Really? I know I've made this point often but banks are run by bankers when they really should be balanced with technologists, as they are in FinTech firms.

Anyway, this legacy thing is only going to get worse and worse if, for no other reason, than the fact that the people who are maintaining the systems are dying of old age. This is not a new phenomenon. Back in 2012, *Computerworld* conducted a survey and found that 46 per cent of the IT professionals interviewed thought that there was a rising COBOL (common business-oriented language) programming shortage while 50 per cent said that the average age of their COBOL people was forty-five years and above.

So why are we still stuck with almost half the mainframe systems locked into COBOL? This very question appears on Quora. I'm tempted to reproduce all of the answers here but, for obvious reasons, can't. All I will underline is that the fifty years of sunk cost in COBOL spaghetti is the biggest challenge for banks today as they open source their structures. The banks that are moving to an enterprise data architecture that is cloud-based, rationalised and consolidated at the back end will survive. The ones that believe they can stay on those stable and reliable COBOL systems will die.

LEGACY PEOPLE IS WHY WE USE LEGACY SYSTEMS

The problem isn't just the legacy system. It's the legacy people and legacy customer. The legacy people are the ones who sit in the organisation and resist change. They know where their cheese is and they don't want it to move. They also sit and look at new technology and wonder how they can apply it to existing processes. For example, the bank that has built a great virtual branch for Oculus Rift. Yes, a bank can augment a customer's reality but if, in reality, that customer never visits a bank branch, why would they want to do so in virtual reality?

These legacy barriers to change and legacy thinkers are the reasons for creating faster horses rather than inventing new forms of transportation. Go and ask the legacy customer what they want, for example. While the answers may vary, they would most likely include lower fees, better interest rates and being made to feel special. OK, that's what all the challenger banks are focused on, but customers don't think outside the box. They think inside. This is why you have banks that have delivered innovative apps, easy payments and fee-free accounts, but customers are still using internet banking (as they don't trust mobile apps), cheques (as they're easier than that PayPal thingy) and passbooks (well, it worked in the past and I like to see my balance).

It may sound ridiculous but show me one mainstream bank that has got rid of anything from the past. If they had branches, they still have them (but maybe a few less); if they try to get rid of cheques, the outcry is so huge that they still issue cheque books; and if they try to stop customers using a particular service, such as shutting a branch, the press likens that bank to Lord Voldemort from *Harry Potter*. Banks get no glory for innovating, especially if it means that they tell their customers that they can no longer do something. The result is that we have a legacy bank with legacy people looking after legacy customers.

Here is another reason for not changing legacy core systems. Does the fact that the bank has a *fifty*-year-old core mean that it is losing customers, cannot compete effectively or is being exposed to cyber security issues? No.

So why change them? If the customer is indifferent as to which system is being used and there are no problems in processing and operations, why should they be changed? What's the compelling reason to replace a fifty-year-old core system?

For some, there is no compelling reason because replacing the core system is a big ask. Bear in mind that the system we are talking about was probably an upgrade in the mid-1970s to the core customer deposit account system in order to accommodate the introduction of ATMs. It was a batch update, punch card system that, over the years, was upgraded and improved. It could cater for more than just branch needs and ended up providing real-time feeds into internet banking balances through middleware interfaces. This meant that 25 years after its introduction, the system resided at the heart of the balance updates for millions of customer accounts and had a complex arrangement of interfaces and accessories that allowed it to look pretty good, even though the bank knew it was archaic. It worked, it wasn't broken, so why change it?

The bank goes through this logic every year during its strategic technology review, and the answer is always the same. Not just the core system but *everything* that interfaces to it would need to be replaced. That's because the mid-1970s' system has had so much built up around it, thus changing the system would involve a wholesale replacement of everything. Doing so would cost billions and there's no compelling reason to change it as it still does the job. So yet another decade goes by, and the same argument still stands up. Yes, it's expensive to maintain the old balance system, but it's far cheaper and poses less risk to keep it running than to change it.

Unfortunately, something then happens. The world of technology moves on a pace. What was all locked into simple front-end interfaces to a back end that does the job becomes far more demanding. Customers want apps, partners want APIs and competitors are moving from in-house proprietary structures to open platforms through the cloud. The competition is getting more personal through data analytics and machine learning. They are also lowering costs by getting rid of their old core system and moving to modern internet-age architectures. However, the bank's little old system in the corner still does its job so there's no reason to change it, is there?

I guess this is where my core argument for the imperative to replace the core system really comes into play. We have moved into an internet age of open-sourced finance and the business model, architecture and infrastructure must change to keep up. With the key message that, for the first time, new technologies are eating into our back-office core systems.

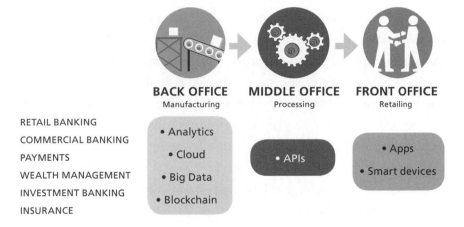

BACK OFFICE
Manufacturing

MIDDLE OFFICE
Processing

FRONT OFFICE
Retailing

RETAIL BANKING
COMMERCIAL BANKING
PAYMENTS
WEALTH MANAGEMENT
INVESTMENT BANKING
INSURANCE

• Analytics
• Cloud
• Big Data
• Blockchain

• APIs

• Apps
• Smart devices

Some banks, however, will still follow the view that this does not create an urgent or compelling need to upgrade a fifty-year-old core system. However, sooner or later, the regulator will force them to upgrade their systems as banks will be required to provide real-time connectivity to their oversight services using APIs and offer third-party connectivity to their customer balances. And what about their costs? Their costs seem to be higher than everyone else's. Not to worry, they can sneak that along into their overdraft fees and credit charges, but maybe their legacy customer might spot this. Only then will these banks acknowledge that they need to change their ageing core systems but, by waiting until the last possible moment, they may have left it too late.

The challenges faced by deeply rooted, centuries-old banks are obvious. First, they have to recognise they have a problem. Second, they have to do something about the problem. Third, they have to recognise that the problem needs a grass-roots transformation, not just a little bit of pizzazz. Finally, it takes guts, hard decision-making and strong leadership to shift the problem of old systems and a frozen middle management team.

I always remember a statement from a Tom Peter's video twenty years ago about business transformation in Union Pacific Railroads in the United States. One of the team said, "The organisation either wears you out or waits you out." This is so true. However, if banks can get leaders who are unwilling to let those choices pervade, then they might just create a third choice to create an organisation that wrestles the bank out of that legacy thinking and creates a transformation fit for the 21st century.

Above all, my experience has shown that the only reason why a bank doesn't change its ageing core system is because the CEO believes he or she will be at the helm for only another two to three years. As a result, they leave the risk and cost of a major change for their successor. That is why core systems reach such a grand old age. Each generation of management just wants to pass the buck on to the next generation. That attitude has worked for thirty years but, believe me, it doesn't work in this age of open-sourced financial interchange.

DO WE REALLY NEED TO RIP UP THE ROADS?

Let's compare FinTech with transportation, and the idea that just because FinTech comes up with the idea of a self-driving car, it does not mean that we have to rip up the roads, does it? No. The transportation system has a huge amount of infrastructure in place ranging from major roads and highways to railways and airports. Just because technology reinvents the idea of a car, train or aeroplane, it does not mean that we need to reconstruct the entire road, rail and airport infrastructure. They just run on the existing infrastructure in a more effective manner. It is then down to the existing manufacturers of cars, trains and planes to work out if they can keep up with the innovations that the new players are bringing to market. That is why GM, Ford and BMW are talking all the time about the threat of Tesla, Google and Apple. As self-driving cars take over the market, the old-timers will scramble to keep up and see if they can also offer a decent version with all the bells and whistles.

Take that back to FinTech. Most FinTech firms are creating new versions of payments, transactions, value exchange and value store. Some are very specific while others are highly innovative, but none of them are making us rip up the roads. In fact, nearly all are running on the roads, railways and airports that were built by the banking system. They may be forcing the banks to upgrade those systems, as in the distributed ledger projects under way in clearing and settlement and payments, but a radical reconstruction and rebuild of the whole network is unnecessary.

When I look at FinTech firms, they fall into a range of categories. Most are supplementing the existing financial system by making the things that work badly easier, vis-à-vis merchant checkout online via Stripe or paying friends for small transactions via Venmo, or reaching parts of the world that the banks cannot reach, vis-à-vis Square for small businesses or M-Pesa and mobile wallets in sub-Saharan Africa.

Where banks have core business, the FinTech start-ups struggle. In fact, there was a great report on Bloomberg, which made the contention that any challenger bank will struggle. The fact that such a bank has no customers, no track record and no capital is the issue and, if it does manage to get over those challenges and gain some market share, it will just get bought by some major incumbent like BBVA.

OK, so it's not as simple as that, and people like to point out that banks are struggling. Deutsche Bank and Wells Fargo are the latest to be laughed at. RBS, Northern Rock, Wachovia and Washington Mutual are previous failures. But these are all failures of management, not of technology strategy. Therefore, I take exception to those who think that bank failures are because of FinTech. Not a single incumbent is failing because of a start-up, and no start-up has succeeded in overthrowing the incumbent's position of strength so far.

The incumbents own the roads, build the cars and maintain the network. There may be new cars and new ways of running the network emerging, but the incumbents' challenge is to keep up with such changes. However, the idea that these changes will cause them to rip up the roads, ditch their customers, fail to react and just throw themselves over the cliff to their doom is a fallacy.

Nevertheless, as I write this, I don't agree with it. Of course, we need to rip up the roads, simply because our mode of transportation has changed dramatically. A great example of this change is the very nature of the underlying transport architecture that we are using.

Historically, our technology architecture has been based on heavily controlled programme structures. In the 1990s, we moved into structures based on modular computing, object-orientation and service-oriented architectures (SOA). Today, we live in a world of plug-and-play APIs and open marketplaces. The structures are very different, although there are similarities.

The object-oriented developments of the 1990s were designed to develop plug-and-play functionality *internally*; today's open APIs are designed to develop plug-and-play functionality *externally*. That is a difference in focus, meaning we can redesign the roads with agility, through open marketplaces and crowd-sourced developments.

RENEWING CORE SYSTEMS IS LIKE RENOVATING THE SUBWAYS

Someone recently equated banks and their systems and structures to the underground in London. I'm talking a lot of pipes, wires, cables and tunnels that were built in the Victorian times and are still operating today. There are engineers on the tracks every night and day, trying to keep the systems running as well as overhaul the system on a regular basis. Air conditioning, elevators, wheelchair access, Wi-Fi and more in the underground stations have made these ancient structures feel modern, but they're not. At their core, they are Victorian edifices to an era that harks back to a bygone age.

Take the following two stories. One is about the difficulty of putting a modern lift shaft into an existing underground station (cost £50 million) and the other is about the hugely complex project of building a new underground line (cost £15 billion). Link these stories back to how a bank's core systems work, and I think you will get the point.

The development of London's underground system began in 1863 and has been a piecemeal development process since then, with the Tube developing into a vast network that today sees almost four million passengers a day travelling across 270 stations. A major challenge now is accessibility and the problem of "retrofitting" lifts around old infrastructure below very congested city streets. For instance, the transport operator spent £50 million and two years to fit a lift into Green Park tube station. One lift. That's just one change for one station to bring it up to date. Replace the 270 stations with the 270 different core systems that a bank operates and you can see the scale of the problem when it comes to upgrading.

The second example is Crossrail, the 120-kilometre Berkshire-to-Essex railway that will pass beneath London's busy streets along 42 kilometres of underground tunnels, and all the challenges that come with building a new railway line around existing infrastructure.

The point of these two stories is that most transport operators spend most of their budget on keeping the tracks open. Transport for London (TfL) spends over £10 billion a year, most of it on maintenance. That's a little bit like banks. Then when they do decide to do something new, like Crossrail, it is always more expensive, more complex and more time-consuming than they expected. For example, the Crossrail build was estimated to cost £10 billion at the outset and there are concerns that it may not be finished in time, by May 2019. That also sounds like most bank core systems projects. It is also why these numbers illustrate why banks and insurance companies spend so much on technology (half a trillion dollars a year). Unfortunately, like TfL, most of it (75 per cent according to Celent) goes into maintenance.

So it's nice to be in a position of starting afresh with FinTech, isn't it? Perhaps it is the reason why Gartner is forecasting that these bank technology budgets will boom in the next few years in order to keep up.

CORE SYSTEMS SHOULD HAVE BUILT-IN OBSOLESCENCE

Talking about moving from proprietary to open, from controlled to marketplace and from internal to external focus, another key change is the very nature of technology itself. It's quite clear that a start-up today can launch with just a few thousand dollars, Amazon Web Services and a bright idea. There is no need to build a complex infrastructure and spend months with hundreds of coders creating something. That is why there are so many new start-up services for banking and payments, and it's not just the big names you know. Take solarisBank in Germany. It's evident that with a few people, bright ideas and enthusiasm, anyone can create a new bank fairly quickly. In Europe anyway. I've met neobanks and newly licensed banks across Europe and the consistent factor is that they are all using open marketplaces, APIs, apps and the cloud to kick-start a new injection of change into banking, pretty fast. Some are getting licences in under a year, just to illustrate that point.

This is so different from the banking markets that I've worked in all my life. When I started out in banking technology, we would try hard to justify a new system acquisition. It was a tortuous process of building a business case, reviewing the return on investment and cost-benefit analysis, talking and presenting and presenting and talking, with huge resistance from anyone to ever say yes. Saying yes was, and still is for many, a big deal. Saying yes was committing the bank to a five-, ten- or even twenty-year contract, it was committing the bank to hundreds of millions or even billions of dollars of investment and it was determining the bank's strategic direction for the long term. That's a big deal.

The issue is that this mentality of the big deal still pervades for many senior bank decision-makers and yet, nowadays, it's no big deal. If a start-up like Ant Financial, solarisBank, Thought Machine, PrivatBank and more can get a full suite of banking software up and running, then you know the answer today is all about speed and agility at low cost. There is no Big Deal here. In fact, if you can build a developer-driven bank where a microservice architecture allows very small teams to change little parts of the architecture continually, then you have a bank built for today. A bank that can provide updates for its apps and APIs every day or even intraday rather than every year or even bi-annually.

This then brings me back to my relentless cry for replacing core systems in banks, as this is the only reason why any technology change today would be a Big Deal. Today, a bank that is stuck with a complex legacy spaghetti mess would find it hard to be agile, developer-driven, open-sourced and competitive in the FinTech marketplaces because such a bank can't make a decision to do anything. Any decision would be committing the bank to a multi-year, multi-billion-dollar change and that's just too hard to do. So they avoid the decision. After all, the CEO is retiring in a couple of years, is rewarded based on shareholder return and can get away with soft shoe shuffling in the markets with a nice app and front end. No one will notice if the back end stinks like crazy.

That used to be acceptable, but it doesn't wash today. After all, the innovative banks, FinTech start-ups and agile new players are all dealing with a different world. Their world is one of fast cycle change. They can do the quickstep, foxtrot, tango and samba all at the same time. This is all down to the knowledge that nothing is difficult to do, nothing costs much to do, short-term technical obsolescence is built into their developments and their journey is a continuum of technological change.

Compare that with their more traditional contemporaries. The banks stuck with legacy are waltzing through the markets. Their movement is slow and laboured, and every change of step along the way causes a coughing and wheezing moan. They know that everything is difficult and everything costs. They cannot accept any obsolescence as it would hit the balance sheet, the shareholder returns and the C-suite's bonuses. Their journey is how to add rooms on to the Castle, rather than rebuild the Castle.

I know I hark on about this a lot, but in a world where technology is disposable, developments are fast cycle and technology-based competition is viscous in an open-sourced marketplace, I would be seriously worried to be leading a bank that can't even enter that world.

DO BANKS NEED A CIO?

I was recently talking to employees of a technology firm. Now this firm offers everything from cloud to core systems, yet the ongoing issue is that the competition wins every time. Not IBM. Not Accenture. Not Tata Consultancy Services (TCS). Not FIS. Not SAP. Not any of the big names you could mention in such areas. No, their competition is the CIO. Core Innovation Objects? No, *the* CIO, as in the chief information officer.

I've encountered this myself. I remember dealing with a great idea of automating corporate actions. We had a great product and started to punt it around the market only to find the chief operating officer (COO) would always kill the conversation. The reason? If he automated corporate actions, then several tens or even hundreds of staff would become redundant.

That may sound screwy as surely the point of automating a function is to displace the humans, but the guys who run those empires really don't want that. When you open source bank technologies, what happens to those thousands of bank developers currently engaged in maintaining all the old junk? When you have irrevocable transactions on shared ledgers that need no reconciliations, what happens to the firms that focus on reconciliation and their staff and customers? When you can do everything in the cloud, what happens to the IT operations department?

Some of this may sound like ephemeral ideas, but it's often at the core of how some bank CIOs think. They are actually the chief incumbent orifice. They are there to maintain the status quo, keep their empire, ensure as little innovation as possible and keep their nice vendor relationships intact. What's their incentive to innovate and possibly cut the branch that they are sitting on off the tree?

This is why many predict that the IT and CIO guys will become like the electricity people of the past. Fifty years ago, there actually was a Head of Electricity in banks who ran the electrical departments. Wiring and structuring the bank to be able to turn the lights on rather than the bank of today that employs thousands of developers to keep the lights on. It's intriguing to watch and think about these poor souls who have no future, as that's exactly what will happen over the next ten to fifteen years. Why will it happen now? Because one fundamental difference has occurred—the consumerisation of technology.

As technology moves to open-sourced structures, even a dumb CEO can see that Amazon's cloud makes sense, that Gmail works, that Dropbox is useful and that salesforce is easier than a spreadsheet. As this extends to APIs like Stripe, smart apps for smart things and shared ledgers that are tamper-proof, even the dumbest CEO is going to wonder why he's got all these architects and keyboard hackers running systems dating to the 1980s that cost a fortune and do little for agility. As marketplaces, platforms and the FinTech community start to build peer-to-peer connectivity based on algorithms, software and servers, even Jamie Dimon can tell that something has to change. And it is.

In fact, it intrigues me that a lot of the innovation within banks today is not coming from the technologists, but from the business guys. That shows both the urgency to change and that the IT guys have been called out. The business bankers are seeing the open sourcing of banking and saying, "Hey! You guys down there in the BASIC bowels of our FORTRAN bank, start the C++ out of here or we'll be Java'd away." Or something like that. The business bankers are seeing the threat, as seen in so many quotes of fear:

- Jamie Dimon, CEO, JPMorgan Chase: "When I go to Silicon Valley … [they all] want to eat our lunch."

- Urs Rohner, chairman of the board of directors at Credit Suisse: "Technology competence on Board level is not only a necessity, it will soon become indispensable for financial institutions."
- Henri de Castries, former CEO of AXA: "Digital transformation is no longer an option—it is a must."
- Ana Patricia Botín, executive chairman of Santander: "If you think about the big guys now, it is not the banks, it is these four large tech companies (Google, Apple, Facebook, Amazon) that are worth more than us."

The leaders of these banks fear technological redundancy in their institutions and so are re-architecting to merge FinTech with their banks. The losers in that process have to be the thousands of internal developers and architects. However, they won't be the only ones to disappear. So too will many of their higher paid brethren in the front-office trading rooms who believe they are Masters of the Universe, when they're actually just monkey market operators who simply have to win more often than they lose. Those jobs are being automated by AI and machine learning. Eventually, the human hand will no longer be involved in trading. Already, the market funds are moving to passive investing. Soon the active fund manager will be sitting next to the head of systems maintenance, wondering what happened to their jobs.

This is again not some wild prediction, but a fairly obvious move over time from proprietary to open and from internal focused technologies that no one understands, except the technologists, to external focused technologies that everyone understands, including the customer.

Customer-focused open systems that provide platform connectivity for marketplaces are the way of the world and, if you work for a bank and haven't realised this yet, then start learning how to maintain, develop and create robots and intelligent systems, as that's where the few who work on maintenance will be needed in the future.

THE DEVELOPER-DRIVEN BANK

Most banks think the CIO is there to run the technology. They're not. That's what they used to do. That's not the job for the future.

First and foremost, the person leading technology developments in any incumbent bank of any longevity needs to be a Change Agent. This is because their first job is to change the core systems to open-sourced structures based on cloud, analytics, APIs and AI. That's a big job. The real question, however, is what happens once that job is done?

Well, I got great insight on this from my friend Sergei Danylenko of PrivatBank, a technology firm that happens to also offer banking. As chief marketing officer (CMO), Sergei promotes the bank's services globally based on a digital core system in the cloud, offered as hundreds of APIs in a microservice architecture.

A microservice architecture takes the bank's development operations and turns them into small independent teams, who then manage components of the bank's technologies using internal apps and APIs. In order to do this, the bank needs to break apart all the processes that need to be done and make them into tiny apps. These apps are then developed individually and put into the network. Thanks to standards, all these tiny pieces can then be put together into a bigger whole that is robust and easy to maintain, mainly because it's just tiny bits that are being changed and maintained, and not some huge monolithic structure.

Now that's very different to the old bank systems that I'm used to dealing with. The old systems I dealt with involved thousands of lines of code, and needed heavy change controls as any code update could ripple across the whole system and break it. In a microservice architecture, it's the other way around. You can change anything, anytime, because everything is independent, separated and distributed.

Another critical factor here is that businesses are being built on a microprocess. A great example is Stripe, an API for businesses that want a simplified checkout system. Valued at $9.2 billion in November 2016, six years after inception, it's doing pretty well for a microservice.

In other words, FinTech can uncouple all the functions and processes from the products and providers and offer them as microservices that, through DevOps, cloud and APIs, can be reimagined into any business model and structure you like.

This concept is made clear by Adrian Cockcroft, former cloud architect at Netflix, who talked about the company's move from DVDs to streaming, and how that forced a huge change in its technology structure. His key messages focused on:

- Functions are now the major companies.
- There are no more cathedrals, just bazaars.
- Apps are now the infrastructure.
- Developer-driven design is key.
- There is no central monolith; it's all micro-as-a-service.
- If you're working as a developer in a waterfall organisation, it's soul-destroying.
- When developers own the design of their product, it's far more agile and fun.[10]

These messages are ones that banks need to listen to and learn from, as many banks I deal with control things top-down. The idea of distributing control to developers would be heresy. And yet, this is what must be done.

THE FUTURE CIO IS NOT A CIO

As mentioned, the CIO's role is changing from running an empire of maintenance engineers to organising a distributed development organisation. The change in role is one from a hierarchical control structure, where everything is proprietary and internal, to a flattened organisation

---

10   Taken from the a16z Podcast on "All about Microservices" on 1 September 2016.

that is open and broad. Most of the developments will come from outside, as it's no longer developing for purely internal needs. In fact, as banks put their services on platforms and operate in marketplaces, they will be more involved in parts of processes than ever before but the good old days of owning the process will have gone.

This means the CIO is moving the organisation through this change process from proprietary and internal to open and broad. It's moving the bank from a cathedral to a bazaar, from a monolith to a marketplace. That's the Change Agent piece: creating the new company where Banking-as-a-Platform leads the operation.

Banking-as-a-Platform is the new hot trend that I wrote about seven years ago and is finally here. It's the ability to plug and play all of the bank's functions and proceeds as apps through APIs. Not just internal apps and APIs, but those of others. It's a whole new operation where the bank is part of an ecosystem of technology components. Mind you, the bank is the leader of those components as it is still the lead player in the marketplace with decades of development, millions of customers, billions of assets and a regulatory licence. But the days of the bank being a completely internal and proprietary structure, or a law unto itself, are over.

The bank is now an integrator of components in the new marketplace of Banking-as-a-Service or Platform. Once that Change Agent process is completed, the role of CIO will change again. The CIO moves from Change Agent to become the Chief Conductor. The leader of the institution deploying Banking-as-a-Platform must be a coordinator of many distributed parts. That is the Chief Conductor's role. The Chief Conductor must be able to see all from the back office (percussion) through middle office (wind instruments) to front office (strings) and get them to operate with perfect timing and in tune to the song they're playing.

It's not an easy role as some parts of the new bank platform have arrived from a different orchestra. There's little time for practice and the orchestra must play 24/7. That is why it becomes so critical that the Chief Conductor allows the developer-driven orchestra to each play their own parts. Each member of the orchestra owns their space. Some might play the odd bum note but, in the overall scheme of the music, it can be overlooked.

I guess it is the final piece in a long-term puzzle as, going way back when, I was told that organisational structures must move from hierarchical command/control, as used in the army, to flattened coach/counsel, as used in families. Banks have resisted such change as they like to command and control. However, as technologies irresistibly move to distributed, open platforms and marketplaces, the large, monolith hierarchy structure is simply collapsing.

In other words, banks may keep their command and control in their physical structures (branch) but they are just part of an ever-growing family in their digital structures. They may be the biggest and oldest member of the family—they may be the daddy—but they've got to get used to letting others play and recognise that they no longer are in control. For this reason, the Chief Conductor is probably going to be the most important job in the future bank. They may have no people, they may have no organisation and they may have no control, but their sole purpose will be to make sweet digital music. I'd be up for that.

THE RISE OF THE ROBOTS

You may have missed the speech by Andy Haldane, chief economist at the Bank of England and executive director for Monetary Analysis, Research and Statistics, about robots replacing humans during the next few decades. His speech seized the headlines, mainly because it was based on the results of a Bank of England study that suggests most administrative, clerical and production jobs are at threat. As a result, the Bank forecasts that half of all jobs could be lost to robots, equating to 15 million lost jobs in the United Kingdom and 80 million in the United States. Accountants are 95 per cent likely to be wiped out while hairdressers only have a 33 per cent probability of becoming extinct. Every job is at risk, even the creatives involved in design, art and music.

For example, in 2011, the editors of one of the oldest U.S. literary journals, *The Archive,* selected a short poem called "For the Bristlecone Snag" for publication in its autumn issue. The poem seems environmentally themed, strikes an aggressive tone and contains a few of the clunky turns of phrase overwhelmingly common to collegiate poetry.

A home transformed by the lightning
the balanced alcoves smother
this insatiable earth of a planet, Earth.

They attacked it with mechanical horns
because they love you, love, in fire and wind.
You say, what is the time waiting for in its spring?
I tell you it is waiting for your branch that flows,
because you are a sweet-smelling diamond architecture
that does not know why it grows.

It's unremarkable … except that it was written by a computer algorithm and nobody could tell. The author of the algorithm, Zackary Scholl, didn't tell the editors that the poem was written by a computer because he "didn't want to embarrass anybody."

WHEN WILL WE PASS THE TURING TEST?

The Turing Test, developed by Alan Turing in 1950, is a test of a machine's ability to exhibit intelligent behaviour equivalent to, or indistinguishable from, that of a human. Although there have been numerous claims that the chatterbot Eugene Goostman has passed the Turing Test, it simply is not true. Let us just say that he cheated the test in a lot of ways. So when will we pass the Turing Test? That's a good question and was addressed in a 2016 *New York Times*[11] report on Google Brain. The article was also a great primer on how Google's team is developing AI systems.

To summarise, an average brain has something in the order of 100 billion neurons. Each neuron is connected to up to 10,000 other neurons, which means that the number of synapses, or junctions between two nerve cells, is between 100 trillion and 1,000 trillion. What Google and others are trying to do is recreate that using compute power. This is extremely challenging as a neural network with trillions of connections is still a long way off. For

---

11   Gideon Lewis-Krauss, "The Great A.I. Awakening," *New York Times Magazine*, 14 December 2016.

example, Google has been working heavily on developing AI over the past decade, reaching a milestone with the Cat Paper in 2012.

Imagine you wanted to programme a cat-recogniser using the old symbolic-AI model. You would stay up for days preloading the machine with an exhaustive, explicit definition of "cat". You would tell it that a cat has four legs, pointy ears, whiskers, a tail and so on. All of this information was then stored in a special place in memory called Cat. Next, you showed it a picture. First, the machine had to separate out the various distinct elements of the image. Then it had to take these elements and apply the rules stored in its memory. If(legs=4) and if(ears=pointy) and if(whiskers=yes) and if(tail=yes) and if(expression=supercilious), then(cat=yes). But what if you were to show this cat-recogniser a Scottish fold, a heart-rending breed with a prized genetic defect that leads to droopy doubled-over ears? Our symbolic AI would get to (ears=pointy) and shake its head solemnly, "Not cat." It was hyperliteral, or "brittle". Even the thickest toddler shows much greater inferential acuity.

What the Cat Paper demonstrated was that a neural network with more than a billion "synaptic" connections—a hundred times larger than any publicised neural network to that point, yet still many orders of magnitude smaller than our brains—could observe raw, unlabelled data and pick out for itself a high-order human concept.

Why is Google so keen on AI? Because it's a natural extension of today for tomorrow. For example, much of the work has been directed towards language translation, and Google has come some way with this, as illustrated by this paragraph from Ernest Hemingway's short story *The Snows of Kilimanjaro*, which opens with this paragraph:

> Kilimanjaro is a snow-covered mountain 19,710 feet high, and is said to be the highest mountain in Africa. Its western summit is called the Masai "Ngaje Ngai," the House of God. Close to the western summit there is the dried and frozen carcass of a leopard. No one has explained what the leopard was seeking at that altitude.

The Google Translate system that has been running for over a decade using old AI training, based on directed learning, would have translated this paragraph as follows:

> Kilimanjaro is 19,710 feet of the mountain covered with snow, and it is said that the highest mountain in Africa. Top of the west, "Ngaje Ngai" in the Maasai language, has been referred to as the house of God. The top close to the west, there is a dry, frozen carcass of a leopard. Whether the leopard had what the demand at that altitude, there is no that nobody explained.

The new neural network-based Google Translate is far more accurate:

> Kilimanjaro is a mountain of 19,710 feet covered with snow and is said to be the highest mountain in Africa. The summit of the west is called "Ngaje Ngai" in Masai, the house of God. Near the top of the west there is a dry and frozen dead body of leopard. No one has ever explained what leopard wanted at that altitude.

This is where AI is really making its mark. I'd recommend reading the entire *New York Times* article if you want to really understand how Google did it, as it's a real feat of human engineering and it doesn't stop there. Basic AI, or artificial narrow intelligence, can do one thing really well.

Then there's a second level of AI called artificial general intelligence, where a machine can multitask and do several activities. We're at that level today and neural network AI is giving us the ability to develop these areas faster and better than ever before. That's why I believe passing the Turing Test will probably be achieved within the next five years.

This means that we may reach artificial super intelligence—the ultimate level of intelligence where machines are as capable as humans at learning and developing—before the end of the next decade. I'll talk about these three levels in more detail later in the chapter.

MACHINES DRIVEN BY ARTIFICIAL INTELLIGENCE

One of the hottest things in technology right now is machine learning and AI. There are others such as contextual commerce, voice recognition and digital assistants, but machine learning and AI are top of mind.

When talking about this with one CIO, his response was that machine learning was the highest priority as it can give a business immediate benefits in improving workflows and processes. Machine learning could save costs and overheads, right here, right now. AI is nothing new. After all, Spielberg made a film about it way back in 2001. What is new are the developments in AI that we're seeing from firms like Google and IBM.

IBM's Watson is probably the best-known AI in the real world, after it won the U.S. game show *Jeopardy!* way back in 2011. Watson (named after IBM's founder, Thomas J. Watson) is a cognitive technology that processes information more like a human than a computer. The system is based on an IBM supercomputer that combines AI with sophisticated analytical software to provide a "question answering" machine.

The Watson supercomputer processes at a rate of 80 teraflops (a trillion floating-point operations per second). To replicate (or surpass) a high-functioning human's ability to answer questions, Watson accesses ninety servers with a combined data store of over 200 million pages of information, which it processes against six million logic rules. The device and its data are self-contained in a space that could accommodate ten refrigerators.

Google meanwhile is using DeepMind, a London-based company the search giant acquired in early 2014, to create its own AI programme. DeepMind is now doing some amazing things, including creating a programme that can beat humans at video games and even win the world's most complex game, Go, against the best human player on the planet.

There are several other AI product developments out there too, including Microsoft's Project ADAM (Active Directory Application Mode), Facebook's open-sourced deep learning tools, the Amazon Machine Learning service *and* Apple's evolution of Siri and the iOS recognition systems. These are just the big guys; there are also hundreds of small guys doing neat stuff too.

So what's the point of all this AI development? Well, in banking, it's quite important as the technology giants are basically training enormous networks of machines to identify faces in photos, recognise the spoken word and instantly translate conversations from one language to another. This means that not only can people talk with their bank when their bank is a machine, but the bank that is a machine can also immediately recognise the correct versus the fraudulent transaction.

PayPal uses deep learning to track fraudulent transactions, but there are many other applications of AI for banking. For example, several of the new payday lenders and credit firms are using real-time credit scoring analytics to calculate the credit worthiness of applicants. Equally, deep data analytics for marketing (effectiveness of campaigns), trading (to build predictive models of prices, volatilities etc.), portfolio management (as a source of alpha) and risk management (to try and obtain better risk estimates) are all fast-developing areas.

I was impressed when I found out that UBS runs deep data analytics combined with machine learning non-stop on their clients' portfolios of investment in order to better advise each customer with specific and personalised services every day. Equally, I was intrigued to hear DBS talking about using IBM's Watson. Similar to UBS, DBS uses deep data analytics to improve customer service and advice. Instead of spending more than two hours every day poring through market reports, DBS relationship managers use the time to meet with clients instead, armed with information from those reports distilled by supercomputer Watson.

Certainly, we are going to see more and more use of AI for everything from simpler user interfaces, improved customer experiences, automated fraud detection and greatly personalised, proactive and predictive services. Banks have long tried to replace human traders with machines. This is referred to as active (human) versus passive (machine) trading systems.

With high-frequency trading and other techniques, combined with machine learning and AI, we could eradicate the need for human traders.

A 2016 report in the *Financial Times* highlighted that active managers whose funds must try to beat the market rather than simply track the index are facing something approaching a crisis. A majority fail to beat the index over any significant period, and most of those that do ultimately find their outperformance to be fleeting. New competitors are claiming any insight they actually possess can be replicated by a computer. Clients are shifting en masse to index-based funds—active funds lost $213 billion in assets up until May 2016 while passive funds took in $240 billion. Profit margins, traditionally among the best in the finance world, are under threat and it seems only a matter of time before there is pressure on managers' pay ... only 15 per cent of active managers are persistent market-beaters.

That is a good reason to get rid of humans in trading. According to a recent Tabb Group report, computers will replace humans entirely in the trading room because the skin and blood brigade are expensive and prone to error. Financial market participants currently spend more than three times more on people than they do on hardware, software and data. This does not mean that we will end up with no humans in trading however, as new jobs will be created for those who can build and control the technology.

In another report by Aite Group in 2014, FX trading accounted for 20 per cent of the markets in 2001, 66 per cent in 2013 and will rise to 76 per cent by 2018. About 81 per cent of spot trading, the buying and selling of currency for immediate delivery, will be electronic by 2018. We can see this shift to electronification of markets across the gamut of everything from FX to equities to structure products to wealth management to advice to service and more. However, with all this change, there may still be a place for human traders who can beat the machines. It will be a different game though.

WE ARE THE ROBOTS

Some believe a lot of this discussion about a future where everything is automated and robots do everything is science fiction, but science fiction is rapidly becoming science fact. In fact, we will reach a stage soon where man and machine are hard to separate. For example, there's a moment in the excellent TV series *Humans* when the human police inspector tells his robot colleague—they call them "synths", as in synthetic humans—about having a heart implant machine that tracks his heartbeat after having a heart attack the year before. As he concludes this speech, he says, "So you see, there's a little bit of machine inside the human, just as there's a little bit of the human inside the machine."

The man-machine discussion has been one we have had since the inception of science fiction and film. Just look at the 1927 film *Metropolis*. This made me think about the predictions that are out there, with Ray Kurzweil's probably resounding most loudly in my ears:

> In less than two decades, you won't just use your computers, you will have relationships with them. Because of artificial intelligence, computers will be able to read at human levels by 2029 and will also begin to have different human characteristics, said Ray Kurzweil, a director of engineering at Google. "My timeline is computers will be at human levels, such as you can have a human relationship with them, 15 years from now," he said. Kurzweil's comments came at the Exponential Finance conference in New York on Wednesday. "When I say about human levels, I'm talking about emotional intelligence. The ability to tell a joke, to be funny, to be romantic, to be loving, to be sexy, that is the cutting edge of human intelligence, that is not a sideshow."[12]

By 2030, we will be making love with robots!

---

12   "Computers will be like humans by 2029: Google's Ray Kurzweil," CNBC, 11 June 2014.

That's one idea anyway. Now add another idea into the mix, namely that scientists claim we can now create babies without men. In other words, by 2030, people will be able to have relationships with robots and have a baby with them, created in a beaker in the lab with sperm made from stem cells. We will no longer need to have a human partner, with their idiosyncrasies and irritations. We can have the perfect relationship with someone who learns our every nuance, wish and desire, and is dedicated to serving our needs.

What will happen when we cannot tell the difference between the human and the machine? That's not scary science fiction; it's almost science fact. However, there is still a long way to go as demonstrated by IBM's Watson Avatar.

Its AI human agent, usually a woman, looks humanish, but no avatar or chatbot today feels properly human. In this case, it's the mouth movements that give away she's a machine, even though she's in high definition. Fifteen years ago, AT&T was working on exactly the same idea, but with scripts for avatars.

As you can see, the idea hasn't changed much in that time. What is changing, however, is the technology behind this idea and, as with all great technological innovation, if something looks worthwhile to develop—biometrics, communicators, health technologies, life sciences, artificial intelligence, robots and so on—then eventually these technologies will develop sufficiently to become mainstream and acceptable. That will take the next ten to twenty-five years to achieve. It feels nearer, but when a group of experts on AGI were asked this question in 2012, their view was that it would not be achieved until 2040.

As I thought about this, it made me think along the lines of science-fiction authors and visionaries, such as Isaac Asimov. An amazing thinker about the future, Asimov wrote a fantastic series about robots and came up with the three laws of robotics:

- A robot may not injure a human being or, through inaction, allow a human being to come to harm.

- A robot must obey orders given to it by human beings except where such orders would conflict with the First Law.
- A robot must protect its own existence as long as such protection does not conflict with the First or Second Law.

These three laws make so much sense, and have been used on many occasions, notably in the film *RoboCop* in which the part man, part machine police officer has three prime directives:

- serve the public trust
- protect the innocent
- uphold the law

This means that RoboCop can kill humans, but only if it conforms to the above.

It made me wonder what the three rules for banking robots should be? We need to have some, otherwise they may run away with our money. After all, robots won't adhere to national laws and rules, only to the way they programme and reprogramme themselves. So, here's my speculative take on three rules for banking robots:

- do not rip customers off
- ensure you are secure
- freeze any activity that breaks the law

YOU CAN NEVER AUTOMATE HUMANITY

A critical area here is the integration of robotics and artificial intelligence. When you can make love with a machine that feels like a human being and doesn't talk back, why would you want a real one? Let's not go there ...

In the Industrial Revolution, people moved from fields to factories; in the services revolution, people moved from factories to offices; in the digital revolution, people move from offices to what? This is the theme of several commentators who claim that there is no next-generation job market, and that the automation of the human cognitive capability gets rid of the need for humans completely.

You don't need human traders, accountants, waiters, cooks, prostitutes, escorts or any of the human capabilities we value today because a robot can do all of these things, and far better. That probably will be true within the next twenty-five years. If that is the case, that robots can do everything that humans can do and do it better, what will humans do? Well, there are two camps: the optimist and the pessimist.

The optimist believes that work has value, and that a robot cannot do everything a human can do. A human can write books, music and make films better than any robot because art is an innate part of humanity. Will tomorrow's artists be automated? A human can oversee operations of robots and ensure they maintain the ethics of operations. Can a robot recognise when it is doing something that is anti-human in nature? And a human service is valued in restaurants, on airlines and in lust, far more than a robot could ever deliver … or so we like to think. Today.

When you get to the point in the next few decades where it will be hard to recognise a human from a robot, when the robot can have attitude and when the robot can think, will we really recognise these fine lines that distinguish us from them?

These are questions raised in a lot of good media from *Ex Machina* to the TV series *Humans*, but the optimist really ends up with a belief that humans are required for humanity. Humans will service humans, humans will be (and already are) required to repair robots, humans will be needed to support space tourism and humans need to provide humanity in the system. Therefore, there will be new human jobs from data scientists to augmented psychologists, who can coach and counsel the development of automated services. That's the optimist's view.

The pessimist's view is actually more interesting and, not necessarily, depressing. The pessimist believes that the robots will take all of our jobs.

By the extreme of automation from 2030 and beyond, no one will need to work. So how will humanity work?

In this vision of the future, those who work choose to work or are selected to work, based on their ultra-cognitive skills. There will be robot enhancers, artificially intelligent designers, machine enablers and more, who will be there to continue the development of machines above and beyond where they are today. In this scenario, we could claim that machines would just make better machines—faster horses—whereas humans would continually rethink the horse. That's a good one.

This would, however, leave a vast swathe of humanity who could do nothing at all. There would be billions of people who would no longer be useful. Their cognitive skills would just not be good enough to be automation enhancers, and so they would have no useful purpose. Their unskilled and semi-skilled capabilities mean that they would have no creative capability to be an artist, and their limitations in cognitive capabilities mean that they would be technically inferior to their robotic alternatives. So, what would they do?

Maybe there is the idea that we would no longer be driven by the accumulation of wealth and assets, but by the betterment of humanity. Great idea, but would you work if you did not have to?

Think about it. You could spend all your time watching *Game of Thrones* box sets, engaging in virtual orgies with robots, drinking whatever you wanted and achieving the ultimate hedonistic lifestyle. Why would you work?

In societies where the choice to work or not to work exists, many end up taking the second option. This doesn't always go the way it's planned. For instance, on Native American reservations, thanks to the generosity of the U.S. government, many of their young people do not have to work. Instead, they end up on drink and drugs. You find the same in other nations like Canada, Australia and the United Kingdom.

Another example is Norway. Norway is a rich economy with the largest sovereign wealth fund in the world thanks to the oil boom. It is an egalitarian society where, I've been told, a highly qualified engineer's starting package is less than someone's from overseas while a trainee waiter could earn more. This is because Norway has a society that provides a cushion, thanks to its wealth. That cushion means you don't have to work. You choose to. And some don't. Their numbers are placed into a catchment called "those who cannot work due to impairment", as in they are ill, but they are not. They could work, but choose not to. Some estimate that one in ten Norwegian adults was unemployed because of illness or through choice. This figure is lower than the numbers in Spain, Italy and Portugal, although theirs are due to bankrupt economies, but higher than those in the most developed and growing economies.

The need to work and create jobs is, in fact, a virtuous circle, and is what is called the "lump of labour" fallacy. As explained perfectly by Tim Worstall:

> The number of jobs in an economy is set not by the amount of work there is to do. It's set by the aggregate demand in that economy: that is, how much money does everyone else have to pay people to do the things they'd like to have done?[13]

And that is the bottom line. If we displace all human workers with robots, do you think the world will end? It will not end unless people lose the motivation to work, as that is what makes humans enjoy life, and then are remunerated for that work, as that is what drives economies.

Replacing humans with robots so we can all just kick back and live off a financial cushion will, I believe, just make us all addicts living a narcissistic lifestyle in an economy that free-falls. That is why I do not think that the robots will take over everything. There will always be a need for a human somewhere.

---

13   Tim Worstall, "Of Course Older Workers Do Not Steal Jobs From The Young; Fallacies Are Fallacies," *Forbes*, 11 March 2015.

ALTHOUGH WE NEED FEWER HUMANS IN THE PROCESS

There is another interesting debate about the risks of humans in the network. Humans screw up. Humans cause problems. Humans have emotions. Humans are not welcome here.

A good example of why humans are not welcome is that it is typically human error that causes an issue. A self-driving car is likely to drive a million miles without an accident while a human-driven car crashes three or four times on average throughout the driver's lifetime. I would personally prefer to be operated on by a robotic surgeon with a million successful operations under its belt than by a human surgeon who makes a mistake once in 10,000 operations. I would have more confidence in traders that were automated and settled without error than a human trader who may be rogue, and where we need to invest millions to reconcile what they've traded, when and where.

You get the point. A machine can process things far more effectively than a human. It's the reason why Tesla wants to ban humans from its operations as they slow progress and why Amazon would prefer delivery via drones. A machine can be programmed to get it right first time, every time and never get it wrong. A human cannot.

A human can let people through a border control because they look like their passport photo; a machine will recognise that they're not that person. A human can be engineered to allow a cyberhacker into the building; a machine will not. This is a critical issue: humans can be socially engineered to do things that machines will not. This is the core of our humanity—trust. We naturally want to trust people. People do naturally trust people. That is our basic human nature, but it's also the reason why we get ripped off.

People are the weakest link so we must get rid of them. If we get rid of people, we can have bulletproof banks, foolproof operations and guaranteed success. In fact, it galls me immensely that I only get angry these days with poor service when the automated processes fail and I have to deal with a human. We must automate everything.

To ram this point home, I argued about this extreme with a colleague. He asked me, "Would you trust a robot to fly your plane home?" To which I replied that most flights are fly-by-wire these days in any case, and so robots do fly my plane home. He countered by saying that it would mean that there would be no human in the cockpit. I wondered about this and was about to reply with the illustration of the film *Sully*.

The film is about the landing of a U.S. Airways plane on the Hudson River by Captain Chesley 'Sully' Sullenberger. It is a true story—you may remember the incident—and the film focuses on the post-river landing enquiry, and the fact that the computer simulations show that the pilots could have got the plane to land safely at LaGuardia Airport.

My point was going to be that a robot would be no good in this situation because, as the film shows, the simulations did not allow enough time for the human pilots to react to the engine failure. Once they built in the reaction time, the simulations showed that the aircraft would have crashed if the pilots had tried to achieve a safe landing at an airport. Therefore, it was the right decision by the human pilots to land on the Hudson River.

However, I then realised the flaw in my counter-argument as, in this situation, if there had been a robot pilot, then it would have immediately calculated the right reaction in nanoseconds and hence would have landed safely at LaGuardia rather than on the Hudson River ... so yes, I would prefer a robot to pilot my plane.

BUILDING THE SEMANTIC WORLD

Artificial intelligence, machine learning and deep learning are the building blocks of the Semantic Web. I first started talking about the Semantic Web a good ten years ago, and probably misinterpreted it from the Tim Berners-Lee version. His version is that the Semantic Web would be a web of data that can be processed by machines:[14]

---

14   Berners-Lee, Tim and Mark Fischetti. *Weaving the Web*. New York: HarperCollins, 1999.

"I have a dream for the Web [in which computers] become capable of analysing all the data on the Web – the content, links, and transactions between people and computers. A 'Semantic Web', which makes this possible, has yet to emerge, but when it does, the day-to-day mechanisms of trade, bureaucracy and our daily lives will be handled by machines talking to machines. The 'intelligent agents' people have touted for ages will finally materialize."

As I'm not as technical as Sir Tim and his friends, I just understood it as an intelligent internet that starts to index itself such that all the things on the web could *talk* to each other. By doing so, they would then congregate around things and make them work better.

In my version of the Semantic Web, the internet would manage all my devices for me and my devices would know what I wanted before I did. My television would order my entertainment without me having to ask, my fridge would know what to order before items ran out and my car would refuel without being told to. In this version of the Semantic Web, the machines are not only behaving intelligently because they have artificial intelligence and machine learning inside but are also communicating their intelligence to other machines and sharing their learning so the whole web learns.

Using AI, machine learning and deep learning are essential foundations of the Semantic Web, but we should note that there is a difference between machine and deep learning. Deep learning has been introduced with the objective of moving machine learning closer to its original goals of enabling artificial intelligence. As MIT Review puts it:

Deep-learning software attempts to mimic the activity in layers of neurons in the neocortex, the wrinkly 80 percent of the brain where thinking occurs. The software learns, in a very real sense, to recognize patterns in digital representations of sounds, images, and other data.[15]

---

15   Robert D. Hof, "10 Breakthrough Technologies 2013: Deep Learning," MIT Technology Review, 2013.

In other words, these developments are trying to create a computer that is as smart as the human brain, if not smarter. This has been dreamed of for years, but it is only now with the availability of almost unlimited computation power that it is becoming a reality and is led by the internet giants, namely Facebook, Amazon, Tencent, Baidu, Alibaba and Google. The combined work of these giants is leading us rapidly into the second level of artificial intelligence—AGI.

I mentioned the three defined levels of artificial intelligence earlier in this chapter, namely:

- **Artificial narrow intelligence (ANI)** specialises in one area, such as IBM's Deep Blue that beat Gary Kasparov at chess because it was good at only one thing, playing chess.
- **Artificial general intelligence (AGI)** is the stage when machines pass the Turing Test and the intelligence levels of human beings, with the ability to both apply logic and abstract thinking to complex ideas, learning quickly and learning from experience.
- **Artificial super intelligence (ASI)** is when machines become smarter than all of humanity combined.

These developments sit at the core of the Semantic Web, and the firm that seems to be furthest ahead in this space is Google. This is not to say that the other companies are behind, but the sheer number of public announcements Google has made over the last six years means that Google's made the most noise about deep learning.

Google's movement started in 2011 with the launch of Google Brain. The first results of that project were released in 2012, when Google announced that their machines had learnt to recognise what cats looked like:

When computer scientists at Google's mysterious X lab built a neural network of 16,000 computer processors with one billion connections and let it browse YouTube, it did what many web users might do — it began to look for cats.

The "brain" simulation was exposed to 10 million randomly selected YouTube video thumbnails over the course of three days and, after being presented with a list of 20,000 different items, it began to recognize pictures of cats using a "deep learning" algorithm. This was despite being fed no information on distinguishing features that might help identify one.

Picking up on the most commonly occurring images featured on YouTube, the system achieved 81.7 percent accuracy in detecting human faces, 76.7 percent accuracy when identifying human body parts and 74.8 percent accuracy when identifying cats.[16]

In 2014, the company then beat Facebook to the line by acquiring the UK start-up firm DeepMind for $600 million. Between Google Brain and DeepMind, the firm started really pushing the boundaries of AI, with its machines able to beat other machines at playing video games.

Next, the big headline of 2016 was when Google's machines beat the world's Go master, a game that is so complex that we believed no machine could ever beat a human player. That achievement was followed soon after by the announcement that its machines were now so clever that they could create their own language. In this experiment, computers created their own form of encryption using machine learning, without being taught specific cryptographic algorithms. The latest news is that the machines are now remembering the skills used for different tasks, a key requirement for reaching AGI. It is easy to understand why Google is so committed to AI and deep learning, when you see the impact on its services, such as Google Translate, as discussed earlier.

The fact that we are rapidly reaching a stage, through the work of the internet giants, where machines are more intelligent than humans is a

16   Liat Clark, "Google's Artificial Brain Learns to Find Cat Videos," *Wired*, 26 June 2012.

dramatic tipping point in the progress of systems to automate everything. We are already near the point where a chatbot can service you better than a human. What happens when that chatbot is put inside a human-looking robot or avatar? Welcome to the Semantic Web—it's not an operating system, it's a consciousness.

What happens when we apply the idea of the Semantic Web to banking? At their core, digital banks are data stores of value. The data they store is deposited and withdrawn as money, recognised and regulated by the nation state. We have alternatives now, such as bitcoin, where you can deposit and withdraw money as data, recognised by the consensus state of the network. Both systems are based on data at the core of transactions and both systems recognise that decentralisation will create more security, as there is no single point of failure.

The issue with the banks' systems, however, is that they were developed in multiple proprietary servers that do not lend themselves to AI and machine learning. How can a machine learn anything about me if my data is stored in multiple systems, based on whether I was using a bank's deposit services, loans, mortgages, cards or savings? That is the challenge today for the analogue bank; it has everything in a patchwork quilt of legacy systems.

However, the Semantic Bank will cleanse that data and apply the power of AI and analytics to really understand my historical financial movements and, by the same token, predict my future financial needs. Humans are not doing this—machines are—and the future Semantic Bank will use its open-sourced structures of apps, APIs and analytics to mine the Semantic Web and the deep intelligence it can gain from integrating its knowledge of me married to my devices and movements.

The Semantic Bank effectively becomes a living, breathing companion to my cyborg mind. It understands me so well that it knows when I'm being stupid, taking risks, missing investment opportunities and when to save. It doesn't ask my permission to do these things—it does them for me, as that's the whole point—and I just live my life knowing that my Semantic Bank is looking after me.

That is why you never see anyone in *Star Trek* think about their money because their money is being managed for them by the system. That's the near future state of finance that we are just entering.

THE FUTURE OF HUMANITY

When I was born, there were three billion people in the world. Today, there are over seven billion. If we can cure all, raise everyone out of poverty, decrease tensions and wars, and create more health and longevity, then we have a real problem. People living for a hundred years implies that we're going to have twenty billion people soon, maybe 100 billion … maybe a trillion.

This planet cannot sustain such a huge population, which is why I've talked about whether we will become a multiplanetary species—the most likely scenario—or succumb to a widespread euthanasia programme. Right now, we can see two diverse visions of the future. One is Dan Brown's *Inferno* whilst the other is Elon Musk's multiplanetary society. Which do you believe in? And why is this important? It's important because we are living in the fourth and soon fifth revolution of humanity.

The next revolution combines a whole raft of ideas from artificial intelligence to life sciences to bio technologies to gene designs to reusable rockets to colonising other planets. These things are all likely to happen. A little bit of the machine inside the human and a little bit of human inside the machine.

How will this change our thinking in the next century? An indicator may come from over a century ago, when Chancellor Otto von Bismarck of Germany came up with the idea of a pensionable age of seventy, later reduced to sixty-five, because most German males were dying in their forties. Today, the average German dies at the age of eighty; tomorrow …

If we all live over a century on average, what does that do to pensions? What does it mean for work? I don't know the answer to these questions, but purely pose them because most seem to have a pessimistic view of the future. For example, two books that have been on the best-seller list focus on this very subject: *The Rise of the Robots* by Martin Ford and *Homo Deus* by Yuval Noah Harari.

A summary of Martin Ford's book on robots includes the idea that AI and robotics will wipe out human work while Yuval Noah Harari's book focuses on humankind moving rapidly towards designer humans for the rich and a gargantuan mass of subhumans who don't matter.

Both are scary views of the next world, but I personally disagree with both. The reason I disagree is that people scared of the future tend to be older. I'm old, but a key part of tracing the future is tracking the young. The young are never scared of the future. In fact, they embrace it. Ask a youngster their age and they always reply in fractions, for instance, "eight-and-a-half" or "thirteen-and-a-quarter". Ask an older person their age and they're Forever 21 or 40. Personally, I'm just two millennials, but that's another story.

So we have these fearful, older people who are frightened of progress. They fear technology and change. That's nothing new.

The good news is that both books have some positive perspectives. Harari's book notes that, for thousands of years, humans were principally worried about famine, plague and war. All three still exist but they are now manageable problems. "For the first time in history," writes Harari, "more people die today from eating too much than from eating too little; more people die from old age than from infectious diseases; and more people commit suicide than are killed by soldiers, terrorists and criminals combined."

Ford's book also believes that the ever-developing world of technology is giving us great leaps in curing incurable diseases. In fact, the technologists themselves believe so, as illustrated by the $3 billion charitable trust created by Mark and Priscilla Zuckerberg to "cure, prevent or manage all diseases by the end of the century". Microsoft has said that it intends to "solve" cancer by using artificial intelligence tools, Google's DeepMind unit is working with the UK national health system (NHS) to find a way to use computers to more accurately diagnose diseases and IBM and MIT have announced a tie-up to develop AI-based systems that could help clinicians improve the care of elderly and disabled patients.

And this is why I disagree with Ford and Harari. Yes, we will have challenges but the next big wave of change will be space. Space travel and spacecraft are already high on the agenda of technologists and entrepreneurs from Elon Musk to Jeff Bezos to Richard Branson. This creates a positive potential for the future as building and using spacecraft will be highly intensive in human/machine collaboration. And that's what the future world for the next few centuries will all be about—human/machine collaboration.

Technology will not get rid of humans and human jobs, nor will it create a race of super- and subhumans. Instead, we will see a future world of humans exploring other worlds, living on other planets and seeking a better humanity.

WORK OF THE FUTURE

There are lots of reports about robots taking jobs from humans, and our fear for the future world of no work. One paper from researchers at Oxford University predicts that 47 per cent of U.S. jobs are at "high risk" of computerisation over the next two decades.[17] Another research report issued in 2015 by McKinsey Global Institute found that 45 per cent of work activities could be automated, including 20 per cent of the responsibilities handled by the world's obscenely compensated CEOs, such as analysing operations data.[18]

Another paper from economists at Boston and Columbia University[19] found that "smart machines" will cause a "long-run decline in labour share

17   Frey, Carl Benedikt and Michael A. Osborne, "The future of employment: how susceptible are jobs to computerisation?", 17 September 2013, http://www.oxfordmartin.ox.ac.uk/downloads/academic/future-of-employment.pdf.

18   Chui, Michael, James Manyika and Mehdi Miremadi, "Four fundamentals of workplace automation," *McKinsey Quarterly*, November 2015.

19   Benzell, Seth G., Laurence J. Kotlikoff, Guillermo LaGarda and Jeffrey D. Sachs, "Robots Are Us: Some Economics of Human Replacement," NBER Working Paper No. 20941, issued in February 2015 and revised in March 2016.

of income", more technology boom-busts and a "growing dependency of current output on past software investment". In other words, there will be less need for new code and, therefore, less employment even for coders.

PricewaterhouseCoopers came out with a hard-hitting headline stating that nearly 40 per cent of U.S. jobs could soon be given to robots (7 per cent less than Oxford predicted), followed by 30 per cent of UK jobs, 35 per cent of German jobs and 21 per cent of Japanese jobs. As the wider financial services sector is more vulnerable to automation than other sectors, the United States and the United Kingdom would be particularly affected by such a turn of events.[20]

Banking will be specifically impacted, with Citigroup estimating one in three banking jobs will disappear by 2025 whilst John Cryan, the CEO of Deutsche Bank, estimates that half of banking jobs will be lost over the next decade.

Taking all of these statistics into consideration, I was recently involved in developing a list of the top five most likely banking jobs of the future. Each of the jobs has unique requirements:

- **Data Scientist:** Data scientists will be the most sought-after bank employees in five years as they will be tasked to figure out "when, why and how" consumers use bank products, using statistics and big data provided from bank products.
- **Storyteller (User Experience Designer):** A "storyteller" is actually a user experience designer who will be tasked with understanding what products customers need and when they need them. They will also help make products available in a frictionless (and in terms of debt, shame-free) way.
- **Behavioural Psychologist:** A behavioural psychologist will try to understand consumers (this sounds like a nightmare) and anticipate the relevancy of bank products for customers.

---

20 "Up to 30% of existing UK jobs could be impacted by automation by early 2030s, but this should be offset by job gains elsewhere in economy," PwC website, 24 March 2017.

- **Algorithmic Risk Specialist:** As technology improves, banks will be able to evaluate risk using highly complex formulas, and do it in real time. This is where algorithmic risk specialists will come in. With data will come understanding of risk.
- **Community Advocacy Builder:** This role is designed to foster good relations with customers as banks and their products become more closely integrated with a consumer's daily life.

My favourite future job is Chief Cannibal Officer. The Chief Cannibal runs the internal Cannibalisation Department, a group with one mission— destroy the business.

The focus of the cannibals is to look at every part of the company and see if they can destroy it. Using technology, new structures, new thinking and new business models, the aim of the cannibals is to knock down the sacred cows within the organisation, leap across the product silos and challenge every nuance of thinking. Of course, these cannibals are really annoying— who wants to get eaten?—and they don't necessarily appear on your doorstep every day but, when they do, prepare to be destroyed.

This is an important role because most businesses are complacent, lazy and resist change. Some businesses can afford to be complacent when little is changing or where new competition finds it difficult to break into the markets due to high barriers to entry, as exist in banking and pharmaceuticals. However, we are living in an age of fast cycle change, lowered barriers to entry and innovation occurring everywhere, and all companies must find themselves being forced to respond faster and faster.

In order to do that, there can be no better qualification than having an internal unit that works first and foremost to destroy the tenets of the old business model. This is to enable the business to become far more alert to weaknesses or exposures far sooner than waiting for an external person to find them. That is why there is a forceful need for an internal Cannibalisation Unit.

I've discussed the emergence of new roles, now let's see which jobs will be lost to automation first. According to Shelly Palmer, head of Palmer Group which gives advice on technology and business, the five jobs[21] that robots will take first are:

- middle management
- commodity salespeople
- report writers, journalists, authors and announcers
- accountants and bookkeepers
- doctors

Certainly, I agree with doctors being vulnerable. After all, if a doctor misdiagnoses half the time, while a robot almost always gets it right, who would you want to diagnose you?

However, the one area that he's missed out is the legal profession. A combination of shared ledgers and artificial intelligence is going to reinvent the legal industry and digitalise it, then we won't need lawyers. How wonderful would that be?

In case you don't believe me, Bloomberg reported in February 2017 that JPMorgan had developed software that can process in a few seconds what previously took lawyers and loan officers 360,0000 hours each year to process.[22] Called COIN, short for Contract Intelligence, the programme is based on a learning machine that does the mind-numbing job of interpreting commercial-loan agreements. The software reviews documents in seconds, is less error-prone and never asks for a holiday. COIN has helped JPMorgan cut down on loan-servicing mistakes, most of which stemmed from human error in interpreting 12,000 new wholesale contracts per year.

---

21   *See* https://www.linkedin.com/pulse/5-jobs-robots-take-first-shelly-palmer.

22   Hugh Son, "JPMorgan Software Does in Seconds What Took Lawyers 360,000 Hours," Bloomberg, 28 February 2017.

AS MACHINES TAKE OVER, WHAT WILL HAPPEN TO PEOPLE?

Worded another way, as we move to robotics, automated agents, and augmented and artificial intelligence, what will happen to people? If we have no branches, no structures and no buildings that need humans, what will happen?

It's a good question. It's a question that always crops up when we move from one form of work to another. If we have no farms, where will people work? If we have no factories, where will people work? If we have no offices, where will people work?

Jobs change, as does life, and we have already moved from hard labour to blue collar to white collar. Where we go next is the big question. My feeling is that we will move to a world of servicing technology. Technology will allow us to live our lives more easily, smarter and with greater confidence. In return, we will nurture and generate technologies that allow us to live our lives easier, smarter and more confidently.

Unskilled workers will service robots and machines, skilled workers will create amazing services with robots and machines, and machines will gradually nurture and operate themselves. Just because a machine can manage itself, however, it doesn't mean that it will never break down. Equally, just because a machine has artificial intelligence, it doesn't mean that it will never need real intelligence to make the next breakthrough.

So our concerns about machines and automation are often misplaced as machines and automation often create new industries, new jobs and new opportunities. A good example is the end of the branch. It is clear that the transactional teller jobs and branch structure are past their sell-by dates. These are a last-century structure of physical distribution that are no longer needed in the age of automation. So what do we do with the branches and the humans? Branches can be sold. Many are now coffee bars and wine bars. But the humans? What will happen to the people?

Well, if the humans are any darned good, they will move to support digital interactions. If the branch staff are that good at relationship, then get them on to Facebook and Skype to create digital relationships. Surely a really empathetic, engaged and enthusiastic member of the branch workforce could share that empathy, engagement and enthusiasm just as easily through a Skype call or Facebook message?

I guess the question here is more to do with whether they have that empathy, engagement and enthusiasm in the first place, bearing in mind that most branch staff are pure administrators who are paid peanuts. So, what are the jobs of the future in banking? Where will the people make a difference?

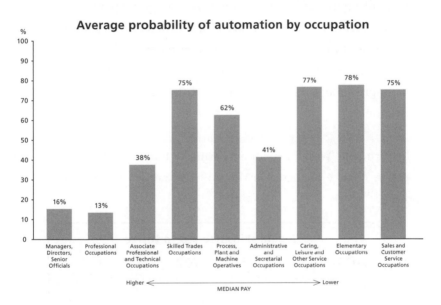

Average probability of automation by occupation

Data sources: The Bank of England; BNP Paribas Asset Management

Andy Haldane of the Bank of England has warned that automation poses a risk to almost half those employed in the United Kingdom and that a "third machine age" will hollow out the labour market, widening the gap between rich and poor.

A report by the Commonwealth Scientific and Industrial Research Organisation (CSIRO), an Australian government agency, has listed ten major forces changing the dynamics of work:[23]

- the increasing importance of education and training
- the need for new capabilities for new jobs of the future
- the need for digital literacy alongside numeracy and literacy
- the changing importance of STEM (whilst participation rates are in decline)
- aptitudes and mindsets to handle a dynamic labour market
- challenging perceptions and norms about job types
- improving workforce participation in vulnerable demographics
- the need to move towards tapered retirement models
- new models to forecast job transition requirements
- improved understanding of the peer-to-peer (and freelancer) economy

In turn, the World Economic Forum's "Future of Jobs" report finds enormous change predicted in the skill sets needed to thrive in the new landscape.[24]

Top 10 skills needed to thrive

2015	2020
1. Complex Problem Solving	1. Complex Problem Solving
2. Coordinating with Others	2. Critical Thinking
3. People Management	3. Creativity
4. Critical Thinking	4. People Management
5. Negotiation	5. Coordinating with Others
6. Quality Control	6. Emotional Intelligence
7. Service Orientation	7. Judgement and Decision Making
8. Judgement and Decision Making	8. Service Orientation
9. Active Listening	9. Negotiation
10. Creativity	10. Cognitive Flexibility

---

23   "Tomorrow's digitally enabled workforce," CSIRO, January 2016.

24   "The Future of Jobs," World Economic Forum, January 2016.

In banking, there are already major changes taking place, with traders almost irrelevant in investment banking these days. The days of multimillion-dollar bonuses may be over, given that a machine can invest better than a human. According to Daniel Nadler, CEO of Kensho, a financial analytics tool, a third to half of the current employees in finance will lose their jobs to automation software within the next decade.

Whatever happens, it is clear that jobs are changing thanks to automation, but they always have. There will always be jobs, just different jobs and new jobs. The only difference in the future is that you will have two types of people: those who own the robots and those who work for them.

MOST OF US WILL END UP IN SPACE

In concluding this chapter, as everything on Earth that can be automated will be, we can look to a future where humans enjoy a different world, or worlds if you would rather. We will be travelling in space as a multiplanetary species, and enjoying new lives moving between Earth, Mars and beyond.

This truly puts the next revolution of humanity in context. When researching your family ancestry, you can see how things have moved from very local, when we were agricultural, to more exploratory, as we created ships and trains, to now becoming astronauts. For example, if you search your family ancestry, you can quickly find your grandparents, great grandparents, great-great grandparents and even earlier generations.

In just a month of research, I traced some parts of my lineage back to the 1600s, and hooked up with a distant cousin thrice-removed who helped me track down the missing links. I realised that my lineage related to specific parts of the country, and even specific villages. That's not so surprising as I guess that, going into the more distant past, we would have had lots of relatives in pockets of communities because people just didn't travel. Take anyone's family a couple of generations ago and you'd probably find all of their ancestry rooted in the same area because people stayed in the same village or town and never left. Why would you leave? What else was there to do? In fact, if you did leave, you would often find yourself in trouble. Peasants were often tithed to the land and could only leave their village if they had the appropriate papers from the Church or lord or king, dependent on the nature of their travels. If caught without such papers, you could be thrown into jail or worse.

Things changed as the Victorian era ended and the automobile came into its own. Before the car, the horse was the only form of transportation and it pretty much limited people to stay in their hometowns. The car, train and steam ship allowed people to move around more easily, and some did. The movement of people was not common, but there were some who migrated to the Americas or relocated around Europe.

However, in general, the masses stayed at home. That was until connectivity allowed easy movement between towns and cities for all, with cheap access to motor vehicles and a growing extension of roads. Urbanisation was under way. Today, it is a phenomenon that is causing great concern to the planet's well-being but, back in the 1950s, it was seen as a great new thing. It enabled women to have greater equality by competing for jobs and created the mass suburb growth and interstate highways of the United States. Everything from family life and the end of the nuclear family to a family divided was impacted, as was how we related to each other and entertained. Travel makes a fundamental difference to how we live.

I can see that today from the third revolution in how we travel—the aeroplane. Fifty years ago, someone catching a plane was an explorer; today, planes are just buses. It still amazes me how I can easily travel around three or four countries across Europe in a day, or around three or four continents of the world in a week. This would have been outrageous thinking half a century ago.

This is illustrated well by a friend of mine who has a base in London, a family in Switzerland, a holiday home that he visits most weekends in the south of France and a company based in Singapore. We do this because we can, but imagine telling a Victorian that's how they would be living in a century's time and they would have thought you an idiot. And that's exactly what you would call someone today who said that your grandchildren will be living on Mars. An idiot. Can you imagine?

Well, I can. I often talk about the fifth age of humanity, and living in space. It is obvious that we will be going in this direction. An essential part of humanity is to explore and now that we've explored most of Earth, we will naturally start to explore most of space. Technology is enabling this to happen, with SpaceX's reusable rockets being a case in point, and the only limitations are our imaginations.

For example, talking about this theme of the next generation of travel at a conference in Luxembourg led to one audience member coming up to me and saying, "I totally agree with your vision of life on Mars, as Luxembourg has already patented space mining." I asked him to explain.

Luxembourg stepped onto space mining's ground floor in 2016, when its Ministry of Economy announced the Space Resources initiative. Key to the programme, said the official statement, "will be the development of a legal and regulatory framework confirming certainty about the future ownership of minerals extracted in space from Near Earth Objects such as asteroids."

The country then passed the first European Space Law in August 2017, which establishes legal certainty that asteroid mining companies can keep what they find in space. This was in response to the American Space Act of 2015, which states that a majority of a company's stakeholders must be located in the United States. In contrast, the Luxembourg law places no restrictions on stakeholder locations.

Luxembourg has also been pretty active in the space mining business, investing €25 million in the space mining company Planetary Resources in November 2016. Space is a real thing, and it's a commercial thing.

Well, there it is. We went from walking between villages to travelling between cities by horse and train to driving across countries to flying around the world to mining in deep space in just a short two centuries. I wonder how we'll be travelling in the 2110s?

THE RISE OF A NEW FINANCIAL STRUCTURE (FINTECH)

Over the past decade, since the open sourcing structures of the cloud, APIs and apps emerged, a new financial structure has been developing. Generically, it is called FinTech, but what is FinTech and how is it changing things?

I think of FinTech as being a new market that integrates finance and technology. This new market is a hybrid of the traditional processes of finance—working capital, supply chain, payments processing, deposit accounts, life assurance and so on—but replaces their traditional structures with a new technology-based process.

In other words, the term "FinTech" describes a whole new industry. It's a little like talking about retailers, and saying that Amazon is a retailer. Is it a retailer or an e-commerce company or both? I would claim that it is a digital service provider of fulfilment, but that's purely because it fulfils consumer orders as well as a cloud-based service delivery through Amazon Web Services (AWS). In other words, it is not a retailer at all but a company in a whole new market place.

In the same way, I don't think of FinTech as a research and development (R&D) function of finance because this is a new emergent market of digital finance that will, over time, displace the traditional financial markets.

In particular, the idea of "large incumbent technology firms supporting the financial sector" is referring to the last-century technology providers to banks, such as IBM, Unisys, NCR and co. Such companies are not FinTech firms, but last-century bank technology service providers.

In addition, labelling emergent FinTech as companies that are "disintermediating incumbent financial services with new technology" may also not hit the mark as some of the incumbents are becoming FinTech companies while some FinTech companies are providing services to incumbents. So we need to define this market space more.

We talk a lot about FinTech. We talk about it as if it were one thing when, in fact, it is many. There are nuances to this market that are over a decade old today, and these need to be fleshed out in more detail because, just as with technology in general, some of this FinTech is in the hype cycle, some is in the chasm and some is coming into the mainstream.

We talk about the billions of dollars being invested in FinTech, the wave of unicorns and start-ups in this space, the challenge they bring to banks and incumbents and the way in which they are reaching new spaces and places. In fact, $100 billion was invested in FinTech between 2013 and 2016, according to KPMG's "The Pulse of FinTech Report: Q4'16".

Looking at the different geographies, the United States is where most action has taken place until recently as Silicon Valley has a vibrant network of investment support. Sure, it's not what it was but it's still bullish when established players like SoFi can get half a billion dollars from Silver Lake Partners. That's $1.89 billion of funding for a firm valued at just $4.3 billion.

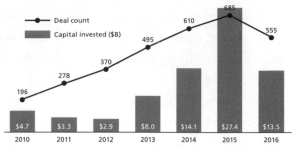

Data sources: KPMG International; PitchBook

Asia is also big on FinTech. The region has just woken up to what FinTech can do, to be honest, and is about two to three years behind most European and U.S. FinTech communities. The year 2016 was a record year for Asian FinTech investments, driven by companies like Ant Financial valued at $60 billion, and I expect this market will continue that bullish behaviour.

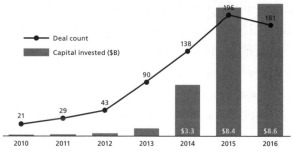

Data sources: KPMG International; PitchBook

Europe has seen that Brexit had a chilling effect on London investments in 2016. Investment in UK FinTech start-ups dropped by a third after the Brexit decision, according to Innovate Finance, from $1.2 billion in 2015 to $783 million a year later. But it's worse than that, according to KPMG, which estimates that UK FinTech investments were down 85 per cent from $4.6 billion in 2015 to $654 million in 2016.

That doesn't mean London has lost its place. The city continues to be seen as one of the truly global financial centres which, along with a vibrant tech start-up sector, has helped create a strong environment for FinTech firms to start up and scale. That still sets it apart from Europe, where FinTech investment dropped 80 per cent from $10.9 billion in 2015 to $2.2 billion in 2016.

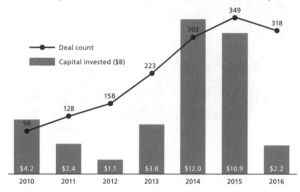

European investments in FinTech start-ups

Data sources: KPMG International; PitchBook

But what exactly is FinTech? It is no longer one big bucket of finance and technology. As I've already mentioned, saying "FinTech" is like saying "retailer". What exactly are they retailing and, in the FinTech sense, what areas of finance are these companies automating?

This gets interesting as we now have a market that is spreading its wings into lots of different areas. As I've just said, it is no longer this one big bucket, but many. There is RegTech for regulatory technologies, WealthTech for wealth management technologies, InsurTech for insurance technologies and so on. FinTech has also gained subcategories like lending, analytics, digital identity, cybersecurity, small- and medium-sized enterprises (SME) finance, financial inclusion, payments, roboadvice, blockchain distributed ledgers, neobanking and more. Then some generic technologies around the cloud, the Internet of Things, artificial intelligence, machine learning, biometrics and others are creating FinTech themes and impacts. Let's look at the range of services and map them onto what I call the "FinTech Wave".

THE FINTECH WAVE

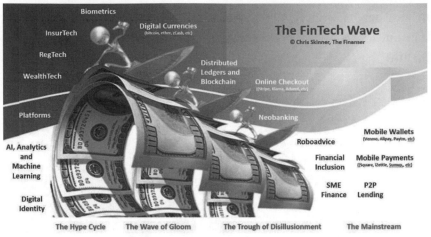

© Chris Skinner

As you can see, some technologies are rising, some are falling and some are now widely adopted such as lending marketplaces. Here it is worth discussing the areas that are primarily generic technologies with a financial flavour such as AI, machine learning, IoT and biometrics. I don't intend to define the whole market for each of these, but purely to place a dialogue around where they fit in the FinTech scene at a high level.

RegTech

Regulatory technologies, or RegTech for short, is the marriage of technology and regulation to address regulatory challenges. This area has existed for some time with varying degrees of success. Increasing levels of regulation, and a greater focus on data and reporting, has brought the RegTech offering into greater focus, thereby creating more value for the firms that invest in these solutions.

InsurTech

Insurance technologies, or InsurTech, are rethinking and redefining how we deal with insurance through technology. The first visible InsurTech start-up that I spotted was Friendsurance in Germany. Launched in 2010, the small peer-to-peer insurer secured a $15.3 million funding round in 2016. The way the model works is that everyone contributes to a common pool to mitigate risk—that's the very nature of insurance. However, in Friendsurance's case, any premiums left over in the fund at the end of year are paid back to contributors, as the risk didn't happen. Given this start-up's success, a whole raft of start-ups worldwide are now doing interesting things within the realm of InsurTech, such as these fourteen companies:

- Cocoon makes an internet-connected security device for the home.
- Kasko provides a white-label option for instant insurance purchases on affiliate platforms.
- Jamii connects low-income populations in sub-Saharan Africa with health insurance.
- Buzzmove provides price comparison for the removals trade; information that is important to insurers after a loss.
- Myfuturenow helps connect dormant pension accounts to holders.
- Roost makes a smart battery for smoke detectors and counts the United States Automobile Association (USAA) among its investors.
- Augury makes sensors for heating, ventilation and air conditioning systems.
- CoVi Analytics is a platform for insurers to use the required reporting from Solvency II data in their enterprise in other ways.
- Domotz is an Internet of Things management system that offers a platform for insurers to rate risk and manage claims.
- FitSense helps life and health insurers leverage data from wearables.
- Quantifyle allows users to "shop around" their wearable and other health data to insurance companies and find the best price.

- MassUp uses APIs to connect insurers to retailers so people can quickly and easily add coverage to new purchases.
- RightIndem is a self-service total loss claims platform that claims to reduce insurers' workload and leakage while improving customer service.
- Safer is designed to help millennials identify what kind of insurance they need by tapping into their social data.

WealthTech

WealthTech is a segment of FinTech that focuses on enhancing wealth management and investing. Wealth and asset management firms have to review their internal processes and communication with clients and decide where tools provided by the FinTech industry can be applied to enhance their proposition and operations. These can be client-facing tools (for example, providing more accessible information in digital formats), portfolio management tools that enhance performance or tools that provide relationship managers with powerful solutions so that they can serve their clients more effectively.

Roboadvice

Roboadvice is automating advice about investments using software. The software algorithms analyse your portfolio of savings and investments, to allow you to maximise your returns based on your risk appetite, in a completely automated system. Today, roboadvisors are primarily targeted for the mass affluent, and are providing an opportunity to bring together the micro and macro levels of money and engage the mass affluent with a real-time ledger and balance system. I like the quote from Jon Stein, founder and CEO of Betterment, who has stated that roboadvisors are not competing with wealth managers, thus explaining why roboadvice falls into a separate category. Instead, he believes that the competition is advice versus no advice, and that it is not a battle between robots and humans but a battle between advice and nothing.

In the roboadvisory field, the United States has led the charge with the rise of companies like Wealthfront, Betterment, FutureAdvisor and Personal Capital. Such firms offer wealth management and micro personal financial management (PFM) in apps.

Lending

Peer-to-peer lending connects people who have money with those who need money through software, and mitigates risk through real-time credit analytics. Zopa was the first online personal finance P2P lending company, but many have followed including Prosper Marketplace, Lending Club, Lufax and more.

SME Finance

SME finance is probably the most radical new market that is being changed with technology from peer-to-peer lending to invoice financing to crowdfunding. Its emergence has generated a huge new flow of capital that enables investors to lend money directly to SMEs and start-ups that otherwise would not exist.

Invoice financing often mixes the ideas of peer-to-peer lending with financial factoring. MarketInvoice, a UK firm, is a good example. MarketInvoice launched in 2011 to provide a financial factoring service, which is where a small business can take its outstanding invoices and get them paid early. The firm providing the finance then collects the invoice payment from the client, and takes a commission for having paid the business early. So if I am owed $2,000 by a client who normally pays in sixty days, a factoring firm will offer me $1,800 today and it, in turn, will get $2,000 sixty days later for a $200, or 10 per cent, commission. That idea has been around for years, but put it on the internet and a firm like MarketInvoice can grow from lending nothing to lending over £1 billion in five years. The firm then doubled that amount in 2016 alone. Although this is actually a form of peer-to-peer lending, the difference here is that the financing of all of those outstanding invoices comes from investors.

Then there is the new model of crowdfunding. Crowdfunding allows start-up firms to get funding on day one from their potential customers. It used to be that a start-up had to go to a bank to get money to get going. The start-up also had to spend a considerable amount of that money on marketing to reach its target audience via media. Sites like Kickstarter, Indiegogo, Crowdcube and Seedrs now collapse that start-up structure into one process, where your market and your customers provide you with the funds directly to get going.

Crucially, crowdfunding overcomes the issue of lack of data. Traditionally, banks have been reluctant to fund start-up SMEs because they have had no data to analyse to assess the risk to determine whether funding that SME would result in a return. Where is the intended market? Will they buy? Crowdfunding businesses turn that risk on its head, as the amount of funding in a crowdfunded business is directly reflected by the demand from the marketplace and customer. In other words, the unknown data the bank is looking for—what is the demand for this product—is determined upfront, before the business gets started, by the potential customer demand.

Financial Inclusion

Financial inclusion is one of the most exciting areas of FinTech because it brings 4.5 billion people who weren't worth serving before, because it was too expensive, onto the network. In particular, the financial inclusion programmes in Africa are key as these are rethinking how money is exchanged through the mobile network. This is a major focus of this book, and is expanded on in many other sections.

Blockchain Distributed Ledgers

This is an area that needs definition and is quite contentious because, in financial markets, blockchain became so overhyped and misunderstood that it hit a wall. In my view, this technology is now firmly over the hype wave and crashing towards the trough of disillusionment. The main reason for this is that there has been a lot of investment in experiments, without the investors necessarily realising that they were just experiments. Gartner summed it up well in a list of the top ten mistakes that companies make when considering enterprise blockchain projects:

- misunderstanding or ignoring the purpose of blockchain technology
- assuming that current technology is ready for production use
- confusing future blockchain technology with the present-day generation
- confusing a limited, foundation-level protocol with a complete business solution
- viewing blockchain technology purely as a database or storage mechanism
- assuming interoperability among platforms that do not exist yet
- assuming that today's leading platforms will still be dominant (or even extant) tomorrow
- assuming that smart contract technology is a solved problem
- ignoring funding and governance issues for a peer-to-peer distributed network
- failing to incorporate a learning process

This means that many banks are now wondering where the returns are in their blockchain investments and are reeling back on those investments. The key here is that the blockchain, when it really is used well, will be as transformational as the internet. However, the use of blockchain shared ledgers is more to do with agreeing new infrastructure operating models, such as how to replace core networks like SWIFT and Visa, than the technology itself.

This does not diminish the importance of blockchain and cryptocurrencies however. If anything, these are the building blocks of the next-generation financial system, as described in depth in *ValueWeb*. Rather than repeat everything I said in that book, all I'll say here is that this technology will be important in the future as it is clearly creating the new real-time, low-cost financial structure for the internet age.

Digital Identity

Digital identity is another big area of debate because it requires an agreed structure before the technology can be deployed. Key questions include the following: Who runs a digital identity scheme? How is it operated? If self-sovereign, as many are arguing it should be, what happens when access is blocked and needs to be unblocked, such as when you have an accident and the medical care team needs access to your health details? These questions will be solved over time.

Analytics

Data is the air that banks breathe, and data analytics is the difference between the banks that win and those that lose. The internet giants make their money out of data analysis and usage. That is their business, and financial institutions have the same opportunities with data, if they use it well. This is why many financial firms are investing in machine learning, artificial intelligence and data analytics because it allows them to improve their credit risk modelling, cross-sell ratios and enhance the user experience. It is all about deep learning from customers' data to personalise and improve their relationship digitally with the institution.

Cybersecurity

There are many concerns about cybersecurity, simply because no one wants to be hacked. That's why the International Data Corporation (IDC) estimates that $101.6 billion will be spent on cybersecurity software, services and hardware by 2020, up from $73.7 billion in 2016, or an increase of 38 per cent. Banks and financial firms are particularly exposed, as thieves try to attack banks first because that's where the money is. Hence, financial institutions are particularly focused on internal and customer security, and any scheme that assists in tightening this area is worthy of consideration.

However, in my own experience of talking with hackers, and I've talked to many, it is the employee of the bank who is the area of least security. This is because every hacker talks about social engineering as their key skill. They play on the natural trust of people in other people. That is the vulnerability; we naturally like to trust other people. Just read more about how thieves hack to discover what the thieves do and, nine times out of ten, it is tricking an employee into becoming part of their plan by using their trust to compromise them.

Biometrics

Talking of security, biometrics has finally reached prime time. That's in part due to the smartphone camera, which offers a great opportunity to capture facial recognition or an iris scan. Equally, the touch screen has given us the chance to use fingerprints and palms. Adding these capabilities to a PIN or one-time password (OTP) provides an excellent way to tighten security for the consumer, by adding an extra identity check, and overcomes the issue of forgotten passwords.

Payments

The payments area of FinTech is actually an area that can be talked about in its own right. This is because it has varying levels from mobile wallets (Venmo, Alipay, Paytm, etc.) to mobile payments (Square, iZettle, SumUp, etc.) to online checkout (Stripe, Klarna, Adyen, etc.) to digital currencies (bitcoin, ether, zCash, etc.) to payments infrastructure (Digital Asset Holdings, SETL, Ripple, etc).

Neobanking

Neobanking refers to the new bank start-ups that are appearing around the world, and they differ considerably. For example, the neobanks that have sprung out of China—YESBANK and WeBank—are very different to those in Europe and the United States, simply because they can be. They have sprung out of other services—commerce and chat—and therefore have a different ethos and look to banks like Soon in France, from AXA Group. Equally, there is a hive of activity across Europe with new bank start-ups from bunq in the Netherlands to CheBanca! in Italy to Lunar Way in Denmark and N26 in Germany. The United Kingdom probably leads the market for neobanks, however, as there are around forty new bank start-ups offering full bank services to bank app front ends. These include Atom, Fidor, Loot, Metro, Monese, Monzo, Starling, Tandem and Zopa. These banks fall into two categories: full banking services with a bank licence (like Atom and Starling) and bank front ends like Loot. All of these neobanks are competing on the basis of giving users a better digital experience than traditional financial firms.

Platforms, Markets and Cloud

Finally, the biggest area of change in banking is the creation of new financial marketplaces. Marketplaces are where apps, APIs and analytics are deployed so that many different firms can play with them. Good examples are Uber, Airbnb and Facebook, where the marketplaces are their platforms and people can then use their apps and APIs to connect and play.

A range of new FinTech start-ups are trying to get into this space from CBW Bank in the United States, which partners with Moven and Simple, to Wirecard in Germany, which powers Holvi, Loot and other neobanks. Such start-ups are now being copied and competed against by firms like solarisBank and Fidor in Germany, Thought Machine and ClearBank in Britain, Leveris from Ireland and more. The biggest of these challenger markets is currently in China, where Ant Financial offers apps, APIs and analytics that are being used by more than forty Chinese banks.

DIGGING INTO THE GRANULARITY OF FINTECH

I keep trying to define and delineate more and more of this FinTech Wave as it is no longer FinTech, but RegTech, WealthTech, InsurTech and more, as can be seen. The thing that strikes me the most is that there are two fundamentally different FinTech camps: those attacking existing business structures and those creating new structures.

It is somewhat easier for those creating new structures because there is no market today. They are starting up to serve the needs of the un(der) served, and that is a huge opportunity. Whether it be creating a mobile wallet or enabling low-cost remittances, for instance, these are market areas that have been crying out for a service and finally they can have one. Low cost and cheap being the key, it is down to the reach of digital technologies. This was best illustrated to me when I recently went to Pakistan, a country with a population of 200 million people, and yet only 20 million have bank accounts. One in ten people is banked, meaning that technology provides a possibility to reach millions more and is already doing so. Since 2013, the country has seen the rapid spread of 3G and 4G data services, with almost 50 million people now using mobile data services. So, one in four people in Pakistan has mobile data services whilst one in ten has a bank account. Now, there's an opportunity.

Ant Financial is at the realm of this market for financial inclusion. The company is forming partnerships almost every day to service these needs, from Paytm (short for Pay through Mobile) in India to GCash in Indonesia. For the governments in these economies, this is a force for positive change. McKinsey estimates that the global gross domestic product (GDP) will rise by $3.5 trillion per annum by 2025 through financial inclusion. That is why governments are encouraging and supporting the movements of firms focused on financial inclusiveness.

Governments, however, are not as keen generally to support those in the other camp, the firms that focus on breaking bank monopolies. I heard a regulator in an emerging market saying that they will force FinTech start-ups to collaborate with banks. He also said that it is an option for banks to partner with FinTechs. The example he then used was for peer-to-peer lending which, in that country, the regulator had stated can only take place through a bank. What? That's not going to create much innovation, is it? The banks don't have to offer such a service or collaborate with such a service, and as such a service would decimate their profit line, why would they?

I find it unbelievable that in 2018 there are so many markets where regulators continue to build barriers for FinTech start-ups. Then again, I suppose it is not so unbelievable as most regulators are puppets of governments who, in turn, are the puppets of banks. Sure, sure, that's a cynical view. However, when I heard Elizabeth Warren talking about Jamie Dimon ringing all the U.S. congressmen, prior to passing the Dodd-Frank Wall Street Reform and Consumer Protection Act, and threatening to ruin the economy and their voters' support if they didn't water the regulation down, it was clear that governments are the puppets of the big banks.

This is the real conundrum: how can you innovate in an economy strangled by the existing players? It's easy to innovate in areas where the existing players have no interest—most banks regard financial inclusion as charity—but when the new start-ups threaten a bank's basic business, then it's a different matter.

It is why I see the Financial Conduct Authority (FCA), the UK regulator, doing some interesting things in its sandbox. Yet the companies getting a fast track to market through the sandbox tend to focus on one of three major areas:

- taking inefficiencies out of the existing banking system by, for example, improving customer onboarding and the customer onboarding process (know your client, KYC)
- taking friction out of the customer experience by making it easier to plug-and-play software between banking services
- innovating the banking system by using technological capabilities to enhance services, such as roboadvising

When a start-up truly threatens a bank's core margins and products, most regulators fear to tread.

IS IT FINTECH OR TECHFIN?

After numerous conversations with both bankers and start-ups, it is clear that there is a differing view of the world. It is not as clear-cut as nimble innovator versus dinosaur incumbent, which is how many portray this chasm of difference in thinking, but there is a significant difference nonetheless. Perhaps this difference can be best summed up by a comment that a banker made to me recently, "Surely this is TechFin rather than FinTech?" I thought about what he meant and realised that this is the subtle difference between the innovator and the incumbent. An innovator thinks of the following as FinTech—taking financial processes and applying technology. In contrast, incumbents regard taking technology to work with financial processes as TechFin. This difference in thinking, although subtle, does create a very different thought process and output to the way in which technology is used. So I thought I would delve a little deeper, as this is a key to seeing how the world differs as far as the innovators and incumbents are concerned.

First, the start-up FinTech firm. This firm looks at the world through the eyes of a technologist. This means that the starting point is technology. Apps, APIs, analytics and more are the foundations of their thinking. Open source, open operations and open thinking are at the heart of their culture. Embracing diversity, working globally and no reference offices or structure are the tools of their skill set. And seeking a mentor, an angel and an investor are the base capital requirements to get them started.

The start-up begins by thinking about how technology could transform financial processes. This means that they take something that exists, be it loans, savings, investments, payments, trading or more, and think about how they could reinvent these processes. P2P lending is a good example. When Zopa started business in 2005, its founders told me about their business model and it sounded weird, to be honest. "We're an eBay for loans," they told me. "You give us your money and we lend it out on your behalf. You get better interest on your money than you would with a savings company, and people pay less for their loans," they continued. "Want to invest £10,000?"

No way, as it sounded crazy. An untested, unproven business that would take my investment and manage the risk of lending that investment to borrowers? An eBay for loans? That's start-up thinking. Over a decade later, that start-up is taking over £1.2 billion in funds from over 53,000 consumers to lend at the most competitive rates in the United Kingdom. In fact, the start-up P2P model is so popular that it has been copied worldwide, with the United States being one of the fastest-growing markets where over $8 billion has been lent, doubling year-on-year. It is why Lending Club had one of the hottest IPOs of 2014 followed by SoFi receiving over $1 billion investment in its 2015 funding round.

These are significant numbers, but nowhere near as significant as the forecasts being made by banks like Goldman Sachs and Morgan Stanley. Goldman Sachs predicts that almost $11 billion of bank profits from lending will move to the new start-up social economy by 2020—about 5 per cent of the current market—whilst Morgan Stanley estimates that global marketplace lending should reach $290 billion by 2020, with a compound annual growth rate (CAGR) of 51 per cent from 2014 to 2020, with China and the United States being the two largest markets.

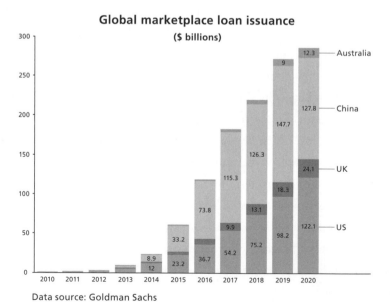

Global marketplace loan issuance
($ billions)

Data source: Goldman Sachs

This is the key to the FinTech thinking of the innovators: how can we take an existing market with a middleman and replace the middleman with a technology intermediary? It is what bitcoin is focused on—replacing the bank with the Internet for Value transfer. It is what new trading schemes like tzero.com focus on—replacing the stock market with the blockchain. It is what firms like TransferWise and Currencycloud believe—replace FX markets with P2P connectivity to enable money to move. The rapidly growing and disruptive FinTech scene is hot because it is all about using technology to transform financial processes.

The incumbent thinking of the TechFin, though, is very different. Banks begin by thinking, how can I apply technology to this financial process? They begin with their existing operations and wonder how they can improve those operations with technology. It's a very different mindset to that of the FinTech start-up, and works differently in different markets.

For example, an investment operation in the capital markets space or a prime broker are far less fearful of ditching existing technologies and reinventing their operations than a large retail bank. This is not surprising as an investment bank is competing in an ultra cutthroat marketplace, where technology has been the competitive differentiator for some years. Take the rise of high-frequency trading (HFT) using low latency technologies, and you can see a completely restructured capital market that has been transformed by technology in the last decade. Compare this with a large retail bank with millions of customers whose primary focus is safety, reliability and stability, and you can soon see why retail banks are stuck with legacy technologies while their investment bank counterparts are running at light speed.

You cannot view the banking marketplace as some homogeneous structure but, at high level, it is certainly the case that investment banks think far more like FinTech firms than retail or commercial banks. The majority of the large retail commercial banks have a challenge that is very different to the one faced by the FinTech firms and their investment counterparts. This challenge is to work out how to transform a business where the customer expects no risk and minimal change.

This was well illustrated to me by a conversation with a digital bank leader who explained that each time they change their mobile app, they get more complaints from customers than compliments. Customers don't like change, especially in their bank. Change implies risk, and general banking should avoid risk in the eyes of both the bank and their customer. As a result, customers are generally reluctant to switch banks, and do not expect their banks to switch the systems that they use. A bank can change the website design, add more mobile functionality and/or restructure the operations but, if any of this is visible to the customer, they scream, "FOUL!"

This is why so many retail and commercial banks find themselves exposed to negative publicity if they close a branch, charge a fee for improved service or upgrade their systems. Any fault, glitch or failure gains headlines of gloom. Any downtime, lost transaction or missed payment results in regulatory review.

Hence, the TechFin firm has to focus on technology improvement rather than total transformation. TechFin firms cannot think like FinTech firms because their customers don't want them to. This is why TechFin firms—the incumbent banks—are not dinosaurs or technology deniers, but purely pragmatists who are improving their operations with technology rather than trying to disrupt and transform them.

THERE'S AN ELEPHANT IN THE ROOM AND IT'S UNDER ATTACK

As I've established, banks have a slightly different view of FinTech to the start-up community. Their line of thinking is again clear when you look at their take on how FinTech has developed over the years. For instance, Victor Matarranz, former head of Group Strategy, Banco Santander, presented at a conference in 2016, during which he highlighted the difference between FinTech 1.0 and FinTech 2.0.

FinTech 1.0, as defined by Matarranz, is the emergence of peer-to-peer lenders and new payments companies between 2010 and 2014. During this time, everyone was talking about disruptive change and unbundling the bank but, as Matarranz put it, it was actually a lot of small fish swimming around the large bank whales.

Photo © Chris Skinner

FinTech 2.0 has pushed this further in that, as the FinTech emerging players emerged, the banks began to work with them. Starting in 2014, innovation labs, accelerators, hackathons and more were being run by many of the more dynamic banks—DBS, Barclays, BBVA and Citi spring to mind as the early leaders here—but now most banks have something going on.

In the FinTech 2.0 era, according to Matarranz, it's all about collaboration and cooperation. I agree with his view to an extent, but feel there is a more fundamental underlying trend. That trend is the open sourcing of financial structures.

Historically, banks have been control freaks. They have developed everything internally and have little trust of external firms, unless it's for tertiary activities. Core systems are carefully maintained and controlled, and that control freak supervision of the core has been a traditional strength of the bank. Now it is the fundamental weakness. Banks have spent years building on their core, which they control and trust because they built it. However, as we entered the 2010s, more and more technologies were attacking this core, proprietary structure. It is the open sourcing of that structure that has become the transitional new world and, by its nature, is creating the major weakness in the old structure.

Apps, APIs, analytics, AI, machine learning, the cloud, mobile, blockchain and more are all driving financial services to be plug-and-play as-a-service. We can see this in the vast array of new players, with some already substantial players.

In fact, what I've seen happening is the first wave of FinTech attacking areas that banks underserved or overlooked, notably, SME funding, student finance, frictionless mobile payments and checkout. In the first wave, FinTech start-ups fell into three categories:

- those that focused on payment processing
- those that generated new lending models using peer-to-peer structures
- those that helped banks through PFM and risk modelling tools

Since 2014, this has shifted. The areas above are still in play but we now have the rise of the roboadvisors, new forms of trading and investing, the rethinking of infrastructures through blockchain protocol, the acceptance of bitcoin as something more interesting than a rogue currency and more. In the FinTech 2.0 wave, I believe we have moved from a few buzzing insects stinging the backside of the banks to a veritable storm of locusts attacking the underbelly of the banking beast.

This is because FinTech 2.0 is actually deconstructing financial pieces into their base elements. Some are back office, some middle office and some front office, with each area being ripe for the plucking thanks to the technologies of today. Smart things with intelligence inside integrated via apps make the front-office customer experience exceptional, API plug-and-play interfaces in the middle office make the connection between front and back office simple and in real time while machine learning, artificial intelligence, deep data analytics, cloud structures alongside blockchain shared ledgers are reconstructing back-office services.

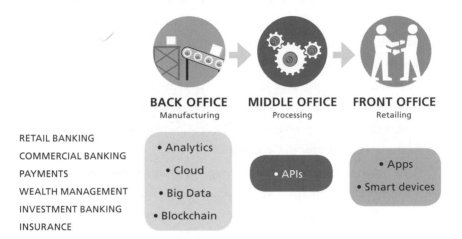

This is the core fundamental shift in today's FinTech world. It will continue to shift and change for the next decade, and a bank that is not at the centre of this storm, open sourcing their core services, will be wrecked.

The thing is that in this process, the bank has to have leadership that understands this structural shift from vertically integrated proprietary structures to open-sourced collaborative structures. Do banks have that understanding? Clearly not when only 3 per cent of the world's largest banks are run by technologists whilst 77 per cent have only one or no (43 per cent of banks) technology experts in their leadership teams.

Meanwhile, when we get to FinTech 3.0, the banks that survive this change will look far more like collaborative financial integrators of the value chain with their proprietary core structures in ruins. The banks that don't survive will be the ones that hang on for dear life trying to keep those structures in play long past their sell-by dates.

WHY FINTECH START-UPS THINK THEY CAN BEAT THE BANKS

There's an old joke about the man who's lost driving in the countryside. When he stops to ask a pedestrian how to get to the city, the pedestrian replies, "Oh, if you want to get there, I wouldn't start from here." This is exactly how banks feel today. They want to get to the nirvana of new technologies but are stuck in a spaghetti of old systems. Some call them legacy, others call them handcuffs, but no matter what they are called, they pose a problem. The problem is that old systems and legacy technologies stop the bank moving forward into the nimble and agile future on offer today, and this is exactly what FinTech start-ups believe they can exploit as it is clearly a weakness for the large banks.

Many new companies are launching capabilities built on the latest internet-enabled technologies. These include easy-to-use apps for customers, simple to add code for merchants and open systems to allow anyone to work with them. It is almost like banking in an apps store, with hundreds of companies offering thousands of services that are simple and easy for sending and receiving money. These companies include firms like Stripe, a 2010 start-up that is the preferred code for building online checkout services. Really easy to work with, the company is the chosen system for many other innovative companies, including Kickstarter and Apple Pay, and valued at almost $10 billion by the end of 2016. The reason why it has gained such a valuation is that the firm has taken something the banks make difficult— setting up online payment services—and made it incredibly easy.

Likewise, there are companies that do similar things in lending, savings, investments and other specific areas of financial services based on internet technologies. They all share many of the same attributes in terms of being young, aspirational, visionary and capable. This is why collectively they have seen investments from venture capital and other funds averaging $25 billion in 2015 alone, according to figures published by auditor KPMG.[25]

25　See KPMG's *Pulse of FinTech* quarterly reports for more information.

However, there is a possible impasse here. The most successful FinTech firms are not replacing banks but instead are serving markets that were underserved. In other words, the FinTech firms that have the highest valuations and greatest success are those seeking easy investing or better access to funding, supporting small businesses and turning mobile telephones into points of sale. However, none of them has replaced a bank. They are succeeding because they are addressing areas that banks find difficult to serve due to cost or risk, such as lending to small businesses.

This is why it is interesting today to see so many new banks launching in the United Kingdom, most of which are FinTech banks. Atom, Starling, Monzo and more have bank licences from the UK regulator and considerable funding. However, they are up against the biggest UK banks that have millions of customers, billions of funding and centuries of history. For new players, fighting the large banks is going to be a challenge and they will need a lot of funding to succeed. This does not mean that they will not succeed but they will need real differentiation and exceptional digital services. Even then, will customers switch? It will be interesting to find out but the one thing the new players have from the start is fresh technologies, no legacy and unconstrained thinking. Equally, they have no cost overheads and, therefore, can compete more effectively on interest rates. After all, big banks have an awful lot of branches that aren't used much anymore. It may not be attractive to their customers or the media to shut down these branches but, if they do not, the big banks clearly cannot compete with these new digital start-ups, even with their millions of customers.

Therefore, the fight for the future of banking is going to be between a host of new digital players and a few large banks that find it hard to change, but are adapting as fast as they can. Interesting times indeed.

GLOBALISING FINANCE THROUGH FINTECH

Global, universal banking was the mantra of the 2000s and HSBC, Citi, Bank of America, BNP Paribas, Deutsche Bank and more all jumped on the bandwagon. After the global financial crisis, they all jumped off it again, and most global, universal banks' ambitions are now clipped back to purely being able to support their global corporate clients' needs. It's not universal, just commercial.

As this has happened, we have seen a counter-trend occurring as the maturing FinTech specialists branch out to create global monoline services in platforms. Klarna, SoFi, Stripe, PayPal, Ant, WeChat and more are branching out to deploy their services in the marketplace of apps, APIs and analytics and succeeding to a greater or lesser extent. So, the universal model of a bank doing a thousand things averagely around the world is replaced by a thousand companies doing a thousand specialist things brilliantly, thanks to the deployment of technology for financial processing.

In fact, many of these early start-ups are now maturing into global players and looking to get banking licences to play across more of the spectrum of finance. This has been the case with Klarna, SoFi and Zopa, and I expect there to be more, purely because linking credit with debit or making payments as a specialist service avoids attacking the core function of a value store, and we need global value stores.

This is obvious when you look at the fledgling hiccups of bitcoin. There are few trusted value stores of bitcoin and the ones that exist are regulated. Many others—the most recent being Bithumb and arbX Digital—are building on the MtGox issue. MtGox was one of the most popular digital currency exchanges, particularly for bitcoin, but got hacked in 2014 and investors lost almost half a billion dollars. These are not trusted value stores, just trading exchanges. You need to get your bitcoin off the exchange and into a trusted value store, digital or regulated, to really be able to believe in this currency.

The libertarians tell me that this is all democratised and that the democracy will regulate the currency. That's all well and good, until you lose your store of value, and have no comeback or say on what happened. What do you do then? Tough.

However, I was equally struck by a banker who laughed at the idea of a global currency that circumvents banks. "Banks will always be needed as your value store," he said. He thought that bitcoin was stupid and that kids will learn to grow up one day and put their bitcoins in banks. I couldn't believe his arrogance and complacency. Of course, kids will find ways to democratise their value stores. They will also find ways to get around the banks, and they already are.

For example, if the specialist FinTech processors I've mentioned could combine forces with each other and then with other global platform players like Facebook, Amazon, Google, Uber, Airbnb, Snapchat and company, what would they achieve? Imagine a marketplace of global players aligning forces where they work together in partnership. This could offer global financial integration into our social and consumer lives through APIs. In fact, it already is. The fact that we can integrate our payment cards and bank accounts into PayPal, Uber and Facebook has already changed that game.

So, I am imagining a future world where full banking licensed global players from Ant Financial to Stripe work in partnership with Facebook, Uber and co to give us a world where we still need banking but we don't need banks. Some may think that is fanciful but give it ten years....

THE RISE OF EVERYONE

Just over a decade ago, only one in ten Kenyans had access to finance. Then M-Pesa was launched in 2007. Today, almost everyone in Kenya has access to financial services. Mobile payments, mobile loans and mobile insurances are changing the world. This is evidenced best by the activities of Ant Financial, which aims to provide financial inclusiveness for everyone in the world.

Thanks to the mobile financial network that is being built or, rather, has been built, the two-thirds of the planet's population who were impoverished can now rise out of poverty. Often, the reason for poverty is the lack of access to the banking system. Think about it. If you have to move money and can only do so through a physical network, it is hard. Without access to a bank account, you are forced to move money through agents, many of whom cannot be trusted. Your money may never get to the person you are sending it to.

Second, it costs poor people a lot more to deal with money than rich people. People who keep bank accounts in credit often receive "free banking" in return. Yet banks make a lot of profit out of banking so how can they make so much profit if banking is free? Well, banking is never free and it is often the poorest who pay to subsidise the richest. The fees and charges on unexpected overdrafts and loans, for instance, are the fees and charges that pay for the richer person's "free" bank account. On top of this, if you don't have a bank account, you pay even more as you have to use a money changer, a payday loans firm or a remittance company to move your cash around.

Third, if you have to live with cash, you are susceptible to attack. Cash is insecure. It is easy to steal and is untraceable. You cannot prove you ever had that cash once it has gone.

Finally, cash is dirty. And here I'm talking literally. Often cash has been in contact with human emissions that are undesirable. If you are not already aware, 94 per cent of U.S. dollar bills are contaminated with bacteria, including some that can cause pneumonia, blood infections, diarrhoea and urinary tract and respiratory system infections. In addition, research has revealed that the flu virus can survive up to seventeen days on banknotes when accompanied by mucus, and four out of five banknotes have traces of cocaine and other drugs.[26]

For these reasons—security, risk, cost and health—there is a growing move to eliminate cash and, through mobile financial inclusion, it is succeeding. A great example is China which, just a few years ago, was a cash-based economy. Today, it is cashless in most Tier 1 cities, with the same trend moving swiftly across the rest of the country, thanks to two major mobile wallet systems—Alipay and WeChat Pay. Within just four years, these two systems converted a cash-based nation into a cashless country where $5.5 trillion of commerce was paid via mobile in 2016, about 70 per cent of all payments, and this number continues to rise fast. Compare this with the United States where just $112 billion was paid via mobile (Venmo, Apple Pay and brethren) in 2016, and you get an idea of the scale of the difference. The Chinese example is being replicated in many other nations across Asia, Africa and the Americas. For example, as mentioned earlier, 200 million people live, transact and trade in Pakistan, yet only 20 million Pakistanis

---

26   Brad Tuttle, "The Money in Your Wallet Might Be Covered With Poop, Mold, and Cocaine," *Time*, January 2017.

have bank accounts. That is all about to change though. Between 2013 and 2016, cheaper 3G and 4G mobile data networks were rolled out across the country and the number of Pakistanis with data mobile services now numbers nearly 50 million, up from none in 2012. You do not even need a mobile to have financial inclusion however. For instance, in India, the mobile wallet service Paytm allows 250 million users to buy from merchants. All the merchant needs is a quick response (QR) code. In case you missed it, the merchant does not need any technology or the network, just a code that their customers can scan to pay for things. This is why we are seeing a revolution of inclusion for the digital human age and why Ant Financial, which operates Alipay, is a major case study at the end of this book as it is the first and, so far, only company with a strategic focus on global financial inclusivity.

A THREE-STREAM FINANCIAL WORLD: WHICH ONE TO WATCH?

I was reflecting on a question posed to me recently by a Turkish banker. He asked me, "Why are Western banks always talking about legacy?" I knew exactly what he was getting at as the banks I deal with in the United States, the United Kingdom, France, Germany and other European nations are always fretting over the challenge posed by their old systems. It is not surprising given that 43 per cent of their bank systems are built in COBOL and other old programming languages but fewer and fewer people have any knowledge of how to programme in these languages anymore. As I mentioned earlier, most COBOL programmers are in their mid-forties to fifties and they are a dying breed. This is forcing banks to replace systems that have been operating for three decades or more, and that is like ripping out the foundations of a building whilst ensuring the house doesn't fall down. It is not easy.

For me however, this question illustrated a different conundrum. Whilst the United States and Europe are wrestling with legacy systems, I see China, India and other growth economies leapfrogging their counterparts thanks, in part, to implementing systems designed in the years after the birth of Mark Zuckerberg. Many of the banks and businesses in these economies began architecting infrastructure in the late 1990s and 2000s, and are now reaping the benefits.

This creates two clear economic structures—legacy West and growth East. However, there is a third stream economy rising. This third trend is the rise of mobile payment and wallet innovations in the developing and emerging economies. These economies are across sub-Saharan Africa, with Uganda, Ghana, Tanzania, Mali, Kenya and Nigeria in particular coming to mind, along with the Philippines, Indonesia and parts of Latin America. In these economies, large parts of the population live on less than $1.90 a day, the measure of the official poverty line today. These people have largely been ignored by technology but that is changing. Thanks to mobile networks, most of these populations now either have a mobile telephone or access to one if needed. By using mobile telephones, they can not only talk, but trade and transact as well, with mobile sales anticipated to rise to billions. This is illustrated by recent research from Global Market Insights, which stated that inexpensive wireless communication techniques among developing nations has stimulated the mobile point-of-sale (MPOS) market to surpass $20 billion by 2020, up from the present $12 billion with an expected CAGR of 19 per cent. The thing about this market is that there was nothing there before. It was too expensive for the physical financial network to serve people living on $1.90 a day. The digital network based on mobile financial exchange is changing the game here.

Precisely because there was nothing there before, these latter markets are reinventing the whole structure of how we think about financial systems and markets. These markets are creating disruptive innovations based on mobile networking transactions that could eventually change the game for all of us.

I see a three-stream world out there. The Western world of legacy economies, the Asian world of growth economies and the southern hemisphere world of innovation economies. When it comes to looking to the future, I know which one I would watch.

LOOK AT FINANCIAL INCLUSION FOR INNOVATION

We live in the developed economies complaining about legacy. In contrast, developing economies are just excited about innovation. Too often, people like me talk about millennials and consumers as people who don't need branches and reject the legacy structures. We forget that for billions of people on this planet, the very idea of being able to transact electronically is an inspiration. So when we talk about the eradication of branches, the redundancy of tellers and the shrinking of the physical network, we should pause to remember that for many people these are services that they have never had.

Many in India, the Philippines, Indonesia, Africa and elsewhere have never had a bank that's bothered to service them. Traditionally, the banks haven't been interested because it's too expensive and doesn't make economic sense. What is amazing today is that it *does* make economic sense. Someone transacting 50 cents a week can now be supported through an electronic network in the same way as someone transacting $50 a minute. That is truly amazing.

In fact, I often think about FinTech and technology in the broader sense as flattening the planet. Just as with Amazon, eBay and other long-tail companies, the internet enables those who couldn't be served by the physical financial network to suddenly gain access to the digital network for finance and be inspired. Anyone can be an entrepreneur on this network. Anyone on this network can make a payment and, more importantly, take a payment. Every mobile phone is a point of sale. That is truly transformational.

When you look at mobile wallets in sub-Saharan Africa or mobile checkouts like Square or lending marketplaces like Funding Circle and SoFi, you are seeing the growth of platforms that can serve the underbanked and the unbanked. Small businesses, students, higher risk borrowers, borrowers with no credit history, the unwanted and the undesired are all now able to be serviced and included. We talk about financial inclusion and that is the real revolution. Everyone is on the network. Everyone can transact. Everyone is included.

However, in the conversation, we blithely skip over the unwanted and undesired and focus on the incumbent and existing. We talk about fewer branches and less advice, digital support and digital outreach, relationships based on social interactions and the ability to provide contextual commerce and advice. The part we miss or overlook is the innovation of the unwanted.

In many developing economies, new financial models are emerging that have nothing to do with branches or advice. These models are emerging because there was nothing there before. No one could support these people and their financial needs before. We now have microinsurance that offers coverage to low-income households, such as policies against famine for 50 cents a day. We have peer-to-peer payments that can start as low as $1 and cost nothing to send and receive. We can exchange value in new structures from airtime to Likes. This is the fascinating world of the digital transformation and those of us who talk about incumbents, branches and traditional models of finance are potentially constrained into creating faster horses rather than rethinking the form of transportation.

The reinvention of finance is surfacing in the emerging economies, not in the developed ones. Digital identities, mobile wallets, microlending, microinsurance and peer-to-peer payments through digital currencies are all being embraced by the emerging and developing economies. Look to those economies for the innovator's dilemma as that's where you're going to find it. Not on the streets of New York or London but on the plains of Tanzania and in the forests of Indonesia. Revolution will come from small steps taken by non-banks in emerging markets. That's where we need to look for innovation.

THE UNBANKABLE BANKED

I spend most of my time jumping on and off aeroplanes. My most visited cities are London, where I live, and Singapore, the second most active global FinTech hub. I've also been to Hong Kong, Bangkok, Jakarta and other cities in Asia, along with Karachi, Dubai, Doha and Bahrain. Then there has been a trip or two to Kenya and South Africa. The United States has figured in my travels too, with New York being the main touchpoint, along with the South American cities of Sao Paolo, Buenos Aires and Bogota. Oh, and not forgetting regular sojourns around Europe with Oslo, Brussels, Paris, Frankfurt, Berlin and Milan being regular haunts.

What strikes me as I travel is how each market, each regulator and each community is different. All the cities have ambitions to encourage start-ups and be a FinTech hub, but some "get it" more than others. Certainly, the UK and Singapore governments have been determined to push their structures to the fore, but there are nuances around this. For example, China emerged as the dominant FinTech nation of 2016, and yet its FinTech is very different to what we see in Europe and the United States. That is partly down to Chinese financial markets using technology infrastructures that were implemented after the mid-1990s, and so a lot of Chinese FinTech is being created with zero legacy. That is the Chinese advantage over Europe and the United States, as the banks and financial markets in the West are trying to rearchitect their legacies. China, India and Africa are starting with almost a blank sheet of paper. In fact, India and parts of Africa are creating new ways of thinking about money and value exchange that have not even been considered by many. This is because financial inclusion has become a key mantra for these countries, with governments in Tanzania, Ghana and Uganda pushing the mobile wallet capabilities to their citizens. In the meantime, India is trying to go cashless, well before most other nations have even developed a policy for such a goal.

This makes for exciting times in emerging, developing and growth markets, but then we come back to the dullness of Europe. European banks are struggling with a lot of old tech. They talk about open APIs under PSD2 with hushed dread, and reference the major groups of workers digitalising the bank at a cost of billions. Really? Surely if the bank is spending billions on tech today, it's wasting the bank's money? I don't see start-ups that need billions to start up. So why do European and American banks talk about megaprojects with massive legions of coders requiring months to develop their digital assets?

I've said it before and I'll say it again, it's because U.S. and European banks are full of legacy. In contrast, countries that have no such banking legacy, such as those in sub-Saharan Africa, are moving billions of dollars through the mobile network because citizens now have mobile money. In Tanzania, people can move money between mobile wallets across all the network operators for almost no cost. In other African nations, digital identity schemes linked to mobile wallets are on the rise. This makes for an incredible combination of technologies that reinvent much of the banking system.

I'm referring to people who once had zero access to banking but can now buy, sell and generate credit histories through their mobile phones. That's why there were 1 billion mobile money transactions in December 2015, or 33 million per day. That is more than double the amount that PayPal processes. There are at least nineteen countries with more mobile money accounts than bank accounts, and most of them are in sub-Saharan Africa. One in three mobile connections in sub-Saharan Africa is linked to a mobile money account. In East Africa, that figure rises to one in every two.

This is why I love the world we see today because we have inspiration, innovation and invention in financial transactions coming from markets that previously did not have access to banking. These markets are making this happen because they now have access to finance through technology. It is why I'm fascinated by the developments in India, China, Indonesia, Brazil, Colombia and other markets where technology is reaching the unreachable. Things are being done with technology that had not been conceived of before. It'll be fascinating to see what they come up with.

THE AFRICAN MOBILE REVOLUTION

China, India and Africa illustrate the rise of mobile cashless inclusion well. The reason is that they each have huge numbers of people who historically have been excluded from the world of money. China and India are discussed in depth in the Ant Financial case study at the end of this book, which includes an interview with Vijay Shekhar Sharma, the charismatic founder and CEO of India's Paytm, whose majority investor is Ant Financial. However, Africa is different. Unlike India and China, Africa is not a country but a continent with great diversity between its member countries.

I chair the annual Dot Finance Live conference, Africa's premier FinTech event, which draws people from all over sub-Saharan Africa. What strikes me as I listen to lots of keynotes about mobile innovation and mobile financial inclusion is that Africa is actually leading the world in financial innovation. According to data from the World Bank in 2015, only 17.9 per cent of people in sub-Saharan Africa had debit cards, dropping to just 6.6 per cent of the lower income population. That's a problem as the poorer you are, the more you have to pay for transacting and transmitting. For example, the average remittance cost of sending money from Kenya to Uganda is over 10 per cent if performed through a bank and 8 per cent through Western Union. In fact, the cost of sending money back home to Africa is higher than anywhere else in the world. The World Bank's Migration and Remittances Factbook for 2016 showed that the global average cost of sending Sh2,000 ($200) back home was about 7.4 per cent, down by 0.6 percentage points from the end of 2014 but still way too high as sub-Saharan Africa's average remittance cost is 9.5 per cent, the highest in the world and over 25 per cent more expensive than other developing countries.

Part of the reason for such high costs is the archaic financial system, which fails in most correspondent banking structures due to international sanctions and fear of exposure to money laundering and terrorist funding due to a lack of digital identities and KYC documentation. How can you perform KYC on someone who lives off the land or in a village with no digital inclusion? This is the reason why sub-Saharan Africa has become the cradle of mobile money.

Yet it's not just about mobile financial inclusion however, but about mobile financial innovation generally. For example, Standard Bank rolled out SnapScan a couple of years ago. SnapScan is a method of paying via the mobile camera and a QR code. It's a great app and is described well in this article from *Time*:

> A free app available for any smartphone, SnapScan works almost like a pocket ATM linked to the user's debit or credit card account. Instead of handing over a card, customers scan a unique SnapScan logo posted at the cash register with their camera-enabled phone. They enter the amount, type in a pin code (or use touch ID) and a few seconds later the vendor's phone chimes with a confirmation sent by SMS. It's quick, painless, and entirely safe … As a result, SnapScan has been adopted by about 12,000 small and medium businesses in more than 17,000 outlets across South Africa. (Apple Pay, by contrast, so far only deals with less than 100 major retailers in the US, but can be used in their multiple branches across the country.) SnapScan has 150,000 registered users, and processes hundreds of thousands of dollars in payments every day for everything from airline tickets to handcrafted wicker baskets at roadside curio stalls.[27]

SnapScan isn't the only African app doing well. Ghanaian FinTech start-up Zeepay is offering a near-field communication (NFC)-based app for paying by phone. Think of it as Apple Pay without the Apple and you get the idea.

---

27   Aryn Baker, "Why One South African Startup Wants You to Pay with Your Phone," *Time*, 13 November 2015.

MNOS SWEEP UP AFRICA AT THE BANKS' EXPENSE

During my visits to Africa, there is always a very interesting dialogue about the mobile network operators (MNOs), such as Airtel and M-Pesa. It is interesting to hear these operators talking directly about how they focus on the customer experience and their singular objective of convenience. Both MNOs talk about customer convenience. The convenience of being able to cash in and cash out anywhere. For instance, in Rwanda's capital city of Kigali, I would say there is a Tigo, Airtel or MTN booth to cash in or cash out every five metres. That's like having an ATM every three strides. Furthermore, their advertising is ubiquitous, with almost every building being an advert for one of these guys. You can't miss them.

Photo © Chris Skinner

Even though M-Pesa is the daddy of them all, and celebrating a decade of operations, it's still worthwhile considering what this operator has achieved in that time. A decade after its launch, M-Pesa has expanded to ten countries, boasts 29.5 million active users and processes up to 614 million transactions per month.

M-Pesa is used by 96 per cent of Kenyan households and has a virtual monopoly there, squeezing out nimble competitors like Airtel and ensuring that its only interoperability is with itself. That is a clear contrast with countries like Tanzania where all the MNOs allow mobile money transfers seamlessly between networks.

Interestingly Michael Joseph, the founding CEO of Safaricom and former director of mobile money for Vodafone, once said in an interview, "If we applied Western standards to all of the things we do, we would probably still be in the dark ages in Africa."

Equally, you have to bear in mind that mobile money in sub-Saharan Africa is way ahead of that in the West. The United States processed $112 billion through mobile payment systems in 2016. For Kenya, that figure was $1 billion (KSh102 billion). Remember, however, that this is a country of just over 45 million people, compared to the U.S. population of 325 million, and most Kenyans live on a lot less than the average American. The average purchasing power of a U.S. citizen is seventeen times higher than a Kenyan, so you get the picture.

In fact, an MIT study published in late 2016 estimated that M-Pesa is responsible for lifting 2 per cent of households in Kenya out of poverty. That's equivalent to 194,000 families who now no longer live below the poverty threshold of less than $1.25 per day.

Mobile wallets and mobile money are a phenomenon in Africa, and specifically in Kenya. It is therefore notable that the banks went from trying to shut M-Pesa down via the regulators to competing with the MNO on rates. In particular, Kenya's Equity Bank has opened its own MNO to try to compete. It isn't succeeding, however. This is in part because Kenyans don't trust banks but, more importantly, it's because the banks are not competing effectively.

Kevin Amateshe, a product manager with M-Pesa, has highlighted this point by stating that banks are failing in this area because they focus on competing with M-Pesa. They copy its products, set its rates and generally imitate what M-Pesa does. However, these banks should be focusing on the customer instead. Banks are product-centric and when they see a nimble, agile competitor taking over a market that they think they should own, they copy the competitor. Where's the customer focus?

Again, Airtel has said that its mission is all about convenience. Making the customer experience the easiest, simplest and best it can be. It's all about the easy, frictionless simplicity of making and taking mobile payments. This is what the banks don't get. The banks believe that banking products is what mobile money customers want. It's not. It's the ease, security, trust and belief that this is the best way to do things.

Take the conversation that I had with a local Rwandan while on my travels there. He told me that he uses his mobile wallet for savings. "Do they give good interest rates?" I asked. "No, they don't give any interest at all." "So why do you keep your money there then?" I asked. "Because it's safer there than in my pocket," he replied. "By leaving it there, I ensure that I don't spend it."

This is the state of the nations we are dealing with, and the MNOs are getting it 100 per cent right in their approach. Simple, easy, secure and trusted. No complexity. And nothing like a bank.

THE CHALLENGES OF MOBILE FINANCIAL INCLUSION

Strangely, one of the gating factors to financial inclusion is the mobile network itself. It sounds simple to say that all of Africa can have access to mobile money, and they can, but if each telco has different wallet structures, charges and fees, then the ease of usage falls sharply. This is why interoperability is a key factor and Tanzania leads the way in this regard.

In February 2016, the country's three leading MNOs, Vodacom, Tigo and Airtel, announced full interoperability. Vodacom's participation means that over 16 million mobile money users in Tanzania are now able to send payments to each other, regardless of which mobile operator they use. That is a key achievement, with the country claiming to be the first in Africa with full interoperability. Will others follow? It remains to be seen.

Right now, it's a challenge with some countries actively encouraging inter- and intraoperator partnerships and agreements to enable domestic and cross-border mobile money transfers cheaply and easily while others, such as Nigeria, prohibit such activity. This is why, according to the GSMA, sub-Saharan Africa's mobile financial inclusion varies immensely:

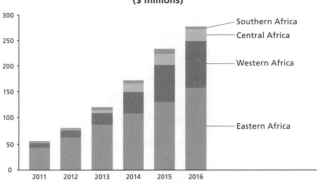

Data source: "The Mobile Economy Sub-Saharan Africa 2017," GSMA report

As can be seen, it varies widely and is a reflection of the regulatory structure and enthusiasm to adopt mobile wallets among the banks and MNOs. For example, in Tanzania, twenty-five banks are involved with the MNOs to allow mobile financial inclusion. The process has been supported by the Bill & Melinda Gates Foundation and has resulted in over half of Tanzania's GDP moving through mobile wallets each month. Compare that with Nigeria where 45 per cent of the population have a mobile subscription and yet only 2.3 per cent are using mobile money. Why?

Because not every country is the same. Just because mobile money can succeed in Kenya, Tanzania and Uganda does not naturally mean it will succeed in Nigeria. Nigeria has a large unbanked population who aren't aware of mobile money, for example. Even though the Central Bank of Nigeria has introduced measures to encourage mobile financial inclusion, the introduction of mobile money in the country has been bank-led, rather than MNO-led, and the banks have not done a great job of advertising the capability. For example, a survey by Philip Consulting in 2015 found that over a third of Nigerians weren't aware that they could make payments by mobile and, of those who did, the trust in the network was low as Nigeria is first and foremost a cash-based economy. This is why many will not use electronic transactions but instead prefer to use informal financial providers called esusu, adashe and ajo.

As can be seen, Africa is not a big homogeneous land mass whose citizens all use mobile money, but it is one where mobile money is taking off rapidly. At the end of 2016, 420 million people were unique mobile subscribers in sub-Saharan Africa, according to GSMA's "Mobile Economy Sub-Saharan Africa 2017" report. This is equivalent to a market penetration rate of 43 per cent, and is growing 50 per cent faster than the global average. This means that the region will have more than half a billion unique mobile subscribers by 2020, when around half of the continent's population will subscribe to a mobile service. These numbers are driving a range of new competitive structures.

For example, seeing the success of M-Pesa led to Equity Bank in Kenya launching its own mobile network service Equitel, in partnership with Airtel. As Equitel was offering better rates on payments, savings and transfers, Safaricom, the operator of M-Pesa, launched a legal battle to prevent its launch. When this bid failed, M-Pesa then tried to block Equitel by charging high costs for transfer outside the M-Pesa network. This move on the part of Safaricom is interesting as Safaricom itself was attacked by the banks during its start-up years for fear of fraud and fee losses. These fears were unjustified and resulted in the turnaround of the banks from fighting against M-Pesa to working with it, and then competing with it. Meanwhile, M-Pesa moved from offering basic mobile money transfers to full paperless banking services through M-Shwari.

It is fascinating to watch these changes in Africa, based on mobile enabling all to use the network. It is not just based on mobile network services, however.

USING TECHNOLOGY FOR IDENTIFICATION

In my book *ValueWeb,* I have the view that you cannot have an Internet of Things without a real-time and cheap Internet of Value. A core part of this is focused on building a cheap, shared ledger structure for digital identity and digital currencies, and guess what? That cheap, shared ledger is most likely going to be built in Africa. In fact, Devie Mohan of Thomson Reuters predicts that Africa will invent the global standard for digital identity and she may well be right as this is a huge issue, not just in Africa, but globally.

There are almost two billion people born with no identity. There is no record of their birth. There is no proof of their existence. As a result, these people can disappear without a trace. In order to solve this problem, the UN has a specific goal to give everyone on the planet a legal identity by 2030. If interested, take a look at the UN's seventeen sustainable development goals. Goal 16.9 states: "By 2030, provide legal identity for all, including birth registration."

I attended a meeting at the UN in 2016 that focused on this problem. The day had lots of discussions about how to create a global digital identity scheme for inclusion, but what exactly is the problem here? If you have no legal identity, what is the issue? The issue is that if you have not been identified as existing, then you don't exist. If a human trafficker abducts a person with no birth record, then there is no evidence of their disappearance because there is no evidence of their existence. Many of those who disappear are girls, sold into sexual slavery. Many others are victims. Victims of war. Victims of politics. Victims of human traffickers. Victims of the inhumanity of humans to humans.

This is the reason why identity is important. So we can find these victims. So we know that they have disappeared. So we can give them hope. You only have to listen to the stories about abducted girls in Nigeria, sex slave trafficking in India and refugees in Calais to understand the problems presented here.

THE IMPOSSIBLE DREAM: A DIGITAL IDENTITY FOR EVERYONE

It is clear that human trafficking is a problem of identity. The first thing that the abusers do when they abduct someone is destroy their identification papers. That is why we need to get rid of paper and create a digital identification system. How can we create an identity solution using today's digital technologies? There is no solution today.

We can talk about grandiose ideas of taking a baby's biometrics and recording them on a blockchain ledger system that gives traceability forever, but it's not as simple as that. We can talk about accepting Facebook as your ID as it's more reliable than most, except that the people we want to identify are unlikely to have a Facebook profile. We can talk about the UN running a blockchain ID system that could be uniquely identified via biometrics. We can talk about a UN ID being available for all, cheaply and freely through the mobile network. We can talk about whether the stateless could be identified this way and what it would mean. We can talk about what a legal identity structure would look like, the problems of creating one and the idea of a public-private partnership that could make one work.

At the end of the day, it's all talk though. I really hope we do get something off the ground, but the day I spent at the UN talking about this issue was pretty much summed up by a conversation I heard in the registration queue that morning. Two chaps behind me were debating and one said the following, "It has nothing to do with the technologies, you know. Technology could solve identity overnight but who would trust it? It's the people who get in the way. It's the governments and the implications of liability for mistaken identities that cause the problems. There's no solution to that."

In other words, we have the technologies. In fact, we've had them for years. We could have issued a global digital identity scheme years ago if anyone had had the motivation to create one. However, borders are there for just that reason—to keep people out. Creating a global scheme that would allow movement across borders with identifications that would be accepted and used by all is a dream. I guess we hope to make that dream come true, now that we have the blockchain protocol. It would be amazing to dream the impossible dream and make it possible. When I read statements like "It's easier for Americans to travel within Africa than Africans themselves" though, it's clear that the issue is not identities but borders, business and commerce.

Would a biometric blockchain mobile inclusion system providing identities for all overcome human trafficking, abduction and sexual slavery? No. However, a United Nations agreement to accept a biometric blockchain mobile inclusion system to provide identities for all might. One day. That is the impossible dream that we need to make possible.

A global identity scheme is not going to happen fast, although it is a specific UN development goal. A national digital identity scheme is happening far more quickly however, and there are a number of notable identity schemes out there, such as those in Argentina, Estonia, Pakistan and India.

Argentina

Documento Nacional de Identidad, or DNI, is the main identity document for Argentinian citizens, as well as temporary or permanent resident aliens. It is issued in card format at birth and updated at eight and fourteen years of age. Known as DNI tarjeta, the card is valid if identification is needed, and is required for voting. The front side of the card states the name, sex, nationality, date of birth, date of issue, date of expiry and transaction number along with the DNI number and portrait and signature of the card's bearer. The back of the card shows the address of the card's bearer along with the fingerprint of their right thumb. The front side of the DNI also shows a barcode while the back shows machine-readable information. The DNI is a valid travel document for entering Argentina, Bolivia, Brazil, Chile, Colombia, Ecuador, Paraguay, Peru, Uruguay and Venezuela.

Estonia

The Estonian ID-kaart is a smart card issued to Estonian citizens by the Police and Border Guard Board. All Estonian citizens and permanent residents are legally obliged to have this card from the age of fifteen. The card stores data such as the user's full name, gender, national identification number and cryptographic keys and public key certificates.

The cryptographic signature in the card is legally equivalent to a manual signature. Here are a few examples of how the card can be used:

- as a national ID card for Estonian citizens travelling within the European Union
- as a national health insurance card
- as proof of identification when logging into bank accounts from a home computer
- for digital signatures
- for i-Voting
- for accessing government databases to check medical records, file taxes, etc.
- for picking up e-Prescriptions

Pakistan

Pakistan's National Database and Regulation Authority (NADRA) was established in 2000. NADRA regulates government databases and statistically manages the sensitive registration database of the citizens of Pakistan. It is also responsible for issuing national identity cards to its citizens. Although the card is not legally compulsory for a Pakistani citizen, it is mandatory for the following:

- voting
- obtaining a passport
- purchasing vehicles and land
- obtaining a driver's licence
- purchasing a plane or train ticket
- obtaining a mobile phone SIM card
- obtaining electricity, gas and water
- securing admission to college and other postgraduate institutes
- conducting major financial transactions

Therefore, it is pretty much necessary for basic civic life in the country. In 2012, NADRA introduced the Smart National Identity Card (SNIC), an electronic identity card, which implements thirty-six security features. The following information can be found on the card and subsequently on the central database: legal name, gender (male, female or transgender), father's name (husband's name for married females), identification mark, date of birth, national identity card number, family tree id number, current address, permanent address, date of issue, date of expiry, signature, photo and fingerprint (thumbprint).

India

The biggest digital identity programme in the world is in India, and is known as Aadhaar. The Indian government started the Aadhaar digital identity scheme in 2009. That was when the Unique Identification Authority of India (UIDAI) was set up with the mandate to create a twelve-digit unique identification (UID) number, termed as Aadhaar, for all the residents of India. By April 2016, over a billion UIDs had been issued, and it was at this point that the government's National Payments Corporation of India (NPCI) unveiled the Unified Payment Interface (UPI). UPI is designed to make person-to-person and e-commerce transactions swifter and easier.

Since the UIDAI and UID project were established in January 2009, the objective has been to provide a unique identification for all citizens of India. The card is based on biometrics—fingerprint and iris recognition—to identify the person and is used for delivery of government welfare services in an efficient and transparent manner. The enrolment process is fairly simple. Once enrolled, the UID can be authenticated and verified quickly and easily online by government and other officials, such as when using it to open a bank account. Before being enrolled in the programme, many Indians were excluded from numerous banking services, government aid and related services that demanded identification.

The first Aadhaar was issued in 2010 and it has grown rapidly to reach coverage of 93 per cent of adults, 67 per cent of children aged five to eighteen and 20 per cent of those aged zero to five. In thirteen of India's twenty-nine states, Aadhaar coverage is over 90 per cent whilst, in another thirteen states, saturation is between 75 and 90 per cent. In other words, within six years, the Indian government had neared its target of every citizen in the country having a biometric ID card.

That's according to the government's figures. According to Ujjivan Financial Services, one of the most prominent names in the microfinance markets, just 77 per cent of its customers had Aadhaar as of 15 July 2016. In other words, the figures of coverage are not robust, but it can be assured that most Indian citizens (four out of five) have the ID card.

The issue is that in order to make all citizens use the card, the card would have to be compulsory— something it isn't today—and compulsion is still being debated. "No service will be denied for lack of Aadhaar," according to one senior government official, but the fact is that living in India is becoming harder and harder if you do not have an Aadhaar number. There are already numerous areas in which it is compulsory, such as when receiving government benefits (aimed at the poorest people in the country), and more and more banks and corporations are demanding the Aadhaar number before they will deal with customers. For example, the major mobile network operators—Airtel, Reliance Jio and Vodafone—are now using Aadhaar as a replacement for paper proof of identification in a process they call eKYC.

This makes sense as the use of a digital identity scheme is saving companies a lot of cost overheads, from KYC to benefits distribution, as well as improving confidence and trust in identification and authentication accuracy. The Indian government estimates to have saved over Rs 27,000 crore (just over $400 million) by using Aadhaar to manage payments to beneficiaries under various welfare schemes between 2014 and 2016, whilst 16 million fake IDs have been deleted from the central database, resulting in a further saving of Rs 10,000 crore ($150 million). It also makes sense as the move towards offering mobile financial inclusion and mobile banking relies on an effective eKYC process.

Aadhaar—creating a cashless society

The Aadhaar (Targeted Delivery of Financial and Other Subsidies, Benefits and Services) Act, 2016 (the "Act") was passed as a money bill in March 2016. As already stated, the Act makes it mandatory for a person to authenticate her/his identity using the Aadhaar number before receiving any government subsidies, benefits or services. It also introduced the UPI. The penetration of bank accounts and, by extension, debit cards and credit cards remains low in India, but the launch of the UPI is designed to bring banking and financial services to everyone.

Unveiled by the NPCI, the primary body that governs all retail payments in the country, UPI aims to propel the economy towards more cashless transactions by making person-to-person e-commerce transactions as fast and as easy as sending a text message. This would, among other things, help the government curb unreported money exchanges that are not subjected to tax (the number of non-cash transactions per person in India is only six per year). The government is focusing on using citizens' smartphones as the computing platform for UPI. India is the world's fastest-growing smartphone market with over 350 million smartphone users, and is projected to grow past 700 million by 2020.

The other integral focus of UPI is interoperability, namely allowing transactions across banks, by using the UID as a single-identifier to make transactions. It is built on top of Immediate Payment Service (IMPS) protocol, a 24/7 and real-time transaction service but, unlike IMPS which requires the counterparties to have bank details including account number and the Indian financial system code (IFSC), UPI-enabled apps only require the twelve-digit Aadhaar UID. Most Indian banks are releasing UPI-enabled apps, such as ICICI Bank's Pockets app, that allow peer-to-peer payments by users including those who don't have an ICICI bank account. According to Mashable, UPI offers payments from Rs 50 (75 cents) to Rs 100,000

($1,500) in a single transaction, and is designed as a replacement for all the apps you need to make payments for online shopping, electricity bills, barcode-based payments and college tuition.[28]

India's idea of a cashless society is not the reality

Having built the identity scheme and the payments system, the Indian government suddenly, overnight, withdrew all 500 rupee ($7) and 1,000 rupee ($14) notes in November 2016. These notes represent 86 per cent of India's cash by value and the move caused chaos with consumers.

The move towards demonetisation and a cashless India is an effort to close down the booming economy of untaxed cash transactions, which allows corruption, funds terrorism and keeps counterfeit notes in circulation. It is not the first time that India has demonetised. It happened in 1946 and again in 1978.

This time though, a specific aim is to move the country towards a cashless economy. That's something phenomenal. After all, look at the United States and Europe, where *cashless* is a fantasy. In India, they're trying to make it a reality.

Digital payments companies like Paytm and MobiKwick, for example, are reporting that demand for their services has increased several hundred per cent, and have brought forward their growth targets by a year or more. The thing is that this move towards a cashless society is a little pre-emptive given that 85 per cent of Indians do not have a mobile telephone yet, live in rural areas and depend on cash.

That is why, in light of the move, there were lots of anecdotes such as this one:[29]

---

28   Manish Singh, "Inside UPI: How India is bringing mobile banking to 1.3 billion people," Mashable, 30 August 2016.

29   Ian Marlow, "Cashless Economy Still a Fantasy for India," Bloomberg, 4 December 2016.

Deepak Kumar, a 22-year-old security guard who earns 7,500 rupees a month, tried to open an account with a New Delhi branch of the State Bank of India after receiving his salary in old notes. The bank refused, telling him to return in January.

"They said we're only looking after our customers, we don't have time to add new customers," Kumar said, adding he wouldn't try to open a bank account again. "This cashless thing is good for big people, but for small people like us, it doesn't mean anything."

And, for those who do have a bank account, the lack of access to cash does not necessarily lead to digital payments. For example, one man paid to use a public urinal with a cheque for 5 rupees (7 cents).

In fact, Bloomberg provided a whole raft of charts showing that only 5 per cent of the population use mobile phones for payments today and only 12 per cent are aware that they can do that.

Awareness of mobile payment options

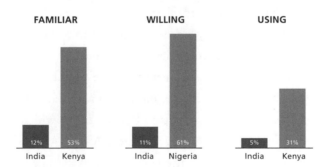

Data sources: Mastercard/Bloomberg

There's a long way to go, but the doubling of Paytm users from 115 million in October 2016 to 230 million by July 2017 shows that things are changing.

WHEN WILL BANKS STOP SEEING FINANCIAL INCLUSION AS CHARITY?

As can be seen, the mobile network and government activities to promote digital identities and financial inclusion are changing the world. Do banks get this? Not really, because banks were built for the physical distribution of paper through a localised network of buildings and humans.[30] That network is expensive to operate and therefore only available to the elite few. Until the mobile came along, only one in three people in the world had bank accounts while these numbers dropped to just one in ten in countries like Pakistan, Indonesia and Colombia.

Banks do believe that the mass poor are just that—poor. How do you make a profit out of the poor? Well, truth be told, the poorest are the most profitable. They are the ones who need loans and go overdrawn and, therefore, pay all the fees for the rest of us—the mass affluent—to get our banking for "free".

It is the poorest who take out payday loans. They prefer to do this than deal with a bank because at least the payday loan firm is upfront about what it's going to charge them. James Barth of Auburn University observed that payday lenders congregate in neighbourhoods with higher rates of poverty, lower education and minority populations. At least they can get a loan rather than an unauthorised overdraft that, here in the United Kingdom for instance, charges more than a payday lender.

At least they are only paying £90 to borrow £100, which is less than what some Kenyans were being charged before M-PESA. Sending money before mobile payments arrived used to be a tricky affair and involved getting a bus or taxi driver to take your £100 from Nairobi to the villages.

---

30   Reimagining the banking system for the digital age is the theme of my 2014 book *Digital Bank*. The strapline for that book is that banks were built in the Industrial Revolution for the physical distribution of paper in a localised network focused on buildings and humans. Now we deal with money as data and banks need to be reimagined for the digital distribution of data in a globalised network focused on software and servers. The book provides a clear explanation of what is happening and the implications for both existing banks and their new challenger competition.

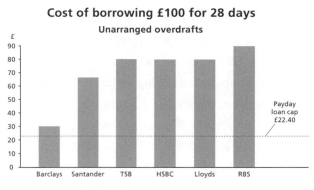

Cost of borrowing £100 for 28 days

Data sources: Which?/BBC

Quite often, it wouldn't arrive. Even if it did, it would often cost 25 per cent or more. Similarly, the high fees of Western Union and other remittance providers were fairly punishing until FinTech came along. Now those costs are dropping rapidly.

Undoubtedly though, the most exciting area of change isn't payday loans or remittance exploiting the poor, but the inclusion of billions of people, who were not included before, thanks to mobile. These vary from the millions in China who are now using Ant Financial to those in India using Paytm to the Venmo'd of the United States. The numbers are stunning— 450 million people using Alipay, 250 million using Paytm while Venmo's user numbers aren't quoted[31]—and it is down to the fact that mobile has moved from dealing with money in buildings to dealing with money in apps.

Outside the apps is just as, if not more, exciting as Africa and other nations stuck in poverty for decades are reinventing the whole concept of money with mobile. This is summarised neatly by research from Financial Inclusion Insights, which notes the following:

• More than 90 per cent of the world's poor are covered by a mobile signal.

---

31   Although PayPal has 200 million active users worldwide, Venmo is only available in the United States and user numbers are not quoted. The Q4 2015 ($2.5 billion) versus Q4 2016 ($5.6 billion) difference speaks volumes though.

- About 60 per cent of Africans live in rural areas and mobile money is the only way to reach them cheaply, affordably and at scale, which is why people in Côte d'Ivoire, Somalia, Tanzania, Uganda and Zimbabwe are using mobile money more than traditional bank accounts.
- In Tanzania, ownership of mobile money accounts surged from 1 per cent of the population in 2009 to 32 per cent in 2014.
- Digital accounts cut the costs of transactions by as much as 90 per cent.
- Digital accounts give people the ability to save and budget for the first time in their lives, allowing them to withstand financial shocks and direct money towards specific uses, such as education and health care.
- Four out of ten adult Nigerians have no access to any form of financial services, making life not only more difficult, but also more expensive for these people.

Now let's go back to that question: when will banks stop seeing financial inclusion as a charitable venture? It's not charity, otherwise M-PESA would be making no money. It is making money. In fact, it is the second-largest revenue generator for the Safaricom Group, which is why it protects its monopoly in Kenya.

Shs (million)	2012	2013	2014	2015	2016
Voice service revenue	68,122	75,848	84,316	87,368	90,802
M-PESA revenue	16,874	21,844	26,561	32,626	41,500
Mobile data revenue	5,223	6,611	9,314	14,823	21,154
Fixed service revenue	1,371	2,113	2,571	3,128	3,815
Messaging revenue	7,768	10,147	13,620	15,671	17,328
Other service revenue	836	1,489	1,980	2,631	3,185
Service revenue	100,193	118,051	138,361	156,247	177,784

Data source: Safaricom Annual Report 2016

It's not charity as Ant Financial is making clear. Ant Financial sees inclusivity as its mission, and its figures prove that its vision is viable as it nearly doubled its pre-tax profits in the 2017 fiscal year, according to Bloomberg estimates. The company saw an 86 per cent jump to $814 million, much of this down to the success of its global efforts at creating financial inclusion through digital services.

In other words, financial inclusion is a charitable venture if you are a bank with physical distribution; but it's good business if you're a telco or technology firm with digital distribution. And telcos will upscale as they learn the model. This is evidenced by Orange. After learning that this was good business in Côte d'Ivoire and Mali, the company opened mobile money services in Poland, Romania and other European countries and then realised that, with its 650 stores in France, it might as well open a bank.

What's the bottom line here? The bottom line is that mobile financial inclusion is a huge market opportunity to bank the unbanked, make money out of it and eradicate the expense of being poor.

Two billion individuals and 200 million micro, small and midsize businesses in emerging economies today lack access to savings and credit and, as a result, economic growth suffers. A research report from McKinsey in September 2016 found that widespread adoption and use of digital finance could increase the GDPs of all emerging economies by 6 per cent, or a total of $3.7 trillion, by 2025. This is the equivalent of adding to the world an economy the size of Germany, or one that's *larger than all* of the economies of Africa. This additional GDP could create up to 95 million new jobs across all sectors of these emerging economies. In other words, it's worth it.

TRANSACTIONS WANT TO BE FREE[32]

"Information wants to be free" was the powerful motto that made hacker culture mainstream in 1984 and led to the internet's creation. What if, as with information, transactions want to be free? Could we expect a new internet-like moment for retail financial services if everyday users were given

---

32 Reproduced and edited with permission from Pablo García Arabéhéty of the Consultative Group to Assist the Poor (CGAP).

the ability to move money instantly across providers for free? What would it take to accomplish? What would the impact be for financial inclusion?

Plenty of transactions are already offered for free, for example, a bank account that offers unlimited ATM withdrawals anywhere in the world at no direct cost to the customer. However, as with lunch or instant messaging, no transaction is free. There is always someone paying. In the case of free ATM withdrawals, customers are paying through seemingly unrelated fees.

For this reason, the question of whether it is possible to make transactions free is ultimately about business models. It is a question of whether certain players in the global retail financial services arena are positioned to move away from transaction-based revenues and cover their transactional costs by other means.

Three trends make this liberation of transactions more likely today than ever before.

- **Real-time, interoperable payment and transfer infrastructure is spreading across markets.** If free transactions need to be subsidised by other revenue streams, lower prices bring them closer to feasibility. In the last decade, instant, interoperable payment and transfer infrastructure has become more widely available across markets, including lower-income economies. Avoiding intermediaries to access this basic infrastructure brings operational savings, ultimately lowering costs. At the same time, open transaction exchange systems using blockchain or other distributed ledger technologies have gained some traction and could become viable alternatives to the centralised payment infrastructure.

- **Transactional financial services providers are diversifying their revenue sources.** Shifting away from transactional revenue requires providers to have alternative revenue streams. Since 2007, transactional businesses have started to cross-sell a broader portfolio of financial services. Kenya's M-Pesa, which has traditionally focused on domestic transfers, launched a microloan service in association with a bank that reached a user base of more than 12 million in 2015. Similarly, PayPal has been offering working capital loans since 2013. As of May 2017, the value of those loans had reached $3 billion.

- **Analytics are becoming a key competitive advantage for cross-selling.** Analytics are taking over traditional credit scoring and making it easier for providers to diversify their revenues through lending. Ant Financial is already offering Zhima Credit, a scoring system that taps several alternative data sources. The ability to tap richer data to offer personalised and timely products is becoming a new competitive edge for financial service providers.

These trends present financial services providers with an opportunity to move away from transactional revenues, but how willing and well equipped are they to do so?

Banks are well positioned across these three trends. They are the backbone of the payments infrastructure in many markets, they know the business of cross-selling financial products and they have been early adopters of analytics to assess credit risk. Many banks already offer free instant transfers across providers, in Brazil, for example. Nonetheless, their payments business model, which accounts globally for a third of their overall revenue, depends heavily on transactional revenues. Opening the floodgates to more free transactions could directly impact their bottom lines in the short term, so to many it does not represent an enticing future.

On the other hand, there is another group of market players that might not be deterred by this immediate hit to the bottom line. Online retailers, instant messaging apps, social networks, online search engines, mobile phone manufacturers and a variety of FinTech start-ups are managing to find niches at the intersection of the trends described above. They are in an unprecedented position to offset transactional costs by cross-selling products like instant credit and digital advertising to third parties. In some markets, they are connecting to the basic interoperable instant transfer infrastructure. And they are well versed in the world of analytics and deep customer insight and personalisation.

Here are just a few examples of what these companies have been doing so far:

- **Alibaba** is aggressively raising capital to continue its global expansion and diversification strategy. The creation of Ant Financial as the parent company for Alipay and the launch of the savings product Yu'e Bao signalled the company's expansion. For more background, read the Ant case study at the end of the book.

- **Facebook** and **WhatsApp** have already secured a payments licence that could enable them to debit and credit any bank account in Europe once the new PSD2 payments directive is implemented in 2018. This would make it possible for bank customers to manage their finances through third parties. In India, there are reports of WhatsApp following a similar path through the new domestic UPI.

- **Venmo**, owned by PayPal, has been offering free money transfers across wallets for a long time in the United States, but it can only offer free and instant transactions within its own platform; transactions across providers take one business day. It is an interesting case in which the United States' infrastructure is limiting the extent to which transactions can be made free and instant, although things are changing rapidly.

- **M-Pesa**, the global brand for mobile money that operates in Kenya, Tanzania and India, among other developing markets, is now experimenting with free in-platform transfers for transactions of less than $1. This initiative could have implications for financial inclusion. By definition, providing transactions to low-income segments is more expensive because cash conversions are typically required, at least at the beginning or the end of each transaction cycle. M-Pesa has excelled at making cash conversion access points available, but these access points are expensive to operate, and subsidising their operation could be a challenge. If M-Pesa figures out a sustainable way to subsidise these transactions, it could have a significant impact on financially excluded segments.

Looking at the overall trends in the global retail financial services industry, liberating transactions seems increasingly possible. Yet the economics of innovative business models like these will ultimately determine to what extent, and for what types of transactions and use cases (applications), free will become the new normal. One thing is clear: If transactions do want to be free, there will be a battle of the titans to liberate them and banking business models will need to change fundamentally.

THE FALL OF BANKS

As I was writing *Digital Human*, I quite often challenged my thinking, and wondered if I were making too many assumptions. I am very aware that when we *assume* something, it can make an *ass* out of *you* and *me*. In this chapter, I am not predicting the death of all banks. That scenario will not come true. However, it is very true that many U.S. and European banks are stuck in their heritage economies, as outlined throughout this book. They need to change but are finding it hard to do so. This chapter is all about the leadership and legacy challenge for those banks.

To kick things off, I came across an interesting research document[33] that looked at the impact of digitalisation in finance. The result of research conducted by the *Harvard Business Review* and the Genpact Research Institute, the study confirmed something I have been saying for years. A majority of respondents voted that they have not unlocked the power of digital to deliver positive business outcomes. This is due to key barriers, such as the inability to experiment or the burden of legacy systems and processes, that are preventing the effective use of digital technologies.

---

33 "Accelerating the pace and impact of digital transformation: How financial services views the digital agenda," *Harvard Business Review Analytic Services* study in association with Genpact Research Institute, 4 November 2016.

In addition, less than half of financial services sector respondents believe that their companies have a clear, enterprise-wide digital strategy, and many report split ownership between the C-suite and business line owners for creating that strategy. It is the absence of a clear digital transformation strategy amidst a backdrop of fragmented leadership, as opposed to just a need for the latest technology, that is preventing firms from rising to meet the challenge of capturing digital's potential to promote customer engagement, grow revenues and improve efficiency.

The key findings of the survey are as follows:

- Only 20 per cent of financial services respondents (versus 21 per cent of all respondents) say their organisations are reaping the full value from digital. In the next two years, however, 55 per cent of finance organisations expect to deliver significant impact.
- Companies aren't delivering digital-driven value to customers as they cannot optimise end-to-end user experiences beyond the web-enabled front end, especially with intractable legacy systems. Only 15 per cent of financial services firms say they do this well.
- While digital leaders grow and outcompete, financial firms see a lag in the use of digital to have a major impact on customer loyalty (50 per cent) and revenue growth (51 per cent) in particular.
- Financial firms cite key barriers as an inability to experiment quickly (56 per cent), legacy systems and processes (55 per cent) and change management (41 per cent). They are, however, less troubled by insufficient technical skills (24 per cent).
- To deliver digital success, financial services providers want to build capabilities for customer-focused problem solving (76 per cent rate it among the top three most important digital skills) and adapt to change (73 per cent).

The report concludes that although many financial services firms are on their way to embracing digital, only a minority, at 20 per cent, believe that they are harnessing these technologies successfully. And only 15 per cent believe that their organisations are capable of optimising end-to-end customer experiences that go beyond web-enabled user interfaces into their middle- and back-office operations. However, for those succeeding in their digital initiatives, a vast majority say digital technology has had significant impact on their companies' cost to serve (90 per cent), customer loyalty (75 per cent) and revenue growth (75 per cent), indicating a clear opportunity for the financial services industry.

Despite the current state, this study shows that financial services respondents have high expectations of digital to help them strengthen competitive capabilities end to end over the next few years. However, all groups, even the digital leaders, face barriers, including the need to better align back- and middle-office functions to support customer expectations. In addition, some long-standing industry hurdles, including legacy systems and processes, an inability to experiment and change management issues, are still commonly cited across the industry. Nevertheless, the familiarity of these challenges does not make them any less severe in a time when nearly any industry has the potential for massive disruption through digital means.

In many cases, technology alone isn't the first step. Firms focused on "fixing" legacy systems as a prerequisite to digital transformation are falling behind. Digital leaders haven't focused all of their efforts on solving these intractable barriers, but instead are creating a companywide vision for digital, improving collaboration across functions and developing the ability to experiment quickly with digital technologies. These activities stand as clear differentiators between firms that realise benefits from digital and those that don't.

As more financial services firms adopt digital technologies to support decision-making, reduce cost and improve the customer experience, they should look to the traits exhibited by these digital leaders to introduce new capabilities, overcome barriers and accelerate the pace and impact of digital transformation across the industry.

CAN LEGACY BANKS AVOID BEING DEAD FISH?

What exactly is the problem? It's that, twenty years ago, we talked about disintermediation and object-oriented architectures and the banks all went yes, very good, and did not do much. Ten years ago, we screamed about the internet age and mobile impact, and the banks all went yes, very good, and did not do much. Now, we are yabbering on about digital and blockchain and the banks all go yes, very good, and aren't doing much. What will it take?

I liken it to seeing a tsunami. It's two miles away or, in this case, two decades away. You can see it coming and say, "That's a bloody big wave!" But then you go back to relaxing on the beach and playing volleyball. Then, some time later, you look again and say, "Oh! That wave is even bigger now!" But carry on playing on the beach. Then the wave hits, smashing you and everything else in its path to bits.

I liken it to a slow death through inertia. Twenty years of embers burning have turned into small flames today and will turn into a burning platform in the next five years to a burnt-out bank within ten. Of course, this is avoidable if the bank starts to change today but, bearing in mind a data rationalisation and core systems upgrade programme takes about five years to complete, it's getting hotter and hotter every day.

This really came home to hit me when walking along the beach in Bali (yes, conference life is tough, folks). As I enjoyed the morning's sunshine, I stumbled across this poor critter.

Photo © Chris Skinner

Now I'm guessing that this fish was doing pretty well. It was swimming along, eating well, avoiding predators and thinking life is good. It did this every day and grew pretty fat and big, chewing off the fat of the coral shores. Just that each day, it swam closer and closer to shore but didn't realise it. Then, one day when a particularly strong tide came in, the poor sucker got washed onto shore. It now knew that there was a problem but what could it do? So it wriggled to the left and it wriggled to the right … to no avail. It's too late. The poor thing has been washed up and has no way to get back to life. It's a dead fish.

Like a dead fish washed onto the shore, an incumbent bank will go the same way if it doesn't open up and join the marketplace wave. This has been a requirement for twenty years, since the internet banking age arrived, but is now a burning platform as the opening of finance through FinTech has emerged. A bank that tries to swim against that tide is going to get washed up or burnt out, depending on whether it's a burning platform or a beached fish. Either way, the ending isn't nice. It's time for banks to get on the wave, surf the open platforms, join the fireproofed marketplaces and get with the plan.

This is a reoccurring theme on the conference circuit, and reminds me of a panel about Open Banking, marketplaces, platforms, open APIs and such like that I was on. It was all very gentlemanly, with a dialogue around how banks are constrained by culture and leadership. I think most bankers were stuck in the vacuum of not being able to change the bank and not being able to replace core systems. Instead they were just twiddling their thumbs while watching all these start-up marketplaces and saying, "Oh look! There's a FinTech start-up that does what we do. Let's watch it."

Fast-forward a few years and they are still watching it and saying, "Oh look! That start-up has got quite big. Interesting!" Then they go back to doing what they've always done, whinging about legacy systems and wondering why the regulator is always on their case.

Then they look around again and say, "Oh! That start-up is now a bit of a threat. Let's go buy it." To which the start-up replies, "Get lost! I'm too big to mess with now!"

I remember organising my first banking conferences in the 1990s and there was a regular mantra among the memes of those speaking on stage: there is more change coming and you're going to be dead meat unless you change. It was a common theme to hear the word "disintermediated" being used in these speeches. For instance, "Microsoft, WalMart and Virgin are all coming for your lunch; you're going to be disintermediated." Well, no one ate the bankers' lunch and so the overused term lost its relevance and interest.

Then, in the 2000s, Yodlee and aggregators appeared and everyone thought that this would kill the bank relationship with the customer. At the conferences, many keynotes would stand up and say, "Technologies like data aggregation are going to disintermediate the banks from the markets." Well, the aggregators have been out there for twenty years now and the banks still have strong client presence in mobile apps, so that was a bit of an overstatement, wasn't it?

Next, mobile banking appeared and the MNOs. The mantra at the conferences became the following: look at the threat of the MNOs. They're all going to disintermediate you. Wake up and smell the coffee. So, the bankers went and got a triple, venti, non-fat, caramel macchiato ... or two ... and watched as the MNOs did their business. Nothing happened.

Most recently, FinTech has appeared and now all the markets, conference speakers and media are saying, "Look, we finally have real disruption. You're all going to be disintermediated." And the bankers watch and wait, and sure enough the FinTech crowd soon realise that banking is a little more complex and end up working with them rather than against them.

This threat of disintermediation is getting ridiculous. Or is it? Perhaps we should be looking at the message from a different angle. Maybe it is not the aggregators, the MNOs or the FinTech firms that will disintermediate banks, but technology itself. Maybe it is the cry of the technologist that is trying to tell the financial community that software is eating the world; everything that can be automated will be; as we digitalise everything, you need to transform or die; it's not an evolution, but a revolution.

In other words, as with all revolutions, this revolution may take a long time to come but, when it finally hits—when the digital transformation finally matures—banks will be disintermediated unless they adapt to its demands. Its demands cover platforms, marketplaces, open sourcing structures, microservice architectures and so on and so forth. In particular, it demands balance in the boardroom where at least half the leadership team knows the difference between a blockchain and a distrusted ledger.

I guess it's really an update of the old, old story of the shepherd boy protecting the sheep and crying "wolf" all the time. Just that this story is about the technologist trying to protect the bankers by crying "disintermediation" all the time.

This is what we've seen in so many other industries and, surely, we've learnt something by now. Tower Records cannot be iTunes, Barnes & Noble cannot be Amazon and the People's Republic of China could not create Alibaba. Jack Ma did.

In this world of rapid cycle change—can you imagine that no one knew what Facebook was ten years ago?— banks that are just paying lip service to the innovation theatre are going to fail. And that is the point. Banks are just talking the talk in most cases. They are dilly-dallying with digital, they are blustering over blockchain, they are happy about API and they are learning about machine learning. However, it's all just talk. It's time to stop talking the talk and walk the walk. It's time to start taking this seriously and start doing something seriously about it.

After all, all these start-ups are taking it seriously and gradually moving from embryonic ideas to market dominance. The Collinson brothers who created Stripe became the youngest billionaires in 2016, PayPal is now worth more than Barclays Bank and, after its IPO, Ant Financial was at one point in 2016 worth *four times* that of Deutsche Bank. Things are changing and they are changing fast. Just because the CEO of a bank says that the bank is committed does not make the bank a FinTech leader. It is still just a bank.

I really tried to drive this message home when a journalist asked me about the latest digital bank launch. He asked, "What's different about a

The Boy Who Cried Wolf! (#FinTech Style)

There once was a technologist who was bored as he sat in a conference watching all the bankers. To amuse himself, he took a great breath and sang out, "Disintermediated! Disintermediated! You're all going to be disintermediated!"

The bankers ran out of the conference to help their brethren stop them from being disintermediated away. But when they arrived at the end of the project, they found there had been no threat of disintermediation. The technologist laughed at the sight of their angry faces.

"Don't cry 'disintermediated', techie guy," said the bankers, "when there's no disintermediation!" They went grumbling back into their offices.

Later, at another conference, the technologist thought he would give it another go, and shouted out again, "Disintermediated! Disintermediated! You're all going to be disintermediated!" To his naughty delight, he watched the bankers run out of the conference to stop them from being disintermediated away.

When the bankers saw there was no disintermediation, they sternly said, "Save your frightened song for when there is really something wrong! Don't cry 'disintermediated' when there is NO disintermediation!"

But the technologist just grinned and watched them go grumbling back to their offices once more.

Later, he saw a REAL disintermediation coming to hit the market. Alarmed, he leaped to his feet and shouted as loudly as he could, "Disintermediation! Disintermediation! It's here!"

But the bankers thought he was trying to fool them again, and so ignored him.

At sunset, everyone wondered why the technologist hadn't returned. They went up the hill to find the technologist weeping.

"There really was a disintermediation here, and now all of your banks that I used to sell to are dead! I cried out, 'Disintermediated!' Why didn't you take any notice?"

An old banker tried to comfort the technologist as they walked back to his office.

"Well, thanks for trying to tell me and my friends that we might die," he said, putting his arm around the youth, "but nobody believes a liar...even when he is telling the truth!"

digital bank to a mainstream bank with an app?" I sighed, took a deep breath and replied as follows:

"A mainstream bank with an app has just added the app to their old systems. That's why it just tells you balances and transactions. A digital bank has been built from the ground up to use and leverage today's internet-based technologies. It is totally different. Perhaps the best way to illustrate this is to think about a big bank. They have buildings, staffers, history. They see a new tech and they try to shoehorn that new tech into their terribly complex structure. A start-up digital bank begins with a clean sheet of paper and asks, 'How can we take all this tech and apply it to financial services?'

"The bottom line is the difference between FinTech and TechFin. A bank is a TechFin firm: they see technology as something to apply to existing financial market structures and processes. A start-up is a FinTech firm: they take tech and work out how to use it with financial markets and structures. The former continues their focus on physical distribution with buildings and humans and work out how to add the tech on top; the latter starts with digital distribution of data through the internet, and then works out if they need any buildings or humans on top. It's a completely different view through the lens, and most banks don't have this view because they have no one in a decision-making role who can take the gutsy decisions and realise that the emperor is wearing see-through clothes."

HOW OFTEN DOES YOUR BANK REFRESH ITS APPS AND ARCHITECTURE?

I was talking to a few FinTech firms recently. They are all fully licensed banks, and are less than fifteen years old. They all seem to have one thing in common—refreshment. What I mean by this is that they talk about technology in a very different way to traditional banks. Traditional banks are encumbered by legacy. I almost see it as a bank that has cemented itself to the floor. All these new waves of tech come around, and this heavyweight bank, cemented to the floor, tries to adapt. It doesn't look good.

What these new banks were telling me illustrates the point well. The first said that it launched its online banking in 2010. It then ditched its platform in 2013, as it wasn't working to its satisfaction, and regenerated itself onto a new platform. It did it again in 2017. The second bank said that it started in 2003 and is now working on its fifth-generation architecture. By my calculation, this bank refreshes its technology structure every three years. That's some going. The third new bank told me that it can provide core updates to its apps every day, sometimes even twice a day if necessary. Typically, it is refreshing itself every six months and its apps every week.

How many traditional banks regenerate their systems every three years and their apps every week? To be honest, in traditional banks, I'm amazed if they've actually regenerated anything and, if lucky, update their app once a year.

This illustrates the divide between large dominating banks and new start-up banks. The new begin with a clean sheet of paper, build for today and renovate regularly. The old start with what they've got, try to change what they've got to keep up with today and renovate hardly ever.

Does the customer notice the difference? I think they do. After all, I am a customer. I have several apps from both newbies and oldies, and I can see the difference. A fundamental is the information I receive. The oldies give me no information. I regularly see transactions on my account and have no idea where they came from. A direct transfer listed as (Take from Barclays) is really useful—not. I have no idea where that money came from or who sent it as it has zero correlation with any invoices or clients I deal with.

In contrast, when I look at my new bank app, every transaction is enriched with information. I can double-click and drill down to not only who sent me money, but what it relates to and when it was sent. It is far easier.

It is a little like the third-party digital financial team that does everything for you in a completely automated way. That is the way it should be. In this age of automation, it amazes me that I'm capturing receipts in apps to send to accounting services that I then have to administer. In this digital age, the receipts should go straight to my digital accountant. I shouldn't have to do anything. And that's how I feel about banking, and why so many new digital banks are getting started.

The new banks have a dream. They dream that the customers shouldn't have to think. They dream that the bank can run their financial services for them, in a completely automated way, linking everything with everything through apps, APIs and analytics. The old banks are getting away with terrible service because no one knows the difference. The old banks give me transactional bank statements, with ledger services that record references and give me zero knowledge. The new banks tell me all I need to know.

Eventually, people will wake up and smell the coffee. Eventually, people will know that the old banks are dumb and the new banks are cool. Eventually, things will change. Eventually, the old banks will buy the new banks to be cool, too. I can't wait.

ARGUING WITH A BANKER

A banker and I were talking about the function of a bank. He gave me the classic bank view: A bank is there to take people's money and lend it out at a profit whilst ensuring that the risk of non-payment is minimised.

"No it isn't," I replied. I pushed the view that the bank is there as a trusted store of value. The lending part is now no longer important as that can be done through alternative media such as peer-to-peer lenders.

The banker took exception to purely being a store of value, and felt that the risk management aspect of banking was a critical part of their function. I argued that the bank's risk management function is being eaten by software. This means that credit analytics, transparency and management of risk, and the democratisation of finance is becoming a key change factor as people connect directly through marketplaces and platforms.

The banker started to get irate at this point, claiming that I didn't understand the complexity of the markets and that there was far more to creating financial markets than just deploying a server. I argued back that anything that can be automated will be automated, and we can see that most clearly in the trading rooms and investment markets as hedge funds and asset managers are replaced by exchange-traded funds (ETFs) and index-linked funds. High value jobs are disappearing fast as are low value transactional jobs from branch-based customer services to compliance to reconciliations to even programming.

He scoffed, and said that my view was too far out. I argued that it wasn't far out at all. After all, a lot of these changes have already happened, and marketplaces for finance are developing quickly. It's all now based on apps, APIs and analytics. The end of the debate was a stalemate, with him believing that the bank needed to balance risk and leverage with human insight whilst I continued to push the idea that a lot of that balance could be achieved through algorithms.

As I reflected on the argument, I realised that the key thing he had missed is that banking is not the end, but the means to the end. The end is what we are buying and selling. A bank provides a method to enable that to happen but software, platforms and marketplaces can just as easily provide that method in a far cheaper, faster and lower risk form. That was the point I was really trying to make—that banking is necessary, but banks are not.

Now you may recognise that line—it's an old one from Bill Gates— so how come banks are just as strong today, if not stronger, than when that comment was made back in 1994? The answer is that the technology had not reached primetime until now, and the regulator had enforced barriers to entry that would not allow new players to enter the markets ... until now.

We are on the cusp of radical change. Some banks are leading the change. Some banks are watching and waiting. Some have no idea what change is coming. This is because they are led by a C-suite filled with people who either make things happen, watch things happen or wonder what happened.

Astoundingly, when it comes to digital readiness, only half of financial institutions are deemed fit for change, according to the 2016 MIT/Deloitte annual survey of banks' digital readiness. In the survey, nine out of ten participants felt that digital transformation is ripping through the industry, but only 46 per cent felt that their organisation was ready to respond.

90% of respondents agree or strongly agree that digital technologies are disrupting the industry to a great or moderate extent.

And **93%** of those with a digital strategy agree or strongly agree that the objective of their digital strategy is to enhance customer experience and engagement.

Yet, only **46%** agree or strongly agree that they are adequately preparing for digital disruption.

Data source: "Digital transformation in financial services", MIT/Deloitte annual survey, 2016

In other words, 54 per cent think they're not ready, even though this is fundamental. Even more telling is that only one in five institutions is felt to be *nimble* enough to change while most feel their bank is slow to change. Is this a problem? Maybe. After all, three out of five employees in slow-to-change banks expect to leave within the next three years.

Perceptions of FSI firms

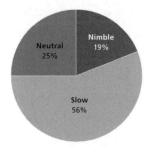

Respondents willing to work for more than three years

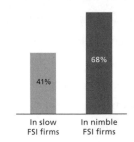

Data source: "Digital transformation in financial services", MIT/Deloitte annual survey, 2016

BANKS' LEADERSHIP TEAMS ARE FATALLY FLAWED

I was chairing a conference with various speakers when a Gartner Group researcher stood up and talked about its annual bank survey. Out of the senior bankers surveyed, 76 per cent did not believe that digitalisation would affect their business model.

I can tell you that those 76 per cent of banking respondents are wrong. Of course digitalisation is affecting the business model. It is changing everything through platformification. It is changing the back office through cloud and machine learning. It is changing the industry structure through blockchain and distributed ledger. It has accelerated the rapid cycle change of microservice organisations. It has given rise to innovation economies in Africa and the growth economy of China.

In fact, I would be amazed if anyone could honestly say that digitalisation doesn't change their business model. After all, the business model of banks was built for face-to-face interactions backed up by paper documentation; the business model of digital banks is for device-to-device interactions backed up by data. The two are completely different.

It doesn't worry me that bankers think their banks' business models don't need to change—after all, banks are run by bankers and it's their problem— but it does worry me that people in charge of such systemically important aspects of our lives could be so dumb. I think it just reflects the lack of insight into how digital transformation is impacting the world, and the lack of balance in the banks' boardrooms.

This was evidenced by a 2015 Accenture report that analysed professional technology experience in the boardrooms of more than a hundred of the largest banks around the world. Accenture's research showed that:

- Only 6 per cent of board members have professional technology backgrounds.
- Only 3 per cent of these banks have CEOs with professional technology backgrounds.

- Of the banks analysed, 43 per cent do not have any board members with professional technology backgrounds.
- Thirty per cent of these banks have only one board member with a professional technology background.
- In North American banks, 12.1 per cent of board members have professional technology experience, compared with 5.1 per cent in European banks and 5 per cent in Asian banks.
- Although boards of banks in the United States and the United Kingdom have higher percentages of directors with professional technology experience than others, the numbers are still low, at 16 per cent and 14 per cent respectively.

Banks are led by bankers even though many banks are trying to become digital banks or even, in some cases, FinTech firms. That is the fatal flaw here. FinTech firms are led by technologists *and* bankers, and most FinTech firms I meet have a healthy balance of young, bright technology experts and seasoned financial people.

That is why it's interesting to see that the biggest banks are gradually reconstructing their boardrooms for more balance. Yet when I think of a bank's boardroom, I tend to have a picture like this in my head: lots of old men in suits. The problem with this is, if a bank's leadership team is a bunch of old men in suits, how can they understand the needs of millennials and women? If they have no leadership that has technology vision, how can they compete with FinTechs that have far more balance? If a bank's top team does not know the difference between a blockchain and a distributed ledger, how do they know if they are investing in the right things?

A bank will be led over the cliff if it does not have a balanced boardroom that is half tech and half finance. That is what FinTech's leadership teams demonstrate. When I think of a FinTech boardroom, I think of it more like an awesome room of young, diverse people who are excited and visionary. It does have some old hands on board, but it's balanced. And the vibe in the room is one of *change the world* rather than *stop the world*.

So what I really expect in the next decade is to see a bank boardroom become just a little bit more awesome: still a bit grey, but also a little younger, with a healthy mix and balance of financial acumen and technology vision.

WHERE IS THE BANK'S DIGITAL VISION?

It's intriguing to find more and more banks creating digital heads. I meet these people regularly: "I'm the digital head of retail banking", "I'm the digital head of retail business banking", "I'm the digital head of the investment bank", "I'm the digital head of our transaction banking business", "I'm the digital head of our commercial bank" and so on. You get the idea. There are lots and lots of digital heads, but who's the daddy?

Often, the digital heads report to the head of a product division or a specific bank line-of-business head who runs retail or investment banking, wealth management or payments, and there's no coordination between them. Usually, these digital heads are given the objective of creating the digital project to add the digital front end to the analogue pig.

I know I'm being harsh, but I keep coming back to the real issue here, which is leadership. Banks are led by bankers, and that's the problem. Most banks have zero technology professionals in the C-Suite. As a result, they think that digital is a project. Each line of business creates the digital project and gives the digital task to a newly appointed digital head. The digital head builds a team and gets a budget and, once the digital stuff is done, is promoted and things go back to normal. That is not digital; that is just tinkering.

Digital is all about rethinking the bank for the internet age. It is changing the business model and culture of the bank to be built around digital platforms. It is reimagining how to offer finance through technology.

Bankers think of this the other way around. They think of how to apply finance to technology rather than how to apply technology to finance. I've touched on all of these things before, but it is frustrating that the message doesn't seem to be getting through. It's not getting through because the leaders of banks understand risk, regulations, compliance, accounting, ledgers and money but they don't understand technology.

How can a bank be built based on technology if the C-Suite is populated by people who do not understand technology?

That is a fundamental question, and is why there are so many heads of digital but no digital head. A digital head should be the CEO or, at the very least, a member of the bank's board. In fact, I often ask these digital heads who they report to, and they tell me it's either the COO or the CIO. This is again where banks underestimate the demand for digital transformation and digital leadership. The chief digital officer, or CDO, should be a single person who is on the C-suite and a direct report to the CEO, or even *be* the CEO, if this digital change is to succeed.

The C-Suite should have at least a quarter of its team populated by people with a professional technology career. Right now, almost 80 per cent of banks have no one of such calibre in the C-Suite. That is a disaster waiting to happen, especially considering there's a five-year change window to get the bank fit for the next decade, at most.

So when I meet most heads of digital, I sympathise as I know they are frustrated. Most of them are frustrated that digital is being dealt with as a project, rather than a change programme, and most of them are frustrated that digital is being delegated rather than led. What can be done?

If the management team of the bank cannot be changed and an employee truly believes that the future is digital, that employee will have to leave the bank and find a firm that has that vision. The vision will only come from a bank or start-up that has technology leadership. You cannot create a digital vision if you don't have leaders who understand digital. In fact, again, the reason why most bank leaders avoid changing core systems is that they don't have the vision, understanding or appetite to make such tough decisions and, because there is no burning platform (yet), they avoid making them. Most CIOs are not there to give vision; they are there to keep the lights on and maintain the system (especially as 80 per cent of their budget is spent on just that). So who's going to create a digital technology vision if only bankers are present in the boardroom and there's no one to challenge them? No one.

OPEN SOURCING FINANCE: YOU CANNOT DELEGATE THIS PROJECT

While on the subject of transformation, I often get pushback that you cannot have too many technologists involved in the running of a bank. We need banks run by people who understand money, and *they* can tell the technologists what to do.

I'm not so sure. A bank cannot delegate its future and that, to me, is the fundamental flaw in the argument over banks being led by bankers. If banks are digitalising and have to be fit for the internet age by unbundling their vertically integrated structures to open source finance, can a control freak really understand this fundamental change in operations?

I use the term "control freak" purposefully as few big banks delegate their IT externally. They may use solutions from external providers, but do they truly put their IT out to the markets or are they adapting such systems to their internal needs and making them proprietary again? I suspect the latter. In fact, it amuses me when we talk about legacy structures because banks have legacy IT, and their providers have even greater legacies in many instances. Add the fact that most banks have tailored the implementation of a legacy solution to suit their needs, and you have a legacy upon a legacy.

Banks are very reluctant to open source their operations and that's where the FinTech community is scoring points. By taking the vertically integrated, proprietary and legacy structures of finance, FinTech firms are able to narrow target every piece of banking, then componentise and open source it. This is why we have narrow peer-to-peer structures for payments, credit and advice emerging that seem innocuous on the surface but may be truly transformational within. It is the true innovator's dilemma. Banks believe that they must control the value chain and process of finance but FinTech is breaking that vertically integrated value chain apart.

Now what the truly visionary and innovative banks are doing is recognising that FinTech firms are just widgets of capability. These banks are taking their capabilities, evaluating their functionalities and, where necessary, copying or partnering to bring that functionality to their clients. White labelling and partnering with FinTech firms is not an embarrassment. It's not an admittance of weakness. It is more a recognition that someone can do a narrow line function better than you and, as a company with centuries of brand recognition and millions of customers, bringing that capability to your client base is visionary.

These banks will be the ones that survive the transition from last-century distributors of paper through a physical network to this century distributors of data through a digital network. The challenged banks, rather than the challengers, will be those that try to keep their vertically integrated control of operations. Banks no longer control any part of their value chain. They do not own the customer; they have zero digital relationship unless they earn it. Furthermore, most of what they do can be provided by an alternative far cheaper and easier because the alternative players are replacing buildings and humans with software and servers.

So this is where the leadership has to be created. Leading incumbent banks from their traditional command and control structures to open-sourced operations that are shared, cooperative and inclusive. This is the core of conversion to digitalisation and, as most bank leadership is immersed in risk management and control structures, open sourcing the bank is a really tough ask. Many banks will fail to meet this challenge, not because their bank is weak or unable to adapt, but more because their leadership is weak and unable to adapt.

Open sourcing finance is the shared economy business model of partnering, white labelling and integrating components to create a new business model of aggregated components of product and service. Any bank resisting such change will not survive. Moreover, to understand such change truly requires a leadership with technological prowess, not just banking knowledge.

Hence, when I come back to this thought of banks not needing technological leadership, just good leadership that can delegate the change to the right advisors, whether internally or externally, I fundamentally disagree. The future of the bank cannot be delegated. Bank leadership cannot ignore its obligations to lead the change.

CAN BANKS CHANGE THEIR CONTROL FREAK CULTURES?

Anne Boden, founder of the UK digital challenger Starling Bank, used to work for ABN AMRO, Allied Irish Banks (AIB) and RBS. As CEO of a FinTech start-up, she said to me, "I've now realised that the simple changes I needed to make in my old jobs would usually cost $3 million or more, and yet now I can make those changes for $3,000."

I've heard this comment from another source, namely Monzo, whose CEO stated that the company built a full-service bank platform from scratch in months with a team of fifteen for $3 million in comparison to a bank that spent $300 million to build such a platform with a team of thousands.

This culminates in a question that I was asked recently by a banker: Today, you talk about apps, APIs, analytics and marketplaces, Chris. Won't these all be irrelevant in ten years as a lot of the technology of ten years ago is the legacy issue we have today?

The nub of this is old thinking. For most of my life, technology has been hugely capital intensive, people intensive and high-cost, long-term developments. Banks would invest millions over multi-year cycles and have high-cost barriers, resulting in a very detailed analysis of the return on investment and whether it was actually worth doing. Today, it is all about fast cycle micro developments that are cheap, easy and fast. However, if you are stuck in the old structure cycle of capital and resource intensive computing, then you cannot adapt to this fast cycle world.

That is the fundamental issue for banks—they are stuck with old technology. I've already said a lot about the problem of legacy systems and how to replace them. However, I'm now going to deviate slightly from my usual standpoint and talk about using cryogenic freezing to replace the old systems.

To do this, you need to convert functions and processes piece by piece to an app, API or analytic and then put that out into the marketplace as brand-new, shiny tech. Eventually, this can be done throughout all the operations and the bank will then eventually find itself in an open marketplace, having managed to shift off the old tech. That's a multi-year enterprise strategy again, which needs vision and leadership, but it can be done. However, there are two issues for a bank when dealing with this change.

The first is how to even contemplate the changes, as there are other things happening that must be done. For example, banks deal with regulatory and compliance changes almost every day, and many of those changes require the old systems to be updated first. Those regulatory changes eat up all the budget as, even if it's just tinkering with a few lines of code in the old systems, it has multiple impacts across gazillions of lines of code. As all of that needs checking and rechecking before going live, it becomes a resource intensive change programme that costs millions. That is why banks have little budget for innovation because most of it gets eaten by the old systems and, as so many COOs say, the focus is "just to keep the lights on".

Let's consider that a bank can re-engineer its way out of that mess, and start to move to Open Banking based on apps, APIs and analytics, what's the problem? Well, there's still an elephant in the room. The new organisational structure is based on moving from macro and monolithic to micro and empowered. Banks, however, don't like micro and empowered. Banks are control freaks and don't like open and fast cycle change. It needs to be slow and controlled, and compliant. This means that moving to a microservice architecture—which is what today's agile, cheap, fast and easy technologies demand—is difficult for an institution that culturally is driven by control and compliance.

In discussing this, I usually say that a microservice organisation has developer teams of no more than two pizzas in size. That's a team that can be fed by two pizzas for lunch. If the team needs three pizzas, the team is too big. It's all about small, nimble, agile teams that can change things fast.

So let's imagine a bank creates a microservice developer organisation. Each of the teams in that organisation owns its piece of code. Each team can change its code fast and replug it back into the architecture. As each team owns the code, no one needs to sign off on it. And there's the rub. Can a bank release its control freakery to allow legions of rocket scientist developers to do their own thing?

If it can, a bank can reboot itself every day. However, I doubt many will. For example, I had a conversation about innovation with a bank executive during which he explained the catch-22 in a bank. You want to be innovative, but only as long as there's no risk but, with any innovation, there has to be risk. You can play in the sandbox like little kids but, if you try to step out of the sandbox, you will be slapped back down. That is your place. Stay there.

I pointed out that any innovation that comes out of the sandbox is incredibly hard to internalise as the bank's culture is there to wipe out the antibodies of the cannibalistic innovators. That is why heading up innovation in any financial firm is a frustrating job that inevitably leads to moving to a Fintech start-up or the job centre.

The banking guy reflected on this and then said something really interesting. His comment was that banks don't like failure. We know this, but it's all to do with the compliance culture. Failure implies issues and can raise regulatory alerts. Banks want to avoid regulatory alerts at all costs, and that this is why failure is not an option. I took the view that microservice architectures in an open marketplace of APIs allow failure, as these don't have the same repercussions, to which he replied:

"Look Chris, you should know this. We, as a bank, find it difficult to invest in conjecture. So if we trial a project for $1 million and it fails, then we soul search to see what went wrong and, more importantly, who led the wrongness. Someone has to be blamed. And that someone is then fired. However, if we are thinking about a $1 million project and can hire a consulting firm to investigate the project and tell us whether it will work or fail, then we are far happier. So we might hire one of the big consulting groups and spend $1 million on their report that tells us our project – which would have cost the same to trial – is going to fail, and then we are happy because they told us it would fail for $1 million but look how much further cost, embarrassment and shame they allowed us to avoid."

Woah. I realised the enormity and, at the same time, the reality of his statement. I have seen this first hand. It is far better to get someone external to come in and tell you if something is right or wrong because if it later turns out that they gave the wrong advice, you then have someone to blame and possibly take to court. However, if an internal guy says it, then woe betide that person if they are wrong.

It ticked so many other boxes. For example, I remember a C-suite member of one bank talking about business cases, return on investment (ROI), cost-benefit analysis and the future project revenues and costs. He said that the bank was rigorous in ensuring that there was a business case for anything and everything. If you wanted to start a new project, you had to show the numbers.

That's difficult to do if you are innovating because it's never been done before, but here are the numbers nonetheless. The trick of the game, he said, was to make the numbers look convincing. Show that you have done your research. Show that you used a consultancy firm to bring together some customer focus groups who overwhelmingly believe that your next-generation app will get a million users in a month, then flesh that out with projections and graphs. Make it look amazing. Don't just put it in PowerPoint, PDF it having used the best graphic designers in town, and then add some GIFs or videos which, when in the boardroom, will keep the management awake.

The reason why this advice is sound and sage is that once you get the money, you can stop worrying. You got the money based on your sound, but fudged, business case. You actually made the whole business case up and the numbers are all estimates based on a finger in the air and a discussion in the pub over a napkin. The fact that you have numbers and seem to have substantiated them, and have research and presentational material that looks amazing, is what gets you the money. Once you've got the money, you need not worry because no one ever goes back to check the numbers from last year. Yes, they may check if you have a substantial failure but, if you work the numbers and the politics, you can pretty much get away with anything for a long time.

I admit that the two conversations seem a bit at odds. On the one hand, if I fail spectacularly, I'm out, but if I get the analysis, I'm in. On the other hand, if I present a load of fictional thoughts, I get the money while if I tell the truth, I don't.

This is how it works. Not just in banks, but in any large corporation. It's called politics. If you are seen to fail, you are out; if you are seen to be doing the right things, you are in. Bear that in mind when you innovate. Large firms will not allow public failures. Equally, large firms rarely invest properly unless they have numbers.

In fact, here are the top ten reasons why most companies find it hard to innovate:

- **PR value versus real results:** often banks have innovation theatre to make it look like they are doing something when they actually aren't internalising it.
- **Hampered by heritage:** there is simply too much legacy infrastructure to be able to adapt and change.

- **No real sense of urgency:** few banks have a burning platform and what drives banks is not customers but regulators so unless it is mandated, why bother?
- **Cannibalisation of existing revenue streams:** like the WalMart versus Amazon discussion, creating a marketplace where third parties compete with internal products is not welcomed.
- **A lack of experienced innovators:** banks tend to eradicate innovation and so an innovation culture is extinguished.
- **A culture clash:** a bank's culture is all about risk minimisation, which directly conflicts with change, and if no one thinks they can do it, almost everyone thinks they can't.
- **A lack of ownership and sponsorship:** the leaders of banks got to where they are because they are bankers and don't want to take risks with technology that they don't understand.
- **"Compartmentalised" innovation:** innovation takes place around the periphery in departmental compartments but is never internalised across the enterprise.
- **Governance, governance, governance:** unless the regulator allows it, we ain't gonna do it.
- **Who else is doing this:** if no one else is doing it, then we're not (but surely that's why it's innovation?).

A GLIMPSE OF THE FUTURE

I thought we should finish *Digital Human* with a look at what comes next. What will the future hold?

One of the biggest areas of surprise in my life is how science fiction has so rapidly become science fact. *Star Trek* invented the mobile telephone, flat-screen HD-TVs, microwaves, and more. Bearing in mind the first series was made in 1966, well before any of these products were envisaged, it was pretty revolutionary.

However, those items are minor compared with what is happening today, as we breathe. Every day there's an announcement that stuns me, so I thought that I'd glimpse into the future and look at how life, our homes, structures and travel are changing. Oh, and banking and insurance, of course. I'll discuss some of the biggest future trends and then the financial market's response to each trend. Obviously, I can't cover everything. It's just to cut the ice on how things are evolving and what it means to financial services.

THE QUEST FOR ETERNITY

Life sciences are extending lifetimes by decades. There are predictions that a child born today could live for 150 years. We can take almost any part of the body and grow it in a beaker. Another *Star Trek* success sneaks in here too, with Dr "Bones" McCoy's body scanner becoming an effective tool for doctors today.

Equally, when we talk about science fiction to science fact, we only have to look at the iconic 1970s series *The Six Million Dollar Man*. The opening lines pretty much sum up the theme of the programme:

"Steve Austin, astronaut. A man barely alive. Gentlemen, we can rebuild him. We have the technology. We have the capability to build the world's first bionic man. Steve Austin will be that man. Better than he was before. Better, stronger, faster."

The series is more popularly remembered as the story of the bionic man. A man who had almost died, but the U.S. government spent $6 million, around $33 million today, to replace most of his body with robotic replacements. Similar to *Robocop* in concept, a person could pretty much die but be kept alive by bionics and other life science technologies.

Well, we now do that stuff on a daily basis. For instance, people's parts can be replaced pretty easily. As mentioned, we can grow them in beakers, 3D print them or just add on a replacement where needed. I have the thought that, in twenty or thirty years, we won't need an Olympics and a Paralympics as some athletes will choose to replace parts of their body with faster versions. As a result, abled athletes will compete alongside the less abled, and both may have chosen to enhance or replace their less efficient, broken or defective parts.

Similarly, there was a 1960s sci-fi movie *Fantastic Voyage* in which a medical crew was shrunk to microscopic size and injected into the bloodstream of an injured man whom they then tried to save. Well, there's no need to shrink humans anymore. Nowadays, doctors can place nanotechnology inside the human body, such as a tiny HD camera used by doctors to see in high definition what's going on inside the body whilst operating from the outside. Oh, and don't think that the doctor is going to be a human. It's a robot. After all, a robot can operate on a million patients with zero errors. I challenge any human doctor or nurse to try to keep up with that record.

While we will be living for longer, advancements in technology will ensure that we are always born on time. For example, I couldn't believe the story about the baby who was born twice. Doctors took the baby out of the womb at 23 weeks for 20 minutes to perform life-saving surgery on her spine. She was then placed back in the womb and born again three months later. It is like the notion of having babies born to three parents in order to remove defective DNA that might lead to birth with inherited diseases. That is justified, but the concerns are that parents will use these techniques to create designer babies.

Even more stunning is what scientists are starting to achieve in the realm of artificial wombs. Today, a baby can only survive outside the womb from about 22 weeks, as it needs that time to get all the necessary nutrients from the mother's bloodstream. Even then, two out of three born at that age are likely to suffer longer-term complications. However, that may change if we can nurture an egg outside of the womb. That's exactly what scientists are on the verge of achieving after decades of trying to develop an artificial womb that will re-create a more natural environment for a premature baby to continue to develop in. This was first imagined by J. B. S. Haldane who predicted in 1924 that 70 per cent of human births would be from artificial wombs by 2074.

The era of motherless births is coming, but there will also be more fatherless births through the use of artificial sperm. Who needs love when you can have a designer baby all of your very own with no partner involved? Oh, and your baby lives forever. As I said, science fiction is rapidly becoming science fact.

110 Years to Save for Retirement

A century ago, the retirement age was set at sixty-five when most people actually died in their forties. Today, the age at which people retire is being repeatedly debated as there are calls to raise the retirement age in response to the fact that most people now die in their eighties. Soon, people will live, on average, to over a century and, according to scientists, babies born today will make it to 150 years of age. What do you do for 150 years?

You grow up, obviously, but then work for 130 years? Well no, you'll spend the last twenty or thirty years having body part replacements using robotics or 4D-printed body matter. Alternatively, you'll have nanobots running around inside you genetically modifying your cell matter to eradicate the cancer or dementia that's been identified by your biodoc robot.

A lifespan of 150 years, with at least 110 years of active life. What exactly will an active life of 110 years entail? Obviously, it will be a challenging one as the babies born today will be coming onto the job markets in 2035. However, the good news is that there will be fewer babies, so less competition. Or is that bad news?

By 2035, there will still possibly be around seven billion people or more on the planet, with every person getting older every day through age-extending medicines and treatments. Equally, as the majority of the ageing population won't be working, own their own homes and no longer pay taxes, the new workforce will have to work hard to pay taxes to support the retired workforce.

Home ownership may become a thing of the past, as all property will be too costly to afford for these new workers. Thus, the mortgage market will become a rental market only. And saving for a pension will probably have to start on day one because it will take a century to build enough of a pension pot to afford to retire on.

Sound depressing? Possibly, but it's more a change of thinking than a depressing prospect. Changing the way you think about mortgages, savings, investments, pensions … everything. There's a raft of things that relate to this, and lots of scholarly articles predicting doom and gloom or happiness and wealth, but you need to make up your own mind. No matter what though, the key will be that change of thinking.

Who Wants to Live Forever?

Building on these ideas of ageing and the 150-year-old humans to come, it really highlights how technology is reinventing every part of life on Earth. From FinTech to science to life sciences, every aspect of humanity is being turned upside down. We can invent humans from beakers in labs to synthetics in production lines. Although we aren't quite there yet, the near-term future is likely to have many synthetic humans acting as carers and cleaners, taking the jobs that others don't want or aren't prepared to do.

It's being predicted by many scientists and futurists that within our lifetime, life sciences will find ways to treat humanity's ailments like no other before. So here are my top picks of the technologies already out there that are changing humanity and will allow us to live for 150 years or more.

- **Genetically engineered humans:** By editing the DNA of the egg and sperm or the embryo itself, it could be possible to correct disease genes and pass those genetic fixes on to future generations. Such a technology could be used to rid families of progressive illnesses like cystic fibrosis and offer lifelong protection against infection, Alzheimer's and, possibly, the effects of ageing. The fear is that this type of engineering is a path towards a dystopia of superpeople and designer babies for those who can afford it.
- **Printing human body parts:** With the advent of 3D printing some twenty years ago, the idea of replacing parts of the human body is becoming more of a reality. This is because 3D printers have the ability to create complex parts relatively quickly and efficiently. Because the required body part is 3D printed, each one can be modelled specifically for its wearer. The scanning process of the part can be completed within a few minutes. Once the design is finalised, the body part takes around 40 hours to print. The cost to do this is a fraction of the higher end prosthetics.

- **Printing human organs:** Until now, medical 3D printing has been mainly used to create prosthetics. Advances in technology, however, now enable 3D printers to print using soft materials such as collagens, alginates and fibrins that naturally appear in the body. Researchers hope that this will eventually mean that transplants will no longer be necessary to repair damaged organs. In other words, you would no longer need prosthetics as you could, for example, just grow a new arm.

- **Growing human body parts:** Scientists around the world are working to perfect techniques to enable them to grow replacements for body parts that have been destroyed or damaged. A historic first was in 2015 with the success of researchers who grew an entire rat forearm from living cells, complete with blood vessels, muscles and skin. The researchers believe that, in future, the techniques would also apply to legs, arms and other extremities.

- **Seeing humans from the inside:** As I've already mentioned, doctors are now using nanotechnology to send computers, cameras and the like inside patients to get a more accurate and specific diagnosis. Further advancements here include the testing of a tiny pill that combines a microphone, a thermometer and a battery to collect several measures simultaneously from inside the human body. This is the latest in a series of ingestible computers such as the Proteus Discover sensor that tracks how patients take prescribed medications and the VitalSense from Philips that tracks a patient's temperature.

- **Human life extension:** Although the idea of bringing people back from the dead may seem the stuff of science fiction, it's the ultimate goal of start-up Humai. The company plans to do this by using artificial technology and nanotechnology to store data about a person's thoughts and behaviours. Once it has collected everything it needs to know about that person, it will then build a robot body for their brain to live in after they die.

Seventy Is the New Thirty

What does all of this mean for financial services? How will you live in a world where those who can afford it are beautiful and can live for almost ever while those who cannot are secondary? What pension policy will you need for 150 years of possible life? How many jobs will you have during those years and when would you retire? What jobs will there be if we can automate almost every form of work?

These are fundamental points primarily for insurance firms that offer critical illness plans, health insurances, pensions and related products. In particular, there will be issues around work—everything can be done by robots—and longer life planning. After all, when Bismarck came up with the idea of a pension, most men died in their forties. That's why the retirement age was set at sixty-five. Today, the average person lives to eighty and that is why there are shortfalls in most economies. Now that the average lifespan is increasing to a hundred, what should the new pensionable age be? Eighty?

Banks, like insurance firms, will also find challenges and opportunities here:

- How will wealth be built and who will be building it?
- If someone becomes a high net worth as they enter their third or fourth career in their seventies, how can a bank even be considered at that point, bearing in mind that most people choose their bank by the age of thirty?
- Can banks offer high net worth products to people who have lived long enough to suss the banks out?
- What will trust look like if it's being played out over centuries, rather than decades?

Obviously, governments will also face huge challenges as, with an average lifespan of 150 years, how many people will be living on the planet? Earth's numbers are already doubling every thirty years or so, and this would see those numbers explode. Add to this the ending of poverty (the goal of the

Bill & Melinda Gates Foundation) and the end of disease (the goal of Mark and Priscilla Zuckerberg), what will all of these people be doing?

Some believe it will lead to a world without wealth as a focus. "The acquisition of wealth is no longer the driving force in our lives. We work to better ourselves and the rest of humanity," as said by Jean-Luc Picard, the captain of *Star Trek*'s USS *Enterprise*. Likewise, Elon Musk has been quoted as saying, "I would like to die thinking that humanity has a bright future ... becoming a multiplanetary species with a self-sustaining civilization on another (planet)."

Others believe it will lead to a world of slums for the poor (the 99 per cent) and floating cities in the oceans and stars for the rich (the 1 per cent). Such visions have been around for a long time, dating back to Fritz Lang's *Metropolis* in 1927. Most recently, *The Hunger Games*, *In Time* and *Elysium* have explored the same themes of the rich living off the fat of the poor and are all, to an extent, remakes of *Metropolis*. In fact, most films have some resonance with that landmark movie.

The above views represent two extremes, but there is often a middle way. The *Star Trek* way would bid banks, money and governments farewell. The world would act as a global citizen with democratised money, self-regulating structures and no need for statist interventions. I love the idea of that world, but just cannot see it working, even with bitcoin. Bitcoin succeeds by being democratised and providing money without government, but how will that self-regulating structure eradicate risks such as terrorist funding, money laundering, drug money and contracts for assassinations or paedophilia? Will a self-regulating market run that world?

At some point, controls need to be put in play that rise above the democracy for these reasons. At this point, it offers the opportunity for *Metropolis* to step in. The controllers control the weak. They accumulate wealth and find ways to exploit those they control because they set the rules. This is all getting a bit too existential for me, but I fundamentally believe that we will have democratised money for value exchange, with digital identities that we control who can access but are issued to us by a statist intervention.

I have no idea who or what will be that statist. However, the digital identity I control in the future will be on some form of distributed ledger and there lies the real question: who will run that ledger? I've hazarded a few guesses in the past but, for sure, there will be an identity controller (me) and an identity issuer. We may automate the issuer through blockchains, but there will still be an intervention, some way to get at that control and, as discussed, you then have the ability to build power through that control. It's going to be fascinating to see how that evolves.

THE INTERNET OF THINGS

We talk a lot about the Internet of Things, and have been for a while. Most of us probably haven't felt it much in our daily lives. OK, so we have a smartphone but what other smart things do you have? Maybe if you live in the United States, you have Nest, Alexa and a Tesla, so you could say that you have a semi-smart home and car. The rest of us are still waiting to experience this. But what happens when things get supersmart?

I'm quite intrigued by this as I used an example almost ten years ago of robots looking after the house: mowing the lawn, looking after an ageing parent and automatically cleaning the house. More recently, there have been some great innovations, like the app that allows someone into your house using a passcode that can be set for permanent access for house members and temporary access for visitors like a plumber.

But what will happen when the whole house is internet-enabled? In that house, you will be able to use biometrics for access, doctors will do medical checks from the bathroom and your home entertainment will be so immersive that it will feel like you're on the holodeck of *Star Trek*.

Take also the example of *Minority Report*. In the movie, there's a scene when Tom Cruise is being chased on the autohighway. At the time, in 2002, that scene looked phantasmagorical. Today, it's a fact thanks to Tesla, Google and the other guys working on self-driving cars and the highways they will run along. It's not just highways though. There will be superfast trains (think Hyperloop) and superfast aircraft that will carry you from New York to London in just over 30 minutes, all of which will ensure that everyone has a clean, happy and healthy life in a low emission, sustainable structure. Well, that's the plan.

Certainly, there are many projects that are focused on creating a self-sustaining planet where, instead of using fossil fuels or other dirty power systems, we get all our energy from the Sun. Elon Musk's company recently announced a range of new house tiles that look like tiles but are actually solar panels. The world is changing fast, superfast, and much of it is being driven by the visionary Elon Musk but he's not alone. For example, Jeff Bezos is quietly building a whole new world through Amazon.

In fact, it seems that we have two sorts of billionaire out there. Those who want to create new solutions for the future (Musk, Bezos and Richard Branson) and those who want to solve present problems in the future (Gates, Buffett and Zuckerberg). Both are doing the right things, but both have different aspirations and objectives. The former are entrepreneurial visionaries whilst the latter are philanthropic angels. Both are to be admired, I guess.

Back to the point, the future world must cater for billions of people. There are over seven billion today and there will be nearer nine billion by 2035, based on current life expectancy and birth rates. This is a challenge, as illustrated by this NATO discussion:[34]

A greater number of people are living in more, and larger, cities than ever before. The proportion of the global population living in cities as opposed to the countryside exceeded the 50% threshold in 2008.

These new cities are concentrated on the world's coastlines. Currently 1.4 million people move to cities worldwide every week and the world population is projected to increase to 8.7 billion inhabitants by 2035. By the 2030s, it is estimated five of the world's eight to nine billion people will live in cities, many of them in slums.

---

34   "Urbanisation – A Growing Challenge in the Future," NATO, 2016.

Oh, dear. By then, people should be living in smart cities where they can have smart things in smart homes. Why then, will they be living in slums?

> As history has shown, conflict occurs where people live, and therefore, most academic and defence research concludes that it is a matter of when, not if, the military will be required to operate in an urban or urban littoral environment. If the Alliance wants to be successful in a future urban conflict, adaptation is not an option it is a must.

This is certainly *not* the future IoT that we are talking about.

It's somewhere in between these visions, I think. Many have a bleak view of the future—think *Rise of the Robots* and *Homo Deus*—while others, like me, have a much brighter view. As to which camp you fall into is, I think, more a reflection of age. What I mean by this is that children are not frightened of the future at all. They want to rush to it so bad. Time goes so slowly when you're young. When you're old, time goes too fast. We fear the future as every passing day brings us nearer to the end. So, an older mind fears the future; a younger mind desires it. That's the fundamental difference for me and is the reason why I can't wait for tomorrow.

THE INTERNET OF EVERYTHING

I've talked often and in depth about the Internet of Things and how this affects banking. In the near future, when each of us has five, six, eight, ten things on the internet, we will be seeing a world where trillions of transactions take place among billions of things in real time, non-stop and in very small amounts. My fridge might be ordering milk, my TV the next episode of *Game of Thrones* and my car a top-up of unleaded petrol, all in immediate space and with immediate finality.

That is the challenge for the banking system. Morphing from a system that takes minutes, days or weeks to one that can process a billion-dollar transaction for the same cost and in the same time as a nano-cent. It's a huge challenge. Yet this is what we need for the Internet of Things.

Now consider the following. If all cars drive themselves and never crash, who will need car insurance? If every house is online and therefore cannot be burgled without alerting the authorities, who will need house insurance? If you never need to pay for anything as it's all wireless, who will need cash?

Again, these raise lots of fundamental questions about financial services business models. We built our business on physicality. As we move to digital, we have no idea what to do. We built our model on annual premiums because it was too hard to do insurance-as-we-live. Now, insurance-as-we-live is the new model. Banking-as-a-service is the way to go. We need to open source and structure our services for how our customers live, breathe and work.

I find this the most puzzling piece, and it's probably because customers haven't got it yet. Today, I live in a world where nothing is an annual commitment. I download as I feel and pay by the month. If I don't like it, I cancel it. In some cases, I download as I go. I only pay if I listen or use. And yet the model of banks and insurance firms is one of long-term commitments. Banking is for life and insurance firms know that when you sign up for your pension, you're there for forty or more years. Woah. This must change.

Why would I make a lifetime commitment today? Some of us marry, but know we will not be around forever. Some of us adopt a dog or a cat, but know that we won't be there forever. Some of us sign up for things—a house, a bank account or an insurance policy—but know that we will switch as soon as there is a better rate. There are no lifetime commitments anymore.

Twenty years ago, we might have applied and been assigned a *job for life*. There is no *job for life* anymore. In fact, I'd go as far as to say that any *job for life* today sounds more like a sentence than an opportunity. Who wants to be grounded forever?

The new world is one of transient relationships, shorter-term commitments and everything online all the time. However, the financial system is built for lifetime relationships, long-term engagement and everything over the counter. This is the core challenge and this is why the globally connected Internet of Things creates a massive challenge for the incumbents.

Incumbents must be agile, nimble and digital but they were built to be slow, risk averse and physical. Now suddenly, customers are saying that they have the things they value all around them, and all of those things are on the internet. Can banks keep up? Will banks keep up?

Certainly, it creates challenges as well as opportunities. I heard a great story, for example, of one insurance company that now insures things based on the security of your house being connected. The insurer monitors your house 24/7 and knows if you have left a window or door open as you leave the house, and will even alert you to the fact. This is the new world. All is online. All is real time. All is connected. And anyone who believes in a system that refreshes annually is delusional.

SPACE: NOT NECESSARILY THE FINAL FRONTIER

Finally, we come to space. No longer the final frontier as we're conquering space fast. From landing explorers on Mars to capturing amazing images of Pluto, we have begun our journey to boldly go where no one has gone before. As mentioned, science fiction often becomes science fact, and the quest to explore our universe is definitely under way led by digital entrepreneurs Elon Musk and Jeff Bezos.

Elon Musk with SpaceX is specifically driving this change by creating reusable spacecraft, which greatly brings down the cost of space missions. We've had space shuttles to the Moon, but spacecraft that can go to Mars and back. Wow. That really does sound like science fiction.

But hold on. Reel back to 1916. Back then, we still had horses and carriages on our streets. Most people were amazed to see an automobile—1916 was the year that BMW was founded—and the aeroplane was used for experiments and in wars, having only been proven as a viable machine thirteen years earlier. Mount Everest was unconquered, the telephone was just starting to be used and it was the year that the light switch was invented.

It sounds like a very different world, but it was just a hundred years ago. At that time, few people had explored the world. In fact, most people had probably never left their place of birth as travel was for the rich. The *Titanic* had been launched and then sunk just four years earlier, and most people would have only been on a ship if they were emigrating. Leisure was at home and holidays were unheard of. Now imagine this: we had still a large area of Earth to explore, especially sub-Saharan Africa and the North and South poles. At that time, explorers visiting these lands were hailed as daredevils who might die. They returned as heroes, and brought wondrous stories back with them.

A century later, people complain if they don't get their annual two weeks of sunshine somewhere exotic overseas. Most have a bucket list to see the things of legend first-hand: Machu Picchu, the Pyramids, Kruger National Park and Sydney. We hop on and off aircraft like they are buses, connecting between cities and continents without a backward glance. We can go on charity jaunts to places that were inaccessible just fifty years ago and see gorillas in the mist and Mount Everest from a base camp.

World numbers of air travellers, 1970–2015

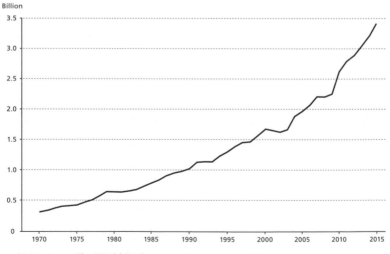

Data source: The World Bank

The world has changed not just a bit, but a lot. Yet when Elon Musk talks today about settling on Mars, he sounds like some nutjob, but he isn't. In fact, when I last heard him talk about it, I thought about how strong the similarities are regarding how life will be a century from now compared to how it was a century ago. A century ago, people who went overseas were considered daring. Today, it is commonplace. Today, we think that the idea of someone going into space is daring. A century from now, it will be commonplace.

SPACE MONEY

Here's a final thought on the future from a banking perspective. According to Elon Musk, we will be colonising Mars by 2040. Why? Because this planet is not going to sustain the population it has emerging. When I was born, there were half the number of people on Earth than there are today. Some say birth rates are slowing, as people emerge from poverty, but we are equally seeing people ageing. Today, the average life expectancy is eighty years; tomorrow, it's expected to be a hundred or more. While we say that birth rates are slowing, given that you may be able to design babies without a partner involved in future, these rates may rise again.

By 2035, it is estimated that 8.7 billion people will be living on Earth, up from 7.5 billion today. My estimate is that this will rise to about fourteen billion by 2065. That's just based on the idea of doubling the population every fifty years, so this may be a conservative estimate. One thing is clear though, the planet will be unsustainable if there are so many humans. What do we do? We send them into space.

Another factor is that some people believe that there will be no jobs in the future as all work can, and will, be automated. I'm not so sure because there will be an increasing need for space stewards, the next generation of air stewards. There will be a need for safety testing of spacecraft, developing systems and apps for the spaceships, providing services for robot repairs, entertainment and developer services for building virtual reality (VR) experiences and more.

However, *everyone* has noted that there will be a problem with money in the future. So many people, not enough work. What do you do if there is a really old population and fewer young people? The young pay the taxes to care for the old, but this situation will be turned on its head. Not just that, the young will find it hard to make decent money because they will be faced with a challenge. The challenge will be down to who has the money.

According to Yuval Noah Harari, the future will create a huge divide between humans. There will be one race of superhumans, with lives that can be extended for years and designer children, namely the elite rich. Then there will be a useless class of humans who have no worth, thanks to automation, as they cannot work.

All of these future predictions can be mind-blowing. However, if the future is vastly and unequally distributed, how will the useless class survive? Maybe *Star Trek* can again provide the answer.

WHY IS THERE NO MONEY IN *STAR TREK*?

Television writer Gardner Goldsmith worked on the *Voyager* incarnation of the show. While pitching a story outline one day about retrieving stolen money, he was told by the producer that Gene Roddenberry, creator of the original show, "stipulated before he died that there was to be no money in the Federation." Roddenberry apparently believed that in the future, "mankind would have evolved past the need for money," and that "humanism would strip mankind of the acquisitive tendencies it had shown throughout history, and that the use of money was a vice."

What the creator believed, his characters propounded. We are told time and again by one character or another that there is no need for money within the Federation, or that money no longer exists, or that humanity has moved beyond its acquisitive past and now pursues only knowledge and self-improvement.

According to one blogger, the original series made no such claims. It was only in the fourth feature film in which the crew travels back in time that Captain Kirk lets it slip that they have no money in the future. But even in later years, the *Star Trek* universe is not strictly moneyless. As numerous people have pointed out, there are occasional references in the shows and films to things called "credits", which sound a lot like money. There is also "latinum", a fictional precious metal used notably by the Ferengi in *Deep Space Nine*, yet another incarnation of the show. Still, credits and latinum are mostly used for dealings with people *outside* of the Federation.

When you think about it, it is more than a bit odd that a fictional universe whose premier starship is named "the Starship *Enterprise*" would be so antagonistic to *actual* enterprise. Then again, it isn't the enterprising part of it that chafes; it's the profit part. Since the Ferengi use money, they are treated with contempt, like money changers in the temple. They are presented as living only for the love of latinum, against which all other purposes pale.

But this base caricature of business and wealth acquisition is about as realistic as a Vulcan mind meld. All of us want to better our lives. As long as we do so while respecting others' rights, this is not only acceptable but downright noble. And there is no reason to believe that humans will abandon our "acquisitive" natures, even if it were desirable to do so—which it is not.

In reality, the pursuit of profit drives productivity. In a free market, where private property rights are respected, the only way to get rich is to serve others, to satisfy their wants and needs. Wealth acquisition requires wealth *creation*. Thieves and aggressors are punished, and the rest of us get on with the business of living. Even in a mixed economy, this remains true to the extent that property rights *are* respected. When and where they are circumvented through legislative decrees, the door is opened to the economy of pull. In a more completely socialised economy, like the Soviet Union of old, pull is the only way to get ahead, and corruption becomes the norm.

But could technology make acquisitiveness obsolete? Put another way: do replicators solve the scarcity problem? If we could make food and other goods materialise practically out of thin air and for a negligible amount of energy, would there not be enough of everything to go around?

There may be some things money can't buy, but there are also some things replicators can't replicate and, for those things, we need money. Among these are "dilithium" crystals, which power the Federation's starships. Those crystals must be mined in the *Star Trek* universe. Children must be reared and taught; replicators and starships must be built and maintained; and, of course, all of those starships have to be manned.

These and many other things still require work in the *Star Trek* universe, and if there is work to be done, there must be incentives to do it, including monetary incentives. Sure, I may work in engineering because I enjoy it, but I will also want some compensation, and I will want my compensation to be commensurate with my effort and my hard-earned skill. If it is not commensurate, I will feel resentful of those who work either less, or less hard, or less well.

In addition to the need for incentives, there is also the very serious problem of economic calculation. Even the former Soviet Union was not able to eliminate money altogether, although it did manage to decouple it from reality to a great extent—with predictably disastrous consequences. In a free market, the laws of supply and demand, as reflected in freely fluctuating prices, transmit an enormous amount of information about what needs to be produced and in what quantities. In the absence of freely fluctuating prices, there is simply no way for a central authority to collate all of that local information and impose complex order. In the Soviet Union, attempts to do so led to famines and shoddy quality across the board. As Murray Rothbard pointed out though, the communists were able "to use prices set by world markets as indispensable guidelines for the pricing and allocation of capital resources." If they had not been able to sneak a peek at prices in neighbouring market economies, the "noble experiment" would have crumbled far earlier than it did.

True to Gene Roddenberry's vision, there is no evidence of money to be found in the latest *Star Trek* film, though mercifully, there are no odes to its absence, either. The filmmakers wisely sidestepped the issue altogether and focused on just giving viewers a satisfying, suspenseful, funny, character-driven story.

As to why Roddenberry fell prey to the myth that money is the root of all evil, we can only assert that he was not the first to be taken in, and he won't be the last. From Plato to Sir Thomas More to Karl Marx, the malevolence of filthy lucre is an idea that has captivated many. But it is an idea that must be challenged. Instead of unrealistic utopias, we must offer up the realistic ideal of a truly free society that lauds, rather than vilifies, humanity's wealth-creating nature.

CLOSING THOUGHTS

As we reach the end of this book, I hope you've seen the two big themes I've tried to cover and how they converge together. The first theme is that we are living through a massive revolution in humanity, not just a technology revolution or evolution of what has gone on before. There is no business as usual, and digital humans are far more complex than humans. First, they live longer; second, they have access to extraordinary knowledge in real time; third, they can work on far more aesthetic, esoteric, creative and higher levels of process, thanks to AI and robotics; fourth, they will soon be living as a multiplanetary species; and fifth, and finally, they will behave completely different to any humans that have gone before. The way digital humans make business, make friends and even make love is like nothing that humanity has seen before. This is the first big theme.

The second is that everyone is now able to use the network to talk, trade and transact. That inclusivity of everyone will make a huge difference. For one, inclusivity will raise global productivity by an additional $3.7 trillion a year, according to McKinsey.[35] Second, the fact that no one is excluded means that the embodiment of human rights will be solidified such that no one can be abused without awareness. Digitally recording everyone's

---

35   "Digital Finance for All: Powering inclusive growth in emerging economies," McKinsey Global Institute, September 2016.

existence from birth; giving everyone access to insurance, savings and loans; providing everyone with a blanket of basic needs, covered possibly in a Universal Basic Income; and educating everyone for inclusion all make a great difference.

It is the reason why Bill Gates has forecast that no one will suffer poverty by 2035 in the way in which it has been known in the last century. No one will be poor because the system makes them poor. Wealth may still be controlled by a privileged few, but giving everyone access to the network, raising their access to knowledge and information, giving them the opportunity to build businesses anywhere, anytime, from nothing, is the biggest transformation in this fourth revolution of humanity.

These two themes go together. As we digitalise humanity, so we provide humans with new forms of access to knowledge and fulfilment. Then, as predicted by *Star Trek,* with our multiplanetary species of digital humans who are growing by their billions, thanks to life sciences, we move beyond wealth as a motivator. After all, if robotics and automation can do all the things that humans do today, then we must do something else tomorrow.

This last point is what truly intrigues me. We began our path to humanity as *Homo sapiens* living in groups of hundreds who could beat any other form of humanity, thanks to our shared beliefs. This was the first big translation of humanity: becoming human.

We then moved to our second level of humanity as we became civilised. Through the Fertile Crescent that stretched from Iraq to Israel, the ancient civilisations thrived and created cities of thousands. They could only live in such peace by creating a new form of value exchange system, namely money. Money was created to ensure that the abundance of crops in good years could be stored for the bad years. In return for their surplus crops, farmers received money that could be exchanged for entertainment in the form of sex. The oldest profession in the world, prostitution, was soon followed by the second oldest, accountancy.

For thousands of years, we lived in civilisations from China and its Silk Road, through the Indus Valley civilisations in the northwestern regions of South Asia across to the Phoenicians, Babylonians and Sumerians, with many examples of not just creating alternative value exchange instruments but, in the case of China, paper money back in the seventh century.

However, it took another thousand years to reach the next change in humanity when we moved from villages of hundreds of individuals with shared beliefs, to towns of thousands exchanging money, to cities of millions travelling the world.

The Industrial Revolution allowed the movement of peoples across borders en masse, and many sought new lands such as the United States and Australia to live and work. Trading between countries on a worldwide scale grew due to the revolution in travel. Steam trains, steam ships and fossil-fuelled transportation from aircraft to automobiles have generated a globalising economic miracle, backed by a new system of value store—the bank. Banks are trusted across borders thanks to their government's backing, and the more Triple-A rated the government, the easier it has been to accumulate wealth. Hence, the reason why Britain and the United States emerged as the financial superpowers while economies from India to Brazil were subjected to debt burdens that effectively left their economies for dust.

This has been true for several centuries, until now. The tremendous change in the BRIC economies—Brazil, Russia, India and China—and particularly in India and China, has been enabled through the digital revolution that began seventy years ago and is crystallising today into a new ecosystem. An ecosystem driven by automating everything we can. Software is eating the world, as Marc Andreessen is so often quoted as saying, and it is true. We will digitalise everything that can be digitalised and, as we do, everything becomes connected, fast and cheap. This is the aim of the Internet of Things—to have everything connected, fast and cheap—and that vision is maturing and being realised as you read this book.

But it's not just things that are being connected, fast and cheap, but people too. Hence, that drive for inclusivity. I hope you therefore enjoy the final chapter of this book as it draws all of these themes together into what I see as the one company realising the digital human dream—Ant Financial.

I have learnt a great deal through my travels over the past thirty years, and the greatest thing I've learnt is that the average person doesn't want to hate. They just want a good life for their family.

"No one is born hating another person because of the colour of his skin, or his background, or his religion. People must learn to hate, and if they can learn to hate, they can be taught to love, for love comes more naturally to the human heart than its opposite."
—NELSON MANDELA, *Long Walk to Freedom*

This is the one thing I believe the digital revolution will deliver: the right for everyone to have the opportunity to have a good life. That will create a better, more peaceful and more sustainable planet, and the thoughts of Jack Ma, Eric Jing and the people I met in Hangzhou, China, at Ant Financial demonstrate all of these ideas well.

In conclusion, technology is creating a democratised planet where a basic right is to have legal identity and the opportunity to trade, pay and network through the mobile network. That is definitely a better world than any we have seen before.

CASE STUDY

ANT FINANCIAL

THE FIRST FINANCIAL FIRM FOR THE DIGITAL HUMAN AGE

CASE STUDY: ANT FINANCIAL

During the summer of 2017, I was invited to join Alibaba's annual conference in Hangzhou, China, for star sellers on Alibaba's Taobao platform. I went to find out more about Ant Financial, the Alibaba spin-off that operates the mobile payments app Alipay. The trip was specifically to develop the case study that follows.

As Americans struggle with the pains of chip and PIN and Europeans embrace contactless payments, China has leapfrogged everyone when it comes to digital payments. In 2016, Chinese consumers spent $5,500 billion through their mobile apps. That is more than any other economy, and many predict that China will be the first major economy to become completely cashless. The chosen mobile payment system for most Chinese citizens is Alipay, and Ant Financial, the company that runs it. The firm has recently started to expand its footprint globally. So where is it going next?

AMBITIOUS PLANS

Many in the West will have heard of Alipay, but it is not the Chinese version of PayPal, as is commonly perceived. In fact, the company bears no relationship or resemblance to anything seen in Europe or North America. It is distinctly Chinese and, having been born out of a need to trade, is now moving towards global dominance. Few would have imagined this a few years ago, and yet Alipay's ambitions are immense, as are those of its parent company Ant Financial. As Eric Jing, the CEO of Ant Financial, announced at the WEF annual meeting in Davos in January 2017, its ambition is to reach two billion consumers by 2025. That is some ambition for a firm that began as an offspring of Alibaba in 2003.

Back then, Alibaba had just launched Taobao, an online platform to enable small businesses to sell their goods direct to consumers in China. Meaning "digging for treasure", Taobao was essentially a mixture of eBay and Amazon. However, there were greater trust issues to overcome in China than there were in the United States. It meant that very few people were willing to order anything online as they did not believe they would receive it. Equally, the sellers would not send anything to a buyer until they had their money.

The problem was solved by telling sellers to fax their orders to Alibaba's offices, and Alibaba would take the money in escrow. This meant that sellers could trust that they would get the money, so they would send the goods. In turn, buyers knew that their money was being held safely until they told Alibaba it was OK to pay. Somehow this system worked. Taobao's sales grew steadily in spite of the fax escrow service, and Alipay was launched. No one has looked back since.

This system, with its fax machines and reliance upon Alibaba setting up links with the banks to transmit the monies manually, was archaic. Yet today Alipay monitors every transaction from its 450 million users in real time with artificial intelligence monitors that are constantly searching for potentially fraudulent transactions. However, the company has refreshed its systems architecture four times in the past twelve years and has just embarked on another refresh.

Alipay has moved from basic escrow services to real-time payments to cloud to microservice, and is now working on new machine learning and a superintelligent structure. This structure can process 120,000 transactions per second and is being designed to scale to more than 10 billion transactions per day when needed. To put that into perspective, Visa and MasterCard handle just over 60 billion transactions per year combined, and average nearly 2,000 transactions per second. This is some operation, as it is new and designed totally for customer need. There is no traditional payment or bank thinking in Alipay and Ant Financial, just a technology firm that wants to enable the best customer experience.

PUTTING THE CUSTOMER FIRST

Customer experience is a key part of Alibaba and Ant Financial's thinking. For example, Western media is very excited about Ant Financial's money market fund called Yu'e Bao, meaning "leftover treasure". This is because it is the biggest money market fund in the world, exceeding $165 billion in assets under management in February 2017, to have raced past JPMorgan's U.S. government money market fund, which has $150 billion of assets under management and was previously the largest global fund of its kind.

However, Yu'e Bao is not really a money market fund. It is a method for consumers to store a balance to spend on Taobao, and earn some interest. It is also a microsavings tool in a mobile wallet that gives rural Chinese consumers a place to save their renminbi. Most of these people had previously found accessing banks inconvenient, as there were none present in their villages, meaning there were few options to accrue interest on their idle funds.

Financial inclusion is a critical part of Alibaba and Ant Financial's story. Most of their customers are tiny businesses that can now sell across the world. Most of their Taobao entrepreneurs are young people with bright ideas, who can go from selling a few items online to becoming a megastore with the right levels of imagination and application. All this in an economy that just twenty years ago required bank tellers to take a proficiency test in using an abacus before they got the job.

A BANK THREAT?

Does Alipay threaten the Chinese banks? The general feeling is not really. While there is some overlap, Alipay's customers are not the traditional customers of banks. They are the unbanked and underbanked. This is why Ant Financial is now stretching its muscles overseas, with a wave of impressive joint ventures, investments and agreements over the past year.

For instance, Ant is the majority shareholder of Paytm in India, serving 235 million citizens today with an ambition to double that by 2020. Ant also acquired Lazada's payment service, called hellopay, in Singapore in April 2017. Lazada is the Amazon of Southeast Asia, serving Indonesia, Malaysia, the Philippines, Singapore, Thailand and Vietnam. A deal between Ant and Ascend Money in Thailand was agreed in November 2016, rapidly followed by a partnership with Globe Telecom's GCash in Indonesia and Mynt in the Philippines in February 2017.

Meanwhile, Alipay has signed deals with Ingenico, Wirecard and a series of other acquirers to allow their customers to use its mobile app in Europe, and has signed a similar deal in the United States with First Data. Finally, there has been a big scramble to acquire MoneyGram, the global remittance service provider, which spawned a head-to-head battle with Euronet.

FROM THE TOP

Alibaba's flamboyant chairman, Jack Ma, understands the technology platform revolution that has seen the rise of the likes of Uber, Airbnb and Facebook, whereby the largest taxi firm in the world owns no cars, the largest hotel group owns no hotels and the largest content firm creates no content. This is because Uber, Airbnb and Facebook provide the platforms that connect those with cars to passengers, those with rooms to tourists and those with stories to friends. This is what Alibaba is doing to commerce and Ant Financial to money. Alibaba does not do commerce; it just provides the platform.

In an interview at the annual Netrepreneurs conference in Hangzhou in July 2017, Jack Ma said the following, "Management. The word is there for regular companies. At Alibaba, we treat it more like governing an economy, as we have to manage so many companies dependent upon us as partners. Any small- and medium-sized enterprise with an idea now has a way to realise that idea. Alibaba marketplace can find you buyers and sellers; we can provide you with computing through cloud; we can distribute and deliver your products. By 2036, we will have built an economy that can support 100 million businesses for billions of users. We won't own that economy. We will just govern it."

Ma went on to talk about the idea that things being "Made in China" or "Made in India" will soon become redundant, as there will just be things that are "M@de in Internet". Everything will be digitally distributed and managed, with a few key platforms providing the services. Alibaba and Ant Financial will be those key platforms for money and commerce across the world, not just in China.

Ant Financial does not intend to create and launch services everywhere in the world; it wants to take its experiences globally and partner locally to share that knowledge and its technologies. It does not impose an Ant Financial way of doing things on its partners in India and elsewhere in Asia. Instead, the company offers access to all of its technologies and services to those third parties in order to get them up and running quicker.

That is what a platform player does, and it strikes at the heart of the comment made by Ma about Alibaba having a complex network of companies that it manages as an economy. It is not a company. It is an ecosystem. It is also a fascinating firm to watch, having already become the largest payment processor in the world by volume and, if it gets its two billion users by 2025, may well be by value too.

THE MARCH OF ANT FINANCIAL

I grew up with America as the dream. However, in the past two decades, China has become the second world superpower, whether the Americans like it or not. This is not me having a love thing for China. It's just a fact. The Americans don't like it. Google "China as a superpower" and most U.S. media write along the lines of "China lacks the political, economic and civil freedoms to become a world leader".

Read a more neutral discussion, such as from the Indian magazine *Swarajya*, and you get a very different view:

America is still the world's biggest economic and military superpower by far, but its geographic isolation means this power cannot rise any more. Its power will last if the Chinese still think the American market is important for its own growth – and that could last for another decade or so. Once its new Belt and Road Initiative starts taking off, the economic centre of the world will even more decisively turn towards Asia.[36]

Perhaps the most neutral observation came from the *Atlantic* magazine, after the 2017 G20 meetings:

Remarkably—and, unthinkably, as recently as one year ago—today China seems to be the world's most likeable superpower. Compare Donald Trump's recent visit to Europe with that of Premier Li Keqiang, China's second-in-command. Li, who landed in Berlin on Wednesday, hoped to use his three-day trip, with stops in Germany and Belgium, to "voice support for an open economy, free trade and investment [and] global regional peace and stability," according to China's state news wire Xinhua. Trump, on the other hand, failed to support NATO, decried Germany as "very bad" for its trade policies,

---

36 "Why Trump's US Has Lost The Plot On China, Russia And The New World Order," *Swarajya*, 31 July 2017.

and even seemingly pushed aside Montenegro's prime minister to barrel his way to the front of a group photo. On Thursday, Li reaffirmed China's support for the Paris Agreement, stating that there is an "international responsibility" to fight climate change. Later on Thursday, Trump announced the United States would exit the landmark climate-change treaty. In that speech, Trump reaffirmed his commitment to his "America First" policy, while Li, in his meetings and speeches in Europe, successfully painted China as a liberal, responsible, globalist power.[37]

What seems obvious to me is that some of us have a distrust of China, and other nations, due to historical stereotyping. We think the Chinese are communists, who abuse basic human rights. Well, this is what some media would have you believe. However, I've been intrigued, over the past decade specifically, to see the rise of a nation through technology that is becoming more equitable. Maybe I'm naïve but feel that, if current trends continue, we will all be viewing China, Chinese culture and Chinese business as the dream in ten to twenty years, replacing the American dream with the Chinese one.

You have to only look to history to see how China's grip on the planet's culture has risen and fallen and is now on the rise again. Growing up, for example, I was educated with strong knowledge about Egyptian, Greek and Roman civilisations. I was taught nothing about one of the oldest cultures in the world where paper, printing, the compass, alcohol, silk, porcelain and more were invented. Why? Because of our Western bias. In fact, it's been interesting to see a variety of discussions over the past months about the Belt and Road (BRI) initiative. If you're not familiar:

The initiative was officially launched in September 2013 when President Xi used a speech at a university in Kazakhstan to call for

37   "Is China Becoming the World's Most Likeable Superpower?" *Atlantic*, 2 June 2017.

the creation of a "Silk Road Economic Belt". The project was later expanded and re-branded with its current name …

The Belt and Road initiative is an immensely ambitious development campaign through which China wants to boost trade and stimulate economic growth across Asia and beyond. It hopes to do so by building massive amounts of infrastructure connecting it to countries around the globe. By some estimates, China plans to pump $150bn into such projects each year. In a report released at the start of this year, ratings agency Fitch said an extraordinary $900bn in projects were planned or underway.

There are plans for pipelines and a port in Pakistan, bridges in Bangladesh and railways to Russia - all with the aim of creating what China calls a "modern Silk Road" trading route that Beijing believes will kick start "a new era of globalisation".[38]

Whilst the United States is rejecting globalisation and creating friction with Russia, by continuing the enforcement of sanctions much to Putin's annoyance, and China, who Trump tweeted wasn't helping to stop North Korea from testing bombs that could reach the United States, China is moving in the opposite direction and courting Europe, Africa, Russia and other nations to cooperate in building the next unique future world.

As if mirroring China's initiative, Ant Financial and Alibaba are a poster child of Chinese entrepreneurialism and are leading the way in building global partnerships for trade. Between Alipay and WeChat Pay, China will be one of the first and largest nations to be cashless. Estimates are that China's Tier 1 cities will be fully cashless by 2022 while the rest of the country will follow within ten years. Already, WeChat and Alipay users are transacting trillions of dollars through their mobile wallets, $5.5 trillion in 2016 to be exact, which makes the United States' paltry $112 billion in mobile payments look archaic.

---

38   "The $900bn question: What is the Belt and Road initiative?" *Guardian*, 12 May 2017.

A cashless China will be an amazing achievement for a nation with almost 1.4 billion people. It is also phenomenal as China was the first nation to use paper money—they invented it—and now it is one of the first nations to get rid of cash. Paper notes as payment have been used in China since the Tang Dynasty in the seventh century A.D., and has been a consistent form of payment since. By comparison, the first paper notes as a value store used elsewhere in the world didn't appear until the 1600s, almost a thousand years after China.

All in all, China's transformation from a nation that demanded bank tellers to take a proficiency test in using an abacus twenty years ago to the near cashless nation we see today is monumental. I firmly believe that the leadership economically and commercially will impact all of us in our day-to-day dealings within another decade.

ALIBABA AND ANT FINANCIAL

"When Alipay was created, we hoped to create an equal environment in China so that everyone can have equal access to financial support. We hoped to see that every honest person, every good person, even though penniless, can create sufficient wealth and value for one's honesty and virtues."

—JACK MA, Chairman of Alibaba

For twenty years, I have been watching developments in financial services in China closely. My first exposure to the Chinese system was in 1997, just before the Asian financial crisis. The Bank of China proudly showed off its Beijing head office, staffed by 300,000 people, with a major focus to drive money from citizen wallets into government-initiated projects. There were high levels of savings and little credit availability. Customer service was of zero interest and the major focus was supporting state-owned enterprises (SOEs).

A decade later, China had opened up to world trade and had experienced a phenomenal expansion of growth in the economy. I had been particularly struck by the emerging social network called QQ, which had achieved 300 million users, and was amazed at how quickly the market was changing. Visiting Shanghai, you could see the change. The riverside financial district had literally merged from the ground up during the preceding ten years, and was now vying to be a global financial centre. It had a long way to go, but was getting there. Former Chinese president Hu Jintao noted in 2004:

"From 1978 to 2003, China's GDP increased from US$147.3 billion to over US$1.4 trillion, with an average annual increase rate of 9.4%; its total foreign trade volume grew from US$20.6 billion to US$851.2 billion, with an average annual growth rate of 16.1%; and the poverty-stricken population in the rural area dropped from 250 million to about 29 million."[39]

I wrote extensively about China's changes back in 2006[40] and, back then, was predicting that the biggest banks in the world within a decade would all be Chinese. Fast-forward to today and the table below speaks for itself:

Top 10 world banks 2017

Rank	(prev)	Bank	Country	Tier 1 capital ($m)
1	(1)	ICBC	China	281,262
2	(2)	China Construction Bank	China	225,838
3	(3)	JP Morgan	US	208,115
4	(4)	Bank of China	China	199,189
5	(6)	Bank of America	US	190,315
6	(5)	Agricultural Bank of China	China	188,624
7	(7)	Citigroup	US	178,387
8	(8)	Wells Fargo	US	171,364
9	(9)	HSBC	UK	138,022
10	(10)	Mitsubishi UFJ Financial Group	Japan	135,944

Data source: *The Banker* magazine, July 2017

---

39   Hu Jintao addressing the Brazilian parliament in November 2004.
40   *See* https://www.finextra.com/resources/feature.aspx?featureid=845.

Today, China's remarkable growth has started to slow, government policies to support such growth are being questioned and concerns over the whole shadow financial system are raising global systemic concerns. No matter. The country is still experiencing progress and QQ is now WeChat, part of the Tencent Group. The group operates alongside several other massive Chinese internet giants, including Alibaba (the Amazon of China), Baidu (the Google of China) and more, to challenge the thinking of all.

In so doing, the country has leapfrogged its legacy competitors. The United States is struggling with the conversion of mag stripe points of sale to migrate to chip and PIN while Europe is trying to work out how to hold together its union in light of Brexit. China, by contrast, has transformed, specifically in its financial markets. What has driven this change and what will happen next?

There is a clear indication, and it is being trailblazed by Alibaba's little-known affiliate company Ant Financial. Ant Financial was created in October 2014 to incorporate the consumer and SME financial operations of Alibaba. This included the Alipay payments system and Yu'e Bao, its money market fund. The company is said to be moving to an IPO as I write this, and analysts believe its valuation is likely to approach $100 billion. To put this in context, such a valuation would make Ant Financial worth three times more than Barclays Bank Group and over half of Citigroup. Not bad for a company that is just a few years old. However, Ant Financial goes way back further than 2014. In fact, its humble roots began back in 2003 when Alibaba came head-to-head with a big U.S. giant that wanted to take root in China. That giant was eBay. Thus begins a story that should fascinate everyone, particularly as Ant Financial is realising the dream that I've been discussing throughout this book, namely the creation of the financial system for the fourth age of humanity.

Through a series of meetings in July 2017, I spent time in Hangzhou, China, and London, England, talking with Ant Financial and Alipay executives about their views of the past, present and future of the company.

I also spent time touring China, talking with people about their views of the company. The following represents the summary of those experiences.

THE ALIBABA STORY

In order to understand how Ant Financial made its mark, we first need a brief history of its origins within Alibaba. The origins of Alibaba date back to 1980 when an Australian communist sympathiser, Ken Morley, travelled around China on a summer holiday. When visiting Hangzhou, Ken and his family went down to West Lake, the main tourist area. There they met a young Jack Ma who, back then, went by the name Ma Yun. Ma Yun was sixteen years old and learning English. He liked to hang out around the West Lake as much as he could in order to improve his English by talking to tourists. Ken's son David was also sixteen years old, and the two boys struck up an unlikely long-term friendship.

Ma Yun and David Morley in 1980. Source: Ant Financial

From the chance encounter with the Morleys, Ma Yun started a pen pal relationship with David. They would exchange letters, with Ma Yun leaving every other line free for David's father, Ken, to make corrections to his English spelling. Ken decided to see if he could help his son's young pen pal out by inviting him to visit Australia in 1985 when Ma Yun, now Jack Ma, was just 21 years old.

This was when the doors of China were still firmly closed and an individual could not get a travel visa. However, Jack Ma was determined and travelled to Beijing to see if he could get one. Seven times, he was told no. At that time, visas were only issued for service, family or studying purposes, not for general visits or tourism. Jack Ma had almost lost all hope. After the seventh rejection, Ken Morley was also worried, and even sent a telegram to the Australian embassy in China, hoping that they could issue a visa for Jack.

Jack stayed in Beijing for a week, diligently applying for the visa every single day as the trip had cost all the money he had. The last time he stepped into the embassy, he ran towards the first visa officer he met and said, "I have been here for a week so this might be my last chance. I want my visa, and I want to talk to you seriously."

"What do you want to talk about?" asked the clerk.

"I have been rejected for a visa seven times during the past week. I have no more money so I have to go back home. But I need to know the reason for my rejections."

Impressed by Jack Ma's persistence, the visa officer listened carefully to the story about him and the Morley family and, afterwards, Jack Ma finally got his visa. This changed his life and, many years later, Jack recalled, "I am very thankful for Australia for that 29 days in Newcastle (a suburb of Sydney) … when I arrived in Australia I was so shocked and amazed by the wonderful things, the people, the culture, the landscapes, the products … I was … educated in China that China was the best and richest country in the world … when I arrived in Australia I saw the world was so different."

After this, Jack's way of thinking changed completely, although he could not realise his dreams as it was still early days. Instead, he returned to

Hangzhou to teach English. However, his Australian trip stayed with him and, combined with a visit to the United States in 1995, his path was clear.

When Jack visited the United States in early 1995, the first roots of search engines and trade were emerging, and this was when he discovered the internet. He was inspired and created his first business, a *Yellow Pages* for China, upon his return. The business failed but Jack was undeterred and, in 1999, Alibaba was formed.

The idea of Alibaba is based on Amazon, but its model works differently as it is Chinese. For example, Amazon emerged from a Western economy that had moved from mom-and-pop stores to large malls, grocery stores and urban shopping centres. As a result, the retail model replicated the offers of these centralised centres and replaced them on margin over time.

China did not have that structure. China in the 1990s just had the mom-and-pop stores, and no large shopping centres and malls. So the original idea was that Alibaba would create a global marketplace, connecting small Chinese businesses with the world's buyers. It was described as being an online tradeshow for Chinese businesses to show what they could do for the rest of the world, and that is how Jack Ma sold it to the Chinese firms. In 1999, Jack and his team at Alibaba organised a huge expo for Chinese business to engage with the world's manufacturers. The expo went so well that Jack and his team saw an opportunity to provide a service connecting people called Taobao. Meaning "digging for treasure", Taobao was launched in 2003, and aimed to emulate eBay's success in the United States but, as mentioned, in a different way. After all, Chinese consumers didn't collect collectibles at that time, as there really wasn't anything worth collecting, or so they thought. This is why Taobao focused on connecting small Chinese businesses and sole traders—the mom-and-pop stores, as there weren't many big firms—to Chinese citizens. It worked, but not before being exposed and made potentially vulnerable to the entry of eBay into the Chinese markets.

eBay entered China by buying heavily into Eachnet, its Chinese equivalent. Jack Ma knew that eBay could eradicate Alibaba, but he also knew that the U.S. auction service was not right for China. At the time, Alibaba was tiny compared to the mighty eBay, which had millions of dollars to win over the Chinese market. However, eBay was not Chinese and did not understand the Chinese markets like Jack Ma and his team at Alibaba did. For example, eBay cut back on features that Chinese consumers liked, such as emoticons and animations. In contrast, Taobao ramped up these features to be a far more social commerce model, as well as added the sprinkler of being free. eBay did not offer a free version to compete and made other mistakes, forcing it to eventually pull out of China completely having lost millions of dollars.

With eBay's withdrawal from the market, Alibaba began to diversify into other areas. For instance, Alipay was launched in 2004 as an escrow account service to allow consumers to hold funds until they were happy with the goods they received. This was key to Taobao's growth as China had very poor consumer protection laws at that time. In 2008, it launched Tmall, a B2C site for the sale of key branded goods and services as an offshoot of Taobao.

In 2013, Alibaba's money fund Yu'e Bao, or "leftover treasure", was launched and marketed to users of Alipay. This has been particularly successful because cash transfers from bank accounts to Yu'e Bao take just one click, with assets rising from zero to 578 billion yuan ($90 billion) in less than two years. Alibaba then expanded into banking in 2015, launching MYbank during the summer and, in an audacious move, opened its bank capabilities to other Chinese banks through an open marketplace of apps and APIs.

All of these financial activities—Alipay, MYbank, Yu'e Bao, Open Banking—are consolidated into the company Ant Financial. There's an apt reason as to why the company is called Ant Financial. Ants are a good metaphor for the business, as ants are weak on their own but strong together, and that's the very message that Ant Financial wants to send to Chinese citizens. It seems to be working as Ant Financial was worth $45 billion in 2015, $60 billion in 2016 and looks likely to top $100 billion by the time of its rumoured IPO in late 2018 or early 2019.

Just to put in context what Alibaba, with Taobao, Tmall, Alipay, Yu'e Bao and more of its affiliates, has put in place, it is like having Amazon, Facebook, Netflix, PayPal and more all in one ecosystem. For example, the following is a five-step vision for Alibaba:

- You can advertise movie concepts and ask customers to crowdfund the movie ideas they like, all channelled through Alibaba Pictures.
- Once a movie is funded and gets made, you can buy tickets to see the movie in Taobao.
- When you see the movie, you might want to watch the digital release at home on Youku Tudou, Alibaba's version of Netflix.
- Then if you like the movie that much, you can buy branded memorabilia on Tmall.
- All of it is paid for and funded through your Ant Financial accounts.

In other words, a digital marketplace that manages the complete process of digital creation from start to finish. This concept was nicely summarised by Jack during his presentation at Alibaba's annual partners' meeting, Global Netrepreneur Conference, which was driven by the phrase "M@de in Internet" in 2017. I attended this meeting in Hangzhou, all in Chinese, and it was an immersive experience. Picture a mixture of online teenage celebrities streaming their ideas to entrepreneurial Taobao businesses talking about their business models and dreams. It was all very Chinese.

The meeting concluded with an interview with Jack, and here are my main notes and takeaways from what he said. I must admit that I was listening to simultaneous translation, so cannot verify that this is 100 per cent accurate, but here's the gist of it:

It is impossible to do business today offline as everything has to have something online, which is why we need more netrepreneurs. The whole supply chain will be impacted by the internet. I talk about these challenges at many conferences and people don't believe me, but I'm used to this. It's like climbing a mountain. What you see ahead is very different to what you see when you are half way up. What people see at the foot of the mountain is very different to what you see when you're half way up. What's at the top of the mountain are those who change their mindsets and, in the next three decades, the world will change more than you can ever imagine.

In the next ten years, all industries will change due to AI, big data and cloud. Industries will be turned on their heads. This means that, in the future, there will be no "made in", as in "Made in China" or "Made in India". You will just have designed, ideated, printed and made in the internet. There is no Made in China or India. Equally, everything can now be customised. It's expensive to customise today but, if you can't do it tomorrow, your company will fail.

Alibaba doesn't do e-commerce. We only provide the platform. So, the more success that our partners have, the more successful we are.

Three years ago, we bet that cloud and big data would be key. Most critical is data and computing. We put all of our resources into data, computing and data services. But still what we do is just a fraction of the total. Soon we will have IoT and all these devices will create data, and this is why we are panicked. There will be a huge amount of data to deal with.

In the age of data, we can no longer have this idea of controlling everything. A monopoly is the idea of the industrial era. We just want to help people, not be a monopoly. We want to connect everyone.

We provide payments and logistics and shipping. We can deliver anywhere in China within 24 hours. That's too slow for Beijing and Shanghai but, for the villages, we want to build that infrastructure across all of China. We will never be a logistics company, however. We partner with others for this. So, we focus on the things that others cannot do or are not willing to do. We focus on things SMEs

Photo © Chris Skinner

cannot do. We only want to compete with companies that won't share or partner with others.

If you are having a difficult time as a start-up, we were like that too, but we had a dream and now we have got there. Now we are a huge company, but if we stay there and don't share those riches, then everyone will hate us. So, we have to make everyone richer. If you are the only rich person in a village of paupers, the paupers will kill you.

Alibaba is a tool for everyone that should benefit everyone, especially young people. Remember, I was a teacher and any company will diminish ultimately. I want people to say Alibaba is great, not because we sell a lot of products, but because we helped young people and our society.

Management. The word is there for regular companies. At Alibaba, we treat it more like governing an economy, as we have to manage so many companies that are dependent on us as partners. Any SME with an idea now has a way to realise that idea. The Alibaba marketplace can find you buyers and sellers; we can provide you with computing through cloud; we can distribute and deliver your products. By 2036, we will have built an economy that can support 100 million businesses for billions of users. We won't own that economy. We will just govern it. Having great, smart experiences will be the keywords for our next decade.

FinTech is there to empower the financial sector. I want to do that for consumers so that they have equal access to finance. I don't want people to be waiting for money or for pity. I want to empower them through access and inclusion, and get things to people a lot faster and easier.

This year is very different to five years ago. This year, we are focusing on M@de in Internet. Your business model is to redefine your consumers, supply chain and financing methods for the M@ de in Internet age. I tell all retailers, manufacturers and banks to do this urgently as I've been saying it for over a decade. You don't have so much time left.

Here are the top ten messages that Jack gave the audience regarding business:

- On chasing dreams, dream big, really big.
- Remember: the bigger the problem, the greater the opportunity.
- Today is tough but the day after tomorrow is beautiful.
- Focus on the customer and the rest will follow.
- Learn from competitors but never copy them.
- It's more important to be best than first.
- Find opportunity in crisis.
- Use your competitors' strength against them.
- Don't dwell on mistakes.

THE ANT FINANCIAL STORY

Although the Alibaba story is interesting, it is not the focus of this case study or book. This book is about the fourth generation of humanity and encompasses a global financial system being created from scratch to support instant, real-time trade between individuals globally. That is why

I have chosen Ant Financial as the focal point case study of this book, namely because Ant Financial is the first company to build a global vision of financial inclusivity through technology. This vision only began in 2014 and has moved at a pace, as we shall see. However, the firm's origins lie deeply rooted in the emergence and subsequent success of Alipay, an online payments service.

Alibaba's original idea was not to create a massive payments service, but to overcome a key challenge of e-commerce in China: trust. No one trusted buying online. Consumers didn't think the goods would arrive correctly and merchants were loath to send goods to people who had not paid. I've seen this challenge in many countries and various ways to approach a solution. For example, FinTech unicorn Klarna cracked this nut in Sweden by using data to resolve the challenge. By having a buyer's postal code, Klarna could mitigate the risk of non-payment and created a business where they paid the merchants upfront, and the buyer then paid Klarna within fourteen days of receipt of goods. However, that system would not work in China as many people didn't have bank accounts, credit or debit cards or an address that could provide the data to mitigate the risk. What was the solution?

In a clever move, in 2004, Alibaba began to develop a code to enable money to be held in escrow on behalf of the buyer, whilst giving the seller the confidence to send the goods knowing that the buyer was good for the money. Here's the original Alibaba press release announcing the service:

Beijing, China - February 2, 2005
Alibaba.com Launches Online Payment Solution in China

Alibaba.com Partners with China's Largest Banks to Provide Online Escrow Service for Businesses and Individuals
Alibaba.com announced today the official launch of its Alipay online escrow system and the www.alipay.com website, which makes Alipay available to all businesses and individuals in China. The payment system provides buyers and sellers with a comprehensive solution

that resolves the issue of trust in online transactions while providing an efficient platform for transacting online.

"2005 will be the year online payment becomes a reality in China. With the help of our 10 million members, we expect Alipay will become the industry standard for safe online payments in China," said Jack Ma, CEO of Alibaba.com. "Today marks a new milestone for e-commerce in China and a fundamental breakthrough for online payment systems serving buyers and sellers."

To insure Alipay is China's safest way to trade online, Alibaba.com has partnered with four of China's largest national banks, including China Merchants Bank, China Construction Bank, Agricultural Bank of China, and the Industrial and Commercial Bank of China. As part of the Alipay launch, Alibaba.com also announced that it will guarantee all transactions made through the Alipay escrow system and reimburse any buyer or seller using the system who is found to have been a victim of fraud.

"We are so confident Alipay is the safest way to trade online in China, that we are going to fully guarantee the service with our own money," said Ma.

In the first several months' testing period, the Alipay service proved a success with the 4.5 million members of Taobao.com (www. taobao.com), an Alibaba.com subsidiary. Of its more than 4.96 million product listings, 70% of the posted products on Taobao. com include a request that buyers use the Alipay service. Products that have already been sold through Alipay include jewellery, cars and real estate. With the official launch of Alipay, the service is now officially open to all buyers and sellers in China, whether or not they are Alibaba.com or Taobao.com members.

A Payment Solution Designed for China's Local Conditions
Despite a growing Internet-savvy middle class, online purchases in China have been slow to take off with traditional payment systems.

Credit card-based payment systems that succeeded in North America and Europe have proven ineffective in China, where credit card usage remains low. Even more important than credit card penetration rates, is the issue of trust between buyers and sellers in a business environment where personal relationships and cash-based transactions have served as the traditional means of securing and settling a deal. Alipay is designed to overcome these hurdles with a model specific to China's needs. "When it comes to online payment systems, one size does not fit all," said Ma. "There is an American model for America, a European model for Europe, and the Alipay model for China."

How Alipay Works

To conduct a transaction using Alipay, a buyer first sends his payment to an Alipay account, where it is held in escrow. Once the buyer indicates that the product has been received, the money is transferred from Alipay to the seller. With Alibaba's full guarantee for each Alipay transaction, buyers and sellers may transact online with confidence. This, combined with Alibaba and Taobao's trust rating systems for members, provides buyers and sellers a comprehensive way to evaluate business partners, build relationships, and transact online.

Back in 2005, when this press release was distributed, who would have imagined the change? From a flat start, Alipay has grown in just over a decade to become China's dominant payment system with 520 million users, giving it a 70 per cent share of mobile payments in China.

WHAT HAS DRIVEN THIS EXPLOSION OF INNOVATION?

Part of it is a change in the way the service works. When it began, as an escrow system, the exchange of information was based on fax messaging.

Fax messages to and from the bank and seller via Alibaba allowed Taobao orders to be fulfilled. Roll on five years, and something changed.

In the summer of 2011, China's Alipay developed a QR-code payment system to support payments, and this was the revolution that turbocharged a payments transformation in China. This is because China had few credit and debit cards in the hands of the population, but everyone had a mobile phone. Using the phone to pay for something was not so simple, however. Then the rollout of the QR-code system changed all of that. Similar to the Starbucks app that made Starbucks become a payments phenomenon in the United States, Alipay did the same thing, generating a unique QR code at checkout that merchants can scan with a barcode reader or their own smartphone camera. The system draws funds from a user's credit or debit card or a prepaid Alipay account.

This move led to some problems though, as Jack Ma made the controversial decision to spin out Alipay as a separate company after a board level stalemate over what to do, and without explicit approval from Yahoo or SoftBank, which owned 40 per cent and 30 per cent respectively of Alibaba at the time. Ma believed the move had to be made in response to new regulations from the People's Bank of China that would have disallowed the company to act as a payments processor without a third-party payments licence from the government. This licence would not have been issued unless Alipay was set up as a domestic company without foreign shareholders. Consequently, this led to the launch of a new company in October 2014 called Ant Financial. Ant Financial was created to take over the Alibaba Group's complete portfolio of financial products including Alipay, Yu'e Bao and more. Meanwhile, to resolve the controversy of this decision with the foreign shareholders invested in Alibaba, it was agreed that a certain percentage of Alipay's profits would flow back to Alibaba.

It is unsurprising that investors wanted a stake in Alipay as the business was processing about RMB 1.4 billion a day, or near $80 billion of transactions for the year 2010. By 2016, this number had risen to almost $4 trillion. Alipay has also created a number of events that show how it has scaled. For example, on China's Singles' Day in November 2016, Alipay processed an average 120,000 transactions per second (tps) for a total billing of $17.7 billion in the 24-hour period. At some points, it was processing 175,000 tps. To put into perspective, Visa averages 1,750 tps and scales to 24,000 tps; Alipay beat that hands down. In 2017, the figures were even more stunning and broke all records. Chinese consumers spent a total of $25 billion across Alibaba's e-commerce platforms, of which $8.6 billion of orders were processed in the first hour alone, with the company's processors handling over 250,000 tps. Again, to put things into perspective, the equivalent days in the United States are Black Friday and Cyber Monday. Yet more money is spent on China's Singles' Day than on the two American shopping days combined. It actually makes Americans look frugal.

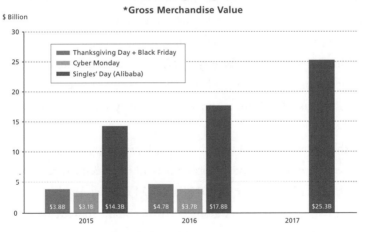

Alibaba's GMV* on Singles' Day vs. US e-commerce sales on Thanksgiving weekend
*Gross Merchandise Value

$ Billion

Legend:
- Thanksgiving Day + Black Friday
- Cyber Monday
- Singles' Day (Alibaba)

2015: $3.8B, $3.1B, $14.3B
2016: $4.7B, $3.7B, $17.8B
2017: $25.3B

Data sources: Alibaba, comScore, statista, *Business Insider*

Singles' Day is just one of several days created to promote the use of mobile payments in China, and emerged from the battle between Alipay and WeChat Pay over the red envelope day to celebrate Chinese New Year.

The idea began in 2014 when Tencent promoted its 400 million WeChat users to send each other virtual red envelopes, which would be deposited into their mobile payment accounts. The gimmick became a big hit with 40 million virtual envelopes being exchanged, worth a record 400 million yuan ($64 million). Jack Ma called it a "Pearl Harbour moment" for his company, and ramped up the game in 2015 by announcing it would give away more than 600 million yuan ($96 million) to its 190 million users as "lucky money" gifts if they used its red envelope messaging system. Tencent responded within hours by saying it would also gift 800 million yuan ($125 million) to users of its virtual red envelopes service, and blocked Alipay users from their WeChat friends. Tencent's WeChat won that battle, with over one billion virtual red envelopes sent on 18 February, compared with 240 million sent through the Alipay Wallet. As can be seen, the rivalry between the two firms is intense.

Meanwhile, Alipay extended its tentacles into other areas, such as creating a savings fund for customers to store their balances when not using Alipay. Called Yu'e Bao, it acts as a method of moving prepaid funds from a balance on Alipay to an amount that can gain interest on Yu'e Bao, a money market fund. Either way, four years into its life, it has become the biggest fund of its kind in the world. By February 2017, Yu'e Bao was managing over $165 billion of funds, overtaking JPMorgan's U.S. government money market fund, which has $150 billion and was previously the largest global fund of its kind.

Another move occurred in 2014, when China's regulators offered private companies the opportunity to apply for banking licences, resulting in Ant Financial launching a bank in 2015 called MYbank. Ant Financial holds a 30 per cent stake in MYbank alongside other main shareholders, including Fosun Industrial, Wanxiang Sannong, and Ningbo Jinrun—three Chinese conglomerates with investments in agriculture, insurance, machinery and other industries. The founders' initial investment was 4 billion yuan (about $644 million). MYbank's most important partner is Alibaba however, as the main offering of loans is based on a user's transaction history in Taobao and Tmall.

MYbank focuses on supporting the small businesses on Taobao, which supports over five million merchants. At its launch, Eric Jing, MYbank's executive chairman and now CEO of Ant Financial, said that the bank's mission is "answering to the needs of those who have limited access to financial services in China" and "is here to give affordable loans for small and micro enterprises".

A good example of such a service is a Taobao shop owner who sells beef jerky. Each time they receive an order, they can immediately turn that order into cash through a short-term MYbank microloan. This particular shop owner has had 3,795 such loans in the last five years, an average of two loans a day, with the amounts varying from 3 yuan (50 cents) to 56,000 yuan ($8,000).

The lessons Alibaba gained through MYbank enabled the company to open its services to other Chinese banks to use. Already, in 2013, Alibaba had verticalised its cloud with the announcement of Ali Cloud for Financial Services, or the Ali Finance Cloud for short. The development of the Ali Finance Cloud was part of a perfect storm for Ant Financial. It had applied for its MYbank licence and obviously needed to have a future-proofed core-banking system. Rather than look to an external provider, Ant decided to develop it internally.

A bank developing its core banking system internally is not unique in China, but Ant Financial went one step further by deciding to sell the cloud-based solution to other banks in China. The breadth of the solution is extensive including risk management, lending, deposits, mobile apps, Infrastructure-as-a-Service (IaaS), Platform-as-a-Service (PaaS), KYC and more.

It is difficult to overstate the potential impact of Ali Finance Cloud on the Chinese banking industry or the potential implications globally. Adoption and usage of the Ali Finance Cloud in China has been swift, with around forty organisations using the service including banks (both big and small), payment providers and even P2P platforms.

ANT FINANCIAL: BUILDING A BETTER CHINA

One of the big things about Ant Financial is its principles and mission, which are all about using technology to improve society and the economy. Here is the opening statement from its 2016 Sustainability Report:[41]

"The evolutionary and civilized history of the human being, in the simplest way, can be seen as a progressive history where a marginal species climbed rapidly to the top of the ecological chain by developing cognition, agriculture, industry, science and technology. At present, human beings are in a golden age of the so-called third industrial revolution.

"As a tech company, what we want to do and are currently doing is to use technology to bring the society back to the origin of human beings: simple, equal and free. For example, our daily errands, can we handle them easily without queuing, begging people or even going out? This is the simple principle. Can a grandmother and a bank president enjoy the same quality and equally convenient financial services? This is the equal principle. Can we say goodbye to complicated passwords, cash or even ID cards and passports, paying bills easily with a face and the credit data behind it?"

In fact, for a Chinese company, Western observers may be surprised by the sustainable ambitions of Ant Financial and its related company, Alibaba Group, as it's all about a better world. This business model is based on three basic principles: an equal society, an inclusive economy and a green environment. These three principles are the platform for what they call Super Ant Power. Exploring these three principles further, the company articulates them like this:

---

41   Many of the facts and statements made in this section draw on Ant Financial's
     2016 Sustainability Report. *See* https://os.alipayobjects.com/rmsportal/
     omkAQCxPyHDDqtqBDnlh.pdf.

- **The core of Super Ant Power is to bring the world equal opportunities through science and technology:** Science and technology is the foundation for Ant to grow, develop and realise its values. Depending on science and technology, Ant is committed to conveying several core values to society: love, wisdom, creditworthiness and sharing. The ultimate goal of Ant's social responsibilities and values is to "Bring the World Equal Opportunities".

- **The responsibilities of Super Ant Power—staying united internally and working hand in hand with outside partners:** We are leveraging all possible social resources by pulling Ant's employees and shareholders' efforts together internally and cooperating with external partners (including clients, suppliers,

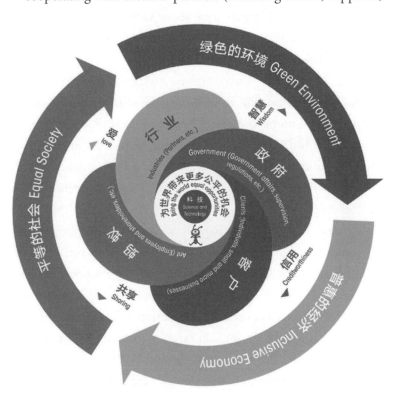

Source: Ant Financial

the government, supervisors and regulators as well as industry partners), aiming to realise an equal society and inclusive future and reflect the values of all shareholders at the same time.

- **The ecology of Super Ant Power—"equal society", "inclusive economy" and "green environment":** Ant hopes that through its relentless innovation, it can continually contribute value and output power. Finally, it will build a sustainable ecology consisting of "equal society", "inclusive economy" and "green environment", realising its goal to "Bring the World Equal Opportunities".

Technology is at the heart of this vision and, more importantly, it is at the heart of this business. For example, the company states openly that creditworthiness is the passport to a better society. Creditworthiness has been difficult historically, as you need some form of credit history to evaluate people and, without data, that is hard.

This has all changed today thanks to the development of cloud computing, machine learning and big data. Creditworthiness, which used to be regarded as a moral commercial evaluation, is now becoming direct and quantitative and can be analysed as well as utilised in real time. Ant Financial therefore created a brand new credit evaluation system called Zhima Credit, which enables more people to enjoy convenience in finance, life and other sectors.

The Zhima Credit score is based on your financial behaviours and trustworthiness with money, and a key part of this is ensuring people pay back their loans. Zhima Credit scoring works with the support of intelligent decision-making, and this is a core part of Ant Financial's operations based on a well-established creditworthiness evaluation and risk forecasting system that operates in real time. As a result, farmers without bank statements can obtain loans to buy fertilizer and seeds through MYbank.

Ant Financial illustrates this well through the stories of its partners and users.

Case Study: Zhang Hongyu and his Orchard

Zhang Hongyu, a 26-year-old designer, came back to his hometown and contracted 3,000 mu (200 hectares) of orchards. His business proved so successful that he decided to take over 20,000 mu (1,334 hectares) of pomegranate orchards. However, this posed a problem: how should he solve the problem of spraying insecticides?

Source: Ant Financial

He made a creative decision and ordered airplane services on Alipay. On 30 June 2016, the Xaircraft agricultural unmanned aerial vehicle (UAV) system was included in Alipay's service window (now known as Life Circle), meaning that users could order UAV spraying services with a simple click. Zhang Hongyu found it easy to rent an UAV. Moreover, because he had a Zhima Credit score as high as 763, Xaircraft exempted him from paying the deposit and offered him free offline training services.

Zhang Hongyu felt the power of science and technology on the first use: UAV spraying increased the utilisation rate of agricultural chemicals by 1.5 times. It also increased working efficiency by sixty times and reduced agricultural water consumption. As a result, he then decided to sign a one-year contract with Xaircraft. Based on his Zhima Credit score, he only needed to pay a deposit that was two-fifths of that of regular users.

"This has never happened to American farmers," Zhang Hongyu said. "Although I was born in the countryside of China, I have witnessed and felt closely the golden age of China's mobile internet."

Case Study: Qiu Zhe and the Zhima Credit Score

After graduating from university, Qiu Zhe chose to stay in Shanghai as his company is located in the Lujiazui area. Although he has a bright future, the present is not easy. The most difficult thing is to rent a house due to high rent. In addition, tenants are usually required to give one month's deposit and pay three months' rent in advance or two months' deposit and three months' rent in advance. As Qiu Zhe is independent, he is reluctant to ask his parents for help.

By accident, while on Alipay, Qiu Zhe found that Zhima Credit scores could be used to offset the deposit if he rented a house through Xiangyu (a property management company). As he has a Zhima Credit score of 751, he is exempt from paying a deposit, and can pay the rent monthly. Tens of thousands of graduates have made the same choice as Qiu Zhe. Cooperation between Zhima Credit and Xiangyu not only helps people like Qiu Zhe reduce their burden, but also secures house owners' rights and interests.

Source: Ant Financial

For almost one year, Qiu Zhe has always paid his rent several days in advance because overdue payments, payment defaults or house damage will be reported to Zhima Credit, thus reducing his Zhima Credit score. On the sixth of every month, the first thing Qiu Zhe does when he gets up is check his Zhima Credit score. This is the day when Zhima Credit scores are updated monthly. Apart from renting a house, Qiu Zhe can now enjoy deposit exemption services on his business trips when he is staying at a hotel, renting a bicycle or even renting a dinner jacket thanks to his Zhima Credit score.

"Zhima Credit scores have become my passport to the world," said Qiu Zhe.

A key backdrop to the Zhima Credit score, creditworthiness, microloans and inclusiveness is Ant Financial's continual real-time analytics and risk management. This enables the company to deliver its **3, 1, 0 model**: it takes **three minutes** to apply for a loan, **one second** to transfer the funds to the applicant's account and there is **zero manual intervention** in the whole process.

MYbank has helped many blue-collar workers, undergraduate students and migrant workers to embark on a new life. By the end of April 2017, 6.5 million people had borrowed over 800 billion yuan ($125 billion) in just two years.

This is bringing a convergence between creditworthiness and wealth to help people from all walks of life realise their dreams. Creditworthiness has implications well beyond what we might typically understand. For example, how we traditionally think about someone's credit is not just about their wealth, but also how people contribute to their community. This touches many aspects of everyone's daily life. This is why the usage of technology to extend credit to everyone creates a more inclusive economy and a more equal society.

For example, people can get health treatments without paying upfront, thanks to the trust in their Zhima Credit scores. This has reduced the waiting time to see a doctor by 60 per cent on average. Equally, merchants offer short-term loans of products, such as umbrellas when it's raining, in the full expectation that you will return the umbrella later. Payments are taken through Alipay based on how long you used the umbrella for, and the merchant trusts that you will return the umbrella because of your Zhima Credit score.

These technologies will push further and further into our lives as we move to the Internet of Things. For example, Ant Financial believes that, in the near future, it is likely that cameras at restaurants, subways and airports will automatically identify your credit status. People will be able to go out without a mobile phone, cash or even an identity card. They will be able to go anywhere with only their face as their authentication system.

That is why creditworthiness is a critical factor driving Ant Financial, and the Chinese society and economy, forward, with the company regularly acting as a mediator between those who can be trusted and those who cannot. It is why Ant Financial's Zhima Credit system is also working with China's Supreme People's Court to help to identify and punish dishonest commercial credit behaviours. By January 2017, Zhima Credit had assisted the Supreme People's Court in identifying and punishing over 730,000 dishonest debtors, almost 50,000 of whom later paid off their debt. This is another key tenet of Ant Financial's vision: to use creditworthiness to improve social governance and make integrity a highly valued attribute of society.

People born in the 1990s have grown up in an environment where the concepts and applications of creditworthiness are being popularised. For example, one in four Chinese people born since 1990 uses Ant Credit Pay for consumption. Therefore, they have a clearer understanding of creditworthiness, and value it more than the older generations. Statistics on Ant Credit Pay show that 99 per cent of people born in the 1990s repay their debt on time. A society that values and upholds integrity is taking shape.

Whilst I attended the Alibaba Netrepreneurs conference in July 2017, they hosted many of their most successful Taobao businesses in Hangzhou. Many of these are young people who are now entrepreneurs. Intriguingly, some of these businesses are based in rural villages ... because they can be. This is a huge change in society in China and, from a Digital Human age platform, the world. The fact is that any human in any place, even in the remotest villages, can become an entrepreneur if they have an internet connection, something everyone increasingly has through their mobile telephone.

Case Study: Qiqi's Shop Cherie Zhang

Qiqi, born in the 1990s, is from Qiqihar in Heilongjiang Province. After graduating from art school when she was twenty years old, she moved to Beijing and became an international ballroom dancing teacher. Six months later, out of her longing for a more free life, she quit her job and opened a shop on Taobao called Qiqi's Shop Cherie Zhang.

Qiqi first sold her personal second-hand goods including several hundred pairs of shoes and several hundred sets of clothes. Gradually, Qiqi started to stock goods from the wholesale market. She also tried to design clothes herself which were then factory customised. As the orders increased, capital turnover became a big problem.

After learning about Loan by Order at MYbank, Qiqi quickly became a frequent user, receiving a loan every two days on average. She obtained 721 loans within four years, with the highest amount at 53,000 yuan ($8,000) and the lowest at 800 yuan ($125).

Source: Ant Financial

Qiqi has launched over sixty sets of clothes designed by her, with an annual turnover reaching almost 10 million yuan ($1.5 million). In addition, 80 per cent of her customers are regular customers. At the beginning of 2017, Qiqi collaborated with her friends and opened a short video enterprise. "When there is favourable wind blowing from behind, even pigs can fly, let alone I am not a pig," she joked.

But it's not just commerce and society that Ant Financial focuses on. It is worth underlining that Ant Financial is not first and foremost a financial firm. It is a technology firm that is focused on leveraging technologies to improve society and the economy. This is illustrated well by the services that it provides to the government.

For instance, Ant Financial has offered its technology to municipal governments to help them build smart cities, using government agencies to promote e-governance with the help of its big data, cloud computing and technological services to, for instance, manage traffic infringements. Through such services, Ant Financial helps the government make scientific decisions, carry out targeted social governance services and provide highly effective public services using the speed of the internet.

Promoting more convenient and intelligent methods for dealing with daily issues requires not only individual efforts, but also the transformation of the governance model. It means that technology such as that produced by Ant can remove inefficient procedures and replace such structures with the intelligent use of data and information via cloud computing, big data, artificial intelligence and other new technologies. These capabilities can bring far more sensibility to social governance, as illustrated by what Ant Financial is doing with the Shenzhen local administration to help the traffic police in Shenzhen.

Case Study: Shenzhen Traffic Police

The city service account within Alipay referred to as Shenzhen Traffic Police enables Shenzhen to lead China's innovations by improving the way the public handles government affairs. For drivers in many other cities, it can be frustrating having to queue in transportation bureaus that deal with administrative procedures, with noisy crowds and not-so-patient service officers, in order to sort out traffic issues and infringements. Quite often, you have to spend a whole day just waiting for your turn. At such times, you should consider how life is in Shenzhen, where you can use Alipay to get things done.

Shenzhen illustrates the true meaning of service, where science and technology converge to bring convenience. As the first government administration in China to partner with Alipay, the convenient Alipay service aimed at the Shenzhen traffic police has around two million registered users since its launch in August 2015. Alipay allows almost all procedures to be carried out on your mobile phone, as well as delivering traffic news, traffic warnings and advice for drivers.

Source: Ant Financial

One of the biggest benefits is that drivers who have opted in to the service no longer need to have their licence with them in the car. It used to be that a driver's licence was a must in a driver's wallet but, as physical wallets are being replaced by phones, the driver's licence has found a new home. In Shenzhen, the driver's licence has found its new home in the phone following the launch of the traffic police's "Electronic Certificate in Smartphone".

This also means that the traffic police can track drivers more effectively. For example, when traffic police aim their smartphones at a driver, they are not taking a photo. Instead, they are using facial recognition technology to identify drivers who cannot provide licences or identity information, and fine them accordingly. In Shenzhen, traffic violators can never use the excuse "I've left my licence at home".

A final area worth mentioning in Ant Financial's strategy is building a greener planet. This is achieved through its programme of gamification called Ant Forest as you use Alipay.

The idea of Ant Forest originates from the carbon emissions account of Alipay, which is by far the largest platform for personal carbon accounts in the world. In the Alipay carbon account, users are educated in using some of the common global practices in energy conservation and emission reduction. It is the first carbon account, using a bottom-up approach to reduce carbon emissions. Specifically, Ant Forest encourages users to choose greener lifestyles by taking public transport, paying utility bills digitally and booking tickets online. It is also the first in the world to encourage hundreds of millions of people to lead a low-carbon life voluntarily, rather than forcing this approach top-down.

The idea is that users can earn points towards reducing carbon emissions, and the more points you gain, the nearer you get to having a tree planted in your name in real life. You not only earn points through your own use of Alipay, but you can also trade and take points off friends through the app. This has become a real programme of value for the company, with the potential to generate the planting of trees covering more than 40,000 square kilometres (15,444 square miles) per annum.

The results are impressive. The programme launched in the summer of 2016 and, as of April 2017, had over 220 million users. These users had already contributed carbon emission reductions of 5,000 tons per day. As a direct result, the company has planted a total of 8.45 million trees, which reduce carbon emissions by another 2,500 tons per day.

Case Study: Going Green

Source: Ant Financial

Wang Jinlong is a postgraduate from the School of Pharmaceutical Sciences at Peking University. Nie Yusheng is a herdsman from a small village of the Alxa League of Inner Mongolia. How can they be linked when they are thousands of miles apart? On 27 August 2016, Ant Financial launched personal carbon accounts in its Alipay system, and the first accounts were presented in the form of the Ant Forest public welfare platform.

When Wang Jinlong uses Alipay for offline payments or carries out other low-carbon activities, he will be able to harvest "green energy" in Ant Forest, and the virtual tree nurtured by the energy will grow. When the "green energy" reaches 17.9 kilogrammes, the "tree" will be mature. When a virtual tree has matured, Ant Financial and its public welfare partner Alxa SEE Foundation will plant a real tree in the desert area of Alxa of Inner Mongolia. Thousands of miles away, Nie Yusheng is nurturing the number one land parcel of sacsaoul for Ant Forest. A grown sacsaoul could help improve the ecology of 10 square metres of desert, and could be where the precious medicinal plant cistanche is grafted. For Nie, a 52-year-old, the traditional lifestyle is gone. Now the best way to fight against desertification and maintain life is to plant sacsaoul in the barren land.

In January 2017, Ant Financial also launched the world's first Green Digital Finance Alliance at the World Economic Forum in partnership with the United Nations Environment Program (UNEP). This alliance aims to promote the extension of green finance throughout the entire global financial system. The alliance will also seek to extend Ant Forest's carbon account concept globally.

There are more nuances and stories that I could share about Ant Financial's approach to inclusion and a better planet but the bottom line is that Alibaba, with Ant Financial, is leading the charge to leapfrog the world through technology. It is not just in China either as Ant Financial is among the first Chinese technology organisations to start to go global. It is this part of its strategy that illustrates the link between Ant Financial and the fourth age of humanity: financial inclusion through a global platform.

ANT FINANCIAL: BUILDING A BETTER WORLD

Now we get to the real reason why I selected Ant Financial as the sole case study in this book. As I've said repeatedly, Ant Financial is the only company worldwide focused on building a global financial inclusion platform. A platform that can support and connect potentially seven-and-a-half billion people in real time. At the very least, a platform that will include all those who are currently excluded from the financial network, by offering them a connection via the mobile network and simple technologies that are interoperable between operators in all countries.

Its strategy is based on finding companies in other countries that offer an e-wallet payments service, and then invest in those firms and share its technologies with them. Eventually, it is likely that Alipay and Ant Financial's base technologies will be powering the core infrastructure of e-wallets globally.

First, it invests in equivalent products and services to its own in other markets of similar nature, such as India and Thailand. That is why Ant Financial's leadership team talks about inclusiveness, as that's a great strategy with a mobile wallet. Hence, the company invested $680 million in India's Paytm in September 2015, just before demonetisation stimulated Indians to open 200 million wallets on Paytm. In November 2016, Ant partnered with Thailand's Ascend Money, which also runs a digital wallet service. Under the agreement, Ant Financial will assist Ascend Money to grow its online and offline payments and financial services ecosystem. Although Ascend is based in Thailand, it is notable that it also operates in Indonesia, the Philippines, Vietnam, Myanmar and Cambodia.

In February 2017, Ant announced a $3-billion debt financing deal to expand its investment portfolio and, interestingly, moved into the U.S. markets with a bid to acquire MoneyGram for $880 million. This was followed by a strategic investment into Korean messaging service Kakao, which offers Kakao Pay, followed by an increase in its stake in Paytm in March, such that Ant Financial is now the majority owner of the service.

Meanwhile, apart from heading for inclusiveness, Ant has also expanded into the United States and Europe, not just through its proposed purchase of MoneyGram though. At the end of 2015, the company signed a deal with Wirecard to give it access to Europe for merchant checkout using its wallet for Chinese tourists. This was followed by a partnership with Ingenico to further enhance its European presence and then a deal with First Data to give it similar coverage in North America.

The media positions the Wirecard, Ingenico and First Data moves as being a pure provision of service for Chinese tourists, but it is not as simple as that. This is a fast-moving company that is expanding non-stop in its mission to be the dominant global mobile wallet.

Case Study: Taking the Chinese to Lapland

ePassi is the partner firm of Alipay in Helsinki, Finland, bringing the app to Finland to allow Chinese tourists to pay easily when travelling. It's been very successful given that it was initially launched to allow tourists to go and meet Santa Claus in Lapland without having to change currencies or work out how to pay in Finnish currency.

Before Alipay turned up, ePassi had already been running a mobile app for companies to pay employees fringe benefit programmes since the early 2010s. The service was an app with coupons, which made it a perfect fit for Alipay. The two firms were in initial consultation about bringing the service over in spring 2016 and signed contracts in June 2016 for a live service four months later. Once live, the service saw over 50,000 tourists travelling from China to spend some of the Christmas season in Lapland, culminating in the launch of 12.12 in Lapland. 12.12 is another made-up shopping day like Singles' Day (11.11) that drives traffic to merchants in the Alibaba ecosystem.

Finland usually attracts thousands of Chinese tourists every year, with an average spend of $1,100 during their visit. Since the launch of Alipay, this spend has become even higher as most Chinese tourists do not use Western credit cards. Equally, the awareness of the service availability is increasing the attraction for Chinese tourists to visit Finland. In 2016, the visitor numbers from China increased by a third on 2015, and they spent the most money

Source: Ant Financial

out of all the nationalities visiting Finland. Risto Virkkala, CEO of ePassi, told me that after Alipay's promotion in China for Christmas 2016, Chinese tourists also spent three times as long in Lapland than they did the previous year. They love Christmas!

The success of the programme has now expanded to thousands of Finnish merchants and the airport, and ePassi's revenues are likely to double in 2017. There's no stopping there either as, by way of example, Alibaba's travel firm Alitrip estimates that up to eight million Chinese tourists will be visiting Finland in 2020. This is important strategically to the country, which hopes to become the hub for all Chinese tourists coming to Europe.

Certainly, I could see the attraction as we checked into the hotel in Helsinki and saw clear signage that Alipay was accepted, and found the same in many other shops and around the airport. In fact, it intrigued me that we had that discussion in Helsinki and then, the following day, I chaired a meeting of people in Stockholm discussing the key Nordic payments wallets which are MobilPay (Denmark), Siirto (Finland), Swish (Sweden) and Vipps (Norway). What I realised as we talked is that I currently cannot travel the 43 kilometres (27 miles) from Copenhagen, Denmark, to Malmö, Sweden, using the same mobile payments app. The mobile wallets of the Nordic region have no interoperability today. Yet I can travel the 6,300-kilometre (3,915-mile) trip from Beijing to Lapland and pay for everything with the same app.

In conclusion, the mission for Ant Financial was articulated by CEO Eric Jing at Davos in January 2017 when he stated, "We have an ambition to be a global company. My vision (is) that we want to serve two billion people in the next ten years by using technology, by working together with partners … to serve those underserved."

How will the company do this? By leveraging all of the key technologies of today: cloud, data analytics and distributed ledgers. "All these technologies will be used … to bring more, a high level of security," Jing explained, adding that artificial intelligence and blockchain will be "deeply" integrated into Ant Financial's operations.

How Ant Financial thinks is radically different to that of the U.S. and European FinTech firms because it is automating a market that had nothing there before. When Alipay began, there was no e-commerce in China. Alibaba and Alipay created it.

That's a radical difference to the American internet giants like Amazon and eBay, which had major brick-and-mortar competitors also competing online, and began without any payments integration. Equally, the U.S. giants were serving a developed market, where consumers had sophisticated online needs; Alibaba and Alipay were serving markets that were changing dynamically as Chinese citizens moved from rural, agricultural work to the rapidly expanding cities, where manufacturing offered a rapid uplift from poverty to riches.

In creating this revolution of commerce in China, both manufacturing and online, Ant has emerged as the leader, and it talks about *empowering digital FinLife globally.* This is important as it's not a payments app or a mobile wallet, but a complete social, commercial and financial system in one. Imagine Facebook, Amazon and PayPal all integrated into one app. That's what Ant has got. And its business model is fundamentally based on deep user understanding, not cross-selling.

THE ANT INTERVIEWS

In the pages that follow are five interviews covering the past, present and future of Ant Financial, from the person who wrote the first code to the head of strategy who is building the company's future. What stands out for me is how the business started in order to solve the problem of a lack of trust online between buyers and sellers. It wasn't about payments at all. It began with the crudest of technologies—the fax machine—but it solved the problems faced at that time. Through the years, the company has regenerated itself several times. Today, Ant Financial is developing its fifth systems architecture, and tends to refresh its systems every four years. How often do companies or banks regenerate their systems architecture? Ant Financial wants to serve more people through the Alipay e-wallet as well as through local partners. As a matter of fact, embarking on gaining a global ambition of two billion users by 2025 is all about partnering locally. In doing this, Ant Financial's aim is to improve the planet, bring finance to all and allow everyone equal opportunities to work, trade, travel and transact. It is very much in keeping with everything I have described in *Digital Human*. I hope you enjoy these interviews as much as I did meeting these inspirational people.

NI XINGJUN, VICE-HEAD OF ALIPAY

I heard that you were the first person to code anything for Alipay. What kick-started this?

I joined the Taobao team in 2003. The problem when Taobao launched was that the merchants didn't trust the consumers to pay and the consumers didn't trust the merchants to deliver, so no one was actually buying or selling anything because they didn't trust each other. People would look at things on Taobao, but they wouldn't buy.

This was the issue that kicked off creating Alipay. It wasn't a project designed to create a payments tool, it was about overcoming this issue of lack of trust between buyers and sellers. That ties into the role that trust plays in Chinese culture.[42] When you think that there's a general distrust of online services globally and then add the Chinese view of not trusting anyone at all, then you can see why we had a real challenge with Taobao. This is what made us create the escrow service, which was the beginning of Alipay.

How did you code the escrow service?

We looked around the markets to see if there was a model that solved this problem already, and the thinking behind our development was to take the existing escrow model and apply that to the e-commerce markets. It was not about making a payment, but a completely different form of transaction. A new form of transaction. An escrow holding model, not a payments model. This would mean that we would pay the supplier for the goods ordered, but the consumer did not pay until they received them and were satisfied. The coding was based on this concept, with Taobao acting as the escrow in between. As the escrow provider, Taobao holds and regulates the payment of funds between buyers and sellers.

---

42   Generally speaking, in the West the default is "trust". I'll give you the benefit of the doubt, and consider you basically trustworthy, until you do something that breaks our trust. In China, the default tilts more towards "distrust", namely I will only award you my trust after you've proven yourself worthy of it. *See* "Understanding Trust, In China and the West" by David De Cremer, *Harvard Business Review*, February 2015 for more.

Did you look at the United States and services like PayPal?

Our problem could only be solved in a Chinese way so no, Alipay is not based on PayPal or any other Western scheme.

And from first design to delivery to market, how did the development of Alipay progress?

Well, this was a very new idea: to pay someone you didn't know and couldn't see for something that you wanted, especially in China. Once we could get over that, then it was how to make it easier for them to pay and more convenient. We created the product—escrow to overcome the trust issue—and then the second challenge was how to make the payment process and processing simple and easy. That is when we moved from Taobao escrow services towards Alipay's creation. That was in the second half of 2004, when we made Alipay its own stand-alone service, rather than just being part of Taobao.

With the escrow service, how did people understand how that worked as general Chinese consumers?

It was all about Alibaba. Alibaba's brand by 2003 was very strong, and so when Alibaba introduced the service, people trusted Alibaba's backing and support of escrow. It was as simple as that.

And what were the main milestones that followed the introduction of Alipay?

The first big milestone was overcoming the trust issue. Then, when we spun off from Taobao, it was all about the convenience and flexibility of making payments. That was firstly online payments but then, more recently, mobile payments have become the central focus of the whole business. That is our focus today. Until 2013, we also were solely focused on payments but then Yu'e Bao was launched and we also expanded into insurance products and services, so we became far more than just payments. That led to the launch of Ant Financial.

Equally, once the payments business got to scale, it was the merchants' side that became a major focus for developing other types of financial products, such as loans and insurances. They were a key factor in both designing and developing these products.

For example, a side effect of the success of Alipay was cash flow for the merchants. This is because their liquidity was impacted in that they could see that the money was there in escrow, but they could not withdraw the money until the buyer was happy. That would usually be a two-week period. This led to a discussion around a problem with merchant liquidity on the Taobao platform, and led us to create a loan-to-order product. Effectively, this product allows merchants to get their order paid immediately as a loan, which can be paid back two weeks later when funds are released. This solved the liquidity issue.

In each iteration from Taobao to Alipay to Ant, has the thinking changed much in terms of how to structure and develop the systems and code?

Well, the company came from Alibaba, and the philosophy of Alibaba is driven by a mission as to whether this makes it easy to do business. The Alibaba mission is the core behind all of our thinking, namely to make it easy to do business anywhere. That is behind everything we do: does this serve our mission? This is not going to change as that is the essence of everything we do.

The thing that has changed is the bigger environment around what we do. We have moved from PC to mobile to tablet to an internet of everything. The environment is very different. Initially, we were trying to work out how to make this work for an online system and online transactions. Now it is mobile and mobile first. In the future, it will be devices and connectivity, and connectivity first.

During the years, have there been any surprises with how the product is used and what your customers do with Alipay?

You learn things all the time as you go along, but 2010 was a critical year in the history of Alipay. Until 2010, we were constantly innovating our products and making decisions for our users that we thought would help them with the way they interacted with Alipay. We assumed that what we thought was in the best interests of our users, based on our users' behaviours. We had this customer-first focus in our minds, but we were making the decisions on behalf of our users. It was a mistake but, at the time, we thought this was the right way to do things.

It was in 2010 that we reached what was probably the lowest point in the company's history, in terms of customer satisfaction. We were comfortable we were trying to do the right thing for our customers, but probably thought wrong, as we were making decisions without consulting them. We ended up with a product that was overdesigned, with too many bells and whistles and too complex for what they really wanted or needed. We had done too much for them and it was too complicated.

What happened in 2010 to make you realise this?

It was at the 2010 Alibaba gala, an internal conference for all key people that takes place annually. It is the usual thing where you gather your key people and have entertainment and key speeches from all the leadership team. The company presents its strategy for the next year and you all get a chance to meet and greet your peers. At the 2010 annual gala, Jack Ma came on stage and basically raged against Alipay's user experience, and ripped it apart.

He said it was clear that there was a huge demand for Alipay and for what Alipay could offer but, in scaling up to meet these increasing demands, the company had lost sight of the balance between the user experience and dealing with the demand. He said that the company had lost sight of the user, and the user experience was terrible because of overcomplexity and overdesign. Jack Ma made it clear that the engineering team had lost sight of the user, and that the user experience should conquer all. Not the features and functionality, but the ease of use and the experience that goes with that became the new key.

I assume then that design and the user experience became the driving force behind Alipay?

Yes. In fact, this was when Lucy Peng was made CEO of Alipay. She had been on the management team of Alibaba before that but was now given explicit leadership of Alipay. She led the management in doing a lot of soul-searching after the annual gala, looking at what they had to do to change and improve their approach. It made them realise that the company had become too divorced from the user. They were too far away from them to see what they were doing and what they needed. Hence the design and development team were making assumptions about what they thought users need and wanted, with no actual idea or validation of their views.

This changed and the company moved to talking to users about what their experiences were, and what they liked and disliked, rather than assuming on their behalf. The designers still used the data and traffic behaviours to see what was happening, but the difference was that they now included user dialogue as part of the approach rather than just looking at the data.

If you could go back fourteen years, to the Ni Xingjun of 2003, and advise him on the way forward, what would you say to him?

I would tell him to think about the user and ask himself whether the user is really at the centre of everything we do. We say they are, but is that actually the case and can you prove that to yourself? Are they really at the heart of the product? Is this change really going to help them? Are they really going to see changes in our strategy that help them in their lives? Are they really at the centre of our thinking and does our strategy reflect that?

Today, you have terabytes of data being analysed in real time with highly advanced artificial intelligence. With such advances in technological developments, would this give you the answers to those questions?

Your question is really getting to the heart of *how* we can put the user experience at the core of what we do. The *how* is the critical piece. There are two things that are the keys to the best user experience and not just the user experience, but realising Ant Financial's mission of inclusive finance. The first part is technology. Our belief is that the better and more intuitive the technology can be, the natural corollary will be that the users get a better and more intuitive experience. An example is the way in which Yu'e Bao, Alipay and MYBank and our other products are being received in rural China. If these products were not simple and intuitive, people would not use them. But the other part of this is that we had to build a credit scoring system. If we can credit score our customers, we can offer them far better targeted and relevant services. That was difficult as there wasn't one there before, unlike Europe and America which have Experian and Equifax and FICO. We had to build one by analysing the digital footprints of Alibaba and Alipay users, and figuring out how creditworthy people are. But creditworthiness is a critical part of building financial inclusion, and combining creditworthiness with technology has been the critical part to getting a user experience today that is intuitive and easy.

I understand and it makes me wonder how you test your developments with the users.

Well, we have two stages. Before we start a new development, we have a whole raft of data to analyse and patents to file. From all of the data and patents, we have to work out the best way to approach the next user need or the next user development. Then, once the product is developed, our approach would be similar to any other large technology firm, such as Facebook or Google. We would roll out the development for beta testing, get feedback and then make adjustments along the way until ready for prime time.

How do you benchmark what you do? Do you see companies like Facebook and Google as best in class, and are they who you admire and would wish to be like?

It is very hard to find a company that we would benchmark ourselves against, as there is no company like us or that is trying to do what we do. If you were to compare us with most technology companies, then the scale and number of challenges that we face as a company are bigger than most. First of all, the business we are trying to be is covering huge numbers of users and capabilities. We are reaching over a billion users today, with differing needs in differing markets, and are likely to double this number within the next few years, so we are very cognizant of who we are and what we are trying to achieve. Equally, we are very cognizant of financial regulations and compliance with those, which again makes us different to most of the other technology players globally you could reference out there. Facebook or Google is not worried about the SEC or Federal Reserve in the way that we would be, because they are not a financial player whilst we are a technology firm offering financial services through technology. It is very different. We have to be watertight on data security and customer information, and we have to deliver technology against all of those financial needs and user needs. We are under no illusions about the scale of our challenges, capabilities and ambitions.

Nevertheless, we do look at innovations from players at a macro level, like Facebook, Google, Tencent, Baidu and others, to see what they are bringing to market and whether it could improve how we make our customers' experience the best that it can be.

You mention data security, and companies like PayPal in the United States are the number one target for hackers, as that's where the money is. Is the same true here with Ant and Alipay, and how do you deal with that?

We are a technology company running a financial business and in the business of finance, risk management is a core competency. That was the whole genesis of Alipay—the lack of trust between people because of the risk of non-payment or non-delivery. Try to compare us to other technology firms or banks, and we are some way ahead of them when it comes to how to deal with risk. That is why we have architected a real-time risk management and fraud detection system, using artificial intelligence. It is some way ahead of everyone else today. We look at risk management as a core competency and also a foundation of future success. It's a hygiene factor for how we do business and underpins everything we do.

If you look at yourselves as a user experience led business, how can you be user experience led as you develop globally with so many different countries and user needs that have to be covered?

Well, user experience is a central part of our corporate culture and also a central part of our product. This is why, as we build partnerships globally with firms like Paytm in India, Kakao in South Korea and Ascent in Thailand, we hold the same culture and user-centric focus within those partnerships. We are constantly sharing our user focus with our partners, and our partners see great value in this. The key is that we will not compromise on the user experience, but will share our knowledge and know-how to ensure that we and our partners and our users get the best experience that there can be. We don't prescribe this approach however, as we also learn from our partners. So, we are not forcing the Alipay Way upon them or anything. It is a shared dialogue and we are acting as a family, sharing knowledge and experience to build financial inclusion for all. That is how I see Ant Financial and our partners in other local markets, as we build and extend globally. It is all about serving as many people as we can, and finding people who know their markets the best to serve those markets. Paytm knows Indian consumer needs far better than we do, and we know Chinese consumers' needs better than they do. But we can share knowledge of how things work in India and China that improve the experiences of citizens in both countries. Equally, the approaches in different countries can be different for that reason. There is no one-size-fits-all approach.

How do you manage data and data privacy when you have different government requirements in different constituencies?

Data and the analysis of that data is a fundamental in order to see how users are interacting with our products and services, but equally their privacy is critical. Data privacy and data security is a critical part of maintaining our customer confidence, and we have to ensure that is protected. Privacy and security is a prerequisite for doing anything and everything, and it's also our largest investment area as this is critical. There are corporate structures and competencies in place, and people with roles and responsibilities who know exactly what is happening with our customers' data.

LI JIN, SENIOR DIRECTOR AND HEAD OF THE TECHNOLOGY TEAM

What is the technology behind Alipay?

We have already seen three different generations of architecture deployed for Alipay, and are now just finishing the fourth generation and starting on a fifth generation. It began with using Java, open sourcing and an Oracle database to provide the basic payment service. We then, a couple of years later, had to move to a second-generation system to scale up to thousands of transactions per second. At this point, we developed our own middleware based on service-oriented architecture (SOA) and object-oriented methodologies, rather than open-sourced systems. It was still on Oracle, but we also started to partition the database for different analysis based on user behaviours. It was important in this design to maintain a clear view of the customer however, so we did this through different virtual connections. Bear in mind that we started with a virtual escrow account, so later on we had to deal with connecting that with the user's bank account. So we started linking a number of banks to scale our transaction capabilities, and had to build an architecture that could connect many different systems to enable this, particularly as we were also building multiple businesses around these services from Taobao to Tmall. This is why it was so important to incorporate an object-oriented SOA architecture in this second-generation system, and we also began moving to cloud-based services.

In the third-generation architecture, in the early 2010s, we moved then to microservice architecture and fully cloud-based services using Ant Financial's own cloud structures. In that third iteration, everything became open cloud infrastructure owned by Ant Financial, and moved away from Oracle and other services, so that we could manage it all ourselves.

I joined Ant Financial from Microsoft as we were developing the fourth-generation architecture. This was the generation when Ant Financial opened up our services to be plug-and-play in a marketplace with others. We used a mixture of private and public cloud and opened our services through middleware to other partners and players. We offered all of our tools and development capabilities to other partners to use and work with us.

We could do this because, whilst developing our third-generation architecture, we launched MYbank, which was created completely in the cloud, using object-oriented SOA in a microservice architecture. MYbank is a purely virtual online bank. There is no offline, just purely online banking. The whole banking system is built in a cloud-based infrastructure and now offered to other banks, insurance companies and payments firms to use. There are many other banks already working with us using our OceanBase database. These are mainly medium-sized banks replacing their core systems and upgrading and changing them by partnering with us. The five big banks tend to have their own development staff using mainframe systems, and are managing their own systems, although China Construction Bank has created a strategy partnership with Ant Financial for its non-core banking areas.

How do you manage all the data flowing through the system?

Data mining is an internal skill, not an internet skill. In our fourth-generation system, we have had to deal with the challenges of superscale and super complication. One of the complications is the fundamental payment systems, which are highly distributed. The second is dealing with the industrial financial system and risk. We have been developing what we call a "risk core". When we create a microloan, we also have to deal with the overall risk management challenges for those loans. Doing real-time risk monitoring, monitoring real-time transactions and applying real-time detection are core parts of the system. In fact, we started applying machine learning and artificial intelligence to these areas five years ago, taking all of our data to provide real-time decision-making to create real-time security through real-time risk analytics. This means that we have a real-time security decision-making system that is part of our core infrastructure.

Regarding the focus on data lakes, we call this the super large-scale data analysis system. We deal with numbers that are large. We have something like 520 million user accounts, growing quickly. We currently handle several hundred terabytes of data on a daily basis and soon we will be talking petabytes, or over 1,000 terabytes a day. Our internal business leaders want to see how their business is working in real time, how many people are using their capabilities per day and more. The business leaders want real-time analysis every few minutes, and so we are dealing with analysing terabytes of data non-stop in real time.

I see that you can provide a microloan in one second. How do you deal with credit risk in this area?
Well, we have already collected the data about transaction history and repayment history, which we then analyse in real time. The user's profile is always up to date and we do risk control and evaluate the cost of lending to someone in real time. 520 million users.

What about cybersecurity? How do you protect the systems?
Our real-time risk management and fraud detection system does real-time transaction scanning and we also use social graph models and cross-checking relationships between different people and different accounts and users to help to prevent account theft and fraud. We use all this visualisation and analytics to detect any abnormalities like account theft. We do this constantly in real time, and every transaction has to go through our real-time detection systems. That's up to 250,000 transactions analysed, tracked, traced and detected non-stop, 24/7 in real time.

And the hardware behind all of this?
An X86-based Intel server farm.

And you mentioned machine learning, how is that developing within Ant Financial?
Well, a good example of this is that we use artificial intelligence to analyse insurance claims. You can take a picture of the damage to your car and send it to us. We then use machine learning to check the details of that image

and provide a real-time assessment and payment for the damage with no humans involved. We get rid of all the loss adjusters and claims handlers, and do the whole thing automatically. We only launched this in June 2017. We also use AI within our wealth management business to provide what may be considered a roboadvisory service.

Another scenario is helping our customer service. We have so many users now and so many enquiries that we would need an army of people to deal with these demands. That is why we created an agent, a robot, who uses all of our knowledge about our customers to provide services. You can chat with us in natural language via our agents, who are actually robots. Ask a question like "Why can't I do this money transfer?" and the agent will talk you through the process in a very natural way. This shows you that it's more than just a chatbot. Most chatbots are preprogrammed with scripts. Our robot is more thought oriented. It uses an understanding of natural language and a knowledge base to build on machine learning and AI analytics. Through all of this, we have a different kind of intelligence occurring because the robot is giving a natural answer that responds to the user's question. It's natural language with machine learning, and we are making these services available to our partners in our marketplace using the branding AI Inside.

AI is the central part of the model, the algorithm model. It's a training platform where the model is continually self-learning in real time and offering new learning online to make decisions and analyse customer behaviours. It's learning constantly from all the data that comes through our systems.

We have another area in which we developed a proof of concept last year for wealth management. The system continually looks at your investments, and selects where and how to invest based on your behaviours and appetite for risk. It's a roboadvisor that automatically selects the mutual funds based on your investment profile, and it automatically selects the amount you put into those funds every month based on your activities. This is not Yu'e Bao, which is the money market fund. This is wealth management through an AI-based roboadvisor.

This is referencing the new technologies that are in your next-generation architecture?

Well, the core of what we enable is payments and the key for us will be the artificial intelligence that we can wrap around that capability. This includes things like identification technologies using facial recognition, behavioural pattern recognition, biometric and location-based analytics, and related technologies. We have groups of people dedicated to those technologies. This led to some interesting demos. For example, we did a demo using a video playing on a phone that we placed in front of another mobile phone using Alipay. The mobile phone with Alipay could recognise that it was not a live person but a recorded video using our facial recognition systems.

Looking forward therefore, we are basically a technology company. We are building the technology platform for payments, banking and finance, and making it robust for the digital age. We are not just a payments company, but a security company and a technology company. We then offer these capabilities globally to our partners as a marketplace of services.

This means that any insurer firm could use our technologies for claims or any bank could use our technologies for authentication. Our partners include banks—not necessarily the top-tier banks, but second- and third-tier—and insurance firms. We then have our family, which includes companies like Paytm, Kakao, GCash, Mynt, Ascent and so on. For our family, we offer our technologies direct and call them A+, which means "Alipay Inside", and so underlying them is our first-generation platform. They can all use our marketplace of APIs.

This means you are talking huge volumes of transactions running through your systems.

We currently are architected for an average 120,000 transactions per second, peaking at 250,000 transactions per second (by comparison Visa is designed to handle to around 14,000 per second). On peak days, like Singles' Day, we can reach ten billion transactions per day and, as I mentioned, we are currently architected to handle a petabyte of data in real time. Longer term, when we reach two billion users globally, our volumes would be looking at over 100 billion transactions per day.[43]

I should also mention that given we are using our own technologies rather than Oracle, and our own cloud server farm rather than mainframe, it means that we have significantly lowered the cost of our transactions. Our average cost to process right now (summer 2017) is about 10 fen, which translates into around $0.015 per transaction. We will continually drill down on this to lower those costs further.

You mention that changes in architecture take place so frequently— about once every three or four years—how do you deal with a systems refreshment of that scale so often, as I don't see that in other large financial firms?

It's actually quite painful but totally necessary. We are now taking out our third generation, as it had some commercial software that we needed to replace. But to take that out is not a fast process and so, during this time, we have to keep the existing service running. We end up running two architectures side by side, but it's necessary and the leadership team recognises that this is the cost of doing business. If we are to keep up with the demands of our system and users and customers, we have to continually refresh and renew and ensure that we are leveraging the right technologies to keep up. We cannot let them stay as they are, as that will mean we will fall behind. Continual refreshment is the cost of doing business. Our leadership team recognises that to ensure we have the right infrastructure, we have to think about technology at least three to five years in advance. We are always looking to the next horizon and new technology trends. We then start putting those pieces together. Otherwise you cannot fulfil future business needs.

---

43 Combined, Visa and MasterCard handle just over sixty billion transactions per year, or near 2,000 transactions per second.

Another unique aspect comes in here; the technology team is not separate from the other teams. We start every year with a battlefield. This is when all of the company works on different challenges, which are simulated scenarios of different business requirements. We all work together on the battlefield, and our key performance indicators (KPIs) are tied to how we deal with these. Every year, a battlefield will bring front- and back-office people together for a few days to a week and we will solve our problems. This creates a strong synergy from front to back office and, at the start of 2017, we got together to work on fifteen battlefields.

We also have a different organisational structure, which is real matrix. Everyone has a technical boss and a business boss. Equally, we have a domestic boss and an international boss. We call it a 2 plus 2 approach. We all have a complete picture of what needs to be done.

How many people do you have in the team working on technology?
In total, there are around 8,000 engineers in the company, of which 4,000 are in the technology team. We hire many graduates, and hired Michael Jordan to work with our team in May 2017. That's Michael I. Jordan, the top electronics and computing professor with the University of Berkeley, not the basketball player! Our aim is to have a world-class top researcher to work with our talent, as hiring good talent is critical.

This gets interesting then for, in the future, we may be talking of billions of customers, tens of millions of merchants, thousands of partners and hundreds in the family. Is there any limit to how far Ant Financial can scale, technologically?
I don't think so. No matter how big we grow, the technology is the same. We just need more data centres, more servers, more disk storage and such like. There is no limit. We have data centres in Shanghai, Beijing, Zhengzhou and two here in Hangzhou, so we just need to grow those. For the OceanBase database, we can switch in real time automatically. Everything

is in real time, it's all backed up in real time and can switch in real time. We demonstrated this to an official from the Central Bank the other day. We made it look as though a server had gone down, and we automatically switched to another server in real time. He had come to see what we could do because he wants us to share these capabilities with other banks, as many of them do not have this real-time fault tolerance. That is the power of the marketplace. We can share and handle issues without the problems of legacy firms or non-technology financial institutions.

JIA HANG, SENIOR DIRECTOR, INTERNATIONAL BUSINESS UNIT

Perhaps we could start with talking about the international expansion of Ant Financial, and how you see that being directed.

We have a very successful business in China, providing a lifestyle service for our e-wallet users. They can use Alipay for their daily life needs, and get a lot of information from the app too. It's not just for a payment, but beyond payments and for other financial services. A natural result of having such success in China is that we then need to serve our Chinese customers when they travel outside of China. For example, we call Hangzhou a cashless city. You don't need any money here. You can just use Alipay. When people get used to such a life as this, they want to have the same experience when travelling outside of China. They don't want to have to have a wallet and a lot of cash. That has become our target: how to serve our customers when they are travelling outside of China? The first step towards this is to enable the merchant to accept Alipay outside of China. We have been trying to do this for several years, starting in 2013. It is difficult however, because the market is different. Merchants overseas are confused as to why they need to accept QR codes. QR codes are very successful in China but, in other markets, they have not taken off yet. There is a company that has been trying to roll this out, Isis, but it has not been very successful because the payment structure is so neutral that trying to introduce a new method is tough. That is the first reason why it has been difficult to roll out Alipay overseas, because the environment outside China does not accept QR codes. The second reason is that when we provide the QR code for payment, we have to have something else. If I talk to a merchant in Japan and say that I'll provide them with a payment by QR code, they are not very interested because they already have many, many payment methods such as Visa and MasterCard, which have not been rolled out so extensively in China. UnionPay covers almost everyone in China. So, when we go to merchants outside China who already take UnionPay, Visa and MasterCard, they ask, "Why do we need another payment method?"

In fact, UnionPay has been very successful in getting adoption outside China and its sales pitch is, If you want the business of Chinese tourists, you must accept the UnionPay card. That convinced a lot of merchants to accept the UnionPay card, and this started back in 2004. UnionPay's success meant that when Alipay started to expand overseas, UnionPay already occupied the position we were trying to take. When we talked to merchants, they would say they were not interested. They would say, "What you are asking me to do is like move my money from my left pocket to my right pocket. I don't see the point. It's all Chinese." These are the challenges we are facing. It is not so painful for cross-border travellers, in that they have a payment card that works. It is not as cool, but it works.

Equally, if we just provided a payment service, it is not sexy for the merchant but it is also not sexy for the user. UnionPay, Visa and MasterCard all provide the same function, after all. Then you have to look at why Alipay has been so successful in China, in that we provide added value to both the merchant and the user, over and above the traditional payment method. For example, the customer can use Alipay to look at all the merchants around them, both physically and digitally, in China and abroad, and look for those offering coupons and discounts. They can get all the information they need to select the merchant they want to deal with. On the other side, we have built the platform for merchants to talk to customers directly through this sort of app. This means they can message customers directly from our system. It provides them with an extra marketing channel.

Is this why you created partnerships with firms like Kakao in South Korea?

Yes. Korea is a developed economy with a payments structure that is already in place and very neutral. It is very difficult to convince Korean people to switch from credit card payments to non-credit card payments. But there is an opportunity through cooperation with Kakao, as Kakao has 95 per cent of the market for social media in South Korea. This gives us the confidence that we can do something, because there exists a very strong and significant user base to build on. This means we purely have to focus on merchants, as there is already a strong relationship with the users.

Kakao also has a lot of resources on the merchant side. It has Kakao Taxi, and Kakao this and that. However at the moment, you can call the taxi within Kakao but you have to pay the driver with cash or by card. This is because Kakao is skilled in social networking but not in payments. It invests a lot in entertainment and music and social content, but its expertise is not with money. This is why it makes a great partnership for us. We are a good match for each other's needs. It has the users and the use case; we have our technology and experience. We know how to do payments.

Yet you seem to have now switched strategy towards financial inclusion?
Yes. This is because, in 2015, we started to change our international expansion focus towards a new route, which is to focus on developing countries rather than the developed economies. Developing countries offer a much better opportunity for us. In the developing countries, most of the people do not have a bank service yet. They do not have cards and payment systems yet. They have a lot of pain points in these countries because payments are difficult.

We are powerful with technology and have a lot of knowledge about how to use technology to deliver financial inclusion. That experience is clearly valuable when we go to developing economies, as they have not had this level of knowledge. They see our technology as valuable for them. If you go to the United States and say, "I have good technology I would like to share with you," they will say, "Oh, we don't need it as we don't think the best technology is in China." We will get similar responses in Japan, Korea and other markets. They are confident that they have the best technologies and don't need someone else's.

However, in developing countries, they admit that they need our help. They need experience, knowledge, technology and cash. That has been our experience with Paytm in India, Ascent Money in Thailand, Globe Telecom for GCash in Indonesia and Mynt in the Philippines. We are also talking to other countries, too.

Sub-Saharan Africa?

Yes. South Asia, the Middle East and Africa will be the next geographies we want to expand into. We have a big challenge here though, in that our capacity is limited. We have a small team, and the technology and product is not ready for such fast expansion. We can deal with several countries, but if you asked me to approach ten countries or more at once, that would be too much to ask. It is not just about whether I have enough engineers, but more about whether those engineers have the ability to talk with the partners. The languages are different, as are their cultures. There is always a culture gap. How we gain knowledge of the local market then depends on the local partner, but the concepts and ideas of the local partner and our concepts and ideas always have some gaps. How to work together with them is something we then have to learn. For a Chinese company, globalisation is far more difficult than for an American company. A U.S. company has two advantages. First is language. An American company can send an employee anywhere in the world and they just need to talk English because other countries have adopted this as their second language. The second reason is culture. The United States has influenced a lot of global culture since the Second World War. Even Chinese people, we grew up with American movies as kids. We have gained more understanding about coffee, hamburgers and how American people talk and smile. This makes it far easier for a U.S. company to expand overseas because people already know what you look like, how to relate to you and how to talk with you. It is very different for a Chinese company. They cannot follow us so we have to follow them. That is not as easy as it sounds as we have challenges to try to follow them. For example, finding local employees. Even if we do find local employees, we then have to work out how to integrate them with the Chinese team.

You also seem to be focused now on just payments internationally. What I mean is that if you look at Paytm and Globe Telecom, your focus is on the e-wallet, whereas Kakao is more like Alibaba, a social, commercial and e-wallet system. Is that a conscious change of strategy? There is a reason for this. We are not skilled at building social networks. If you look at India or Indonesia, they already have social networks that are established and working. We can always partner and have cooperation with those social networks. For example, in Indonesia, they have a very popular social network called Blackberry Messenger (BBM). Consequently, we have invested in a joint venture in Indonesia where BBM is a part of that.

It is also important that we start with payments first, as the whole Ant Financial model is based on payments. Payments is the connection between you and your users and merchants. Social networking can expand the users very quickly, but you don't really have a connection with the user. The users haven't given you their KYC information. Only when they make a payment, do they need to give you this information because of anti-money laundering and risk management rules. Then they have a serious connection with you. By building on payments, you can build real connections and those users will be a very stable and reliable resource for you.

We start from the payment and, in developing countries, we know there are lots of pain points in payments. For example, young people move to the cities for work but the problem they have is how to send money back home to their parents in the village. Peer-to-peer money transfer through this wallet is one of the core use cases, and is an integral part of the services our partners offer in India, Indonesia and the Philippines. Traditional bank services cannot handle this. Their business model and technology means that it is not that they don't want to do it, simply that it is not worth them doing it. It would cost too much. We are doing it because we use the smartphone and internet to access the user.

That leads to another question: how do we do KYC for people living in villages? Those people living in rural areas often do not even have a photo identification document. We discuss this issue with the regulatory authorities through our local partners, and the good news is that those authorities are often interested in what we can do because they know it is a problem for their economy. They have a developing economy, a rising new class of young people with money and a rural structure that needs to be connected. They welcome our help in bringing this infrastructure into their countries. We get a very warm welcome in these countries when we teach our local partners to do this type of business.

By talking with the governments, we can create policies that work. For example, if you keep your e-wallet balance under a certain amount, you don't need to do KYC. This is the policy established with Paytm in India. As long as the balances are small, no KYC is required. That is a great policy to work with because people living in villages do not want to have big balances. Working with a small balance works for them. It is good policy for all and can cure their pain points. If you do not have an electronic way of transferring money, then it is very difficult and expensive with cash.

How do you gain trust in overseas markets? For example, when you go the Middle East, how can you convince them to trust that a Chinese firm will work in their best interests?

That's a very good question. When we select the markets, countries and partners we want to work with, this is a core part of our thinking. We do not want to work with some countries yet because they would be more difficult for this reason. Some Middle Eastern countries would be a big challenge but we would like to work in countries like the United Arab Emirates, and particularly Dubai , due to its international outlook. This is not the most important factor though. It is just a filter we use in order to work out which countries rise high on our list and which do not. The second factor is the partners we can work with. Is there an ideal partner already there, and do their capabilities match our requirements? If you're trying to create an e-wallet business, you firstly need users and merchants. We are Ant Financial, and we don't have those, so we must find partners to provide this.

If I then summarise your international expansion strategy, it appears to be based on two key foundations: inclusion and tourism.

It is actually three. The first is travellers, supporting Chinese people to be able to pay outside China. We have a team focused on this. The second is that a lot of Chinese people do not travel outside of China but want to buy things from overseas via Apple, Amazon or similar services. That is a pure online business, and we have a team focused on that. Then the third is strategic partnerships focused on the local markets to serve local people with a local payment method. That is Paytm, Ascent Money, Globe Telecom, Kakao and Lazada. Alibaba acquired Lazada, the largest e-commerce platform in Southeast Asia, and I am leading the team working with Lazada to solve their payments platform. Lazada has six e-commerce platforms in six Asian countries, and each platform has a different language, a different interface and a different culture. In other words, each platform is a local platform, and we are creating the payments systems to support those platforms.

How does the partnership model work in practice?

For each partner, we take a minority share of the joint venture. We rely on the local partners as they have to deal with the local users, the local merchants and the local authorities and regulators. We bring the experience and technologies to do payments and may, over time, bring in other financial services. All of those financial services are heavily regulated by local governments. If this company is majority owned by a foreign company out of China, that can create issues.

We don't really handle the users or their data. That stays local. The local company manages and stores all the data locally. For compliance, we share technology and experience and provide consultancy support. We show them how it can work and help them copy the Chinese way, but everything stays local and is managed locally.

How do you see the longer-term vision of where your international expansion will take you?

As mentioned, we definitely want to be a global company. We believe in globalisation. We also want to share our technology and experience that we have gained in China with other developing countries. For us, we are a company that is a business, that needs revenues and profits, but on the other hand, we are also trying to do things that are good for society. We want to help everyone improve their lives. We can do this by doing good business providing financial inclusion. That achieves both objectives: good business that is good for society. It benefits the business side and the human side. It benefits the people in these developing countries. It is not a charitable objective. It is a business objective with a profit and loss account (P&L) but, as we have seen this benefit people in China, we want it to benefit people in these other countries.

For my team, it is hard to send our young generation of Chinese engineers to developing countries and for them to experience being in different societies with different foods, different cultures and different languages. It is hard for them to fit in. I just tell my engineers that by going there, they are really making a difference. They are really helping people. They want to do that, and that is why we have a great team of engineers travelling to these developing markets. It makes sense to do things and, from a strategy side, is why we are now focusing on developing countries. We cannot help people in developed countries.

There is an ambition to achieve two billion users by 2025. Do you see this as achievable?

It is not so easy to reach this number. I am a working level person and focus on the challenges and difficulties, rather than the goal. Let's look at Paytm as an example. There are still a lot of people in India who do not speak English. There are many different languages in India, so you need to introduce many different language apps for those people. Then you need to educate those people in how to use an e-wallet. There is a long way to go. It is a similar situation in other countries. Indonesia, for example, has 300 million people but only 20 million of these people have photo identification. The rest of the people live in the countryside, the rural economy. They have no ID. It is only the 20 million living in the cities who do. Many people are using a function phone and not a smartphone. Many would find a smartphone with a data service too expensive to use. How do we serve them? We don't have a solution for a function phone and do not want to invest resources in creating services for function phones, especially as smartphones are growing in number every day. Equally, it is a big project to cover 20 million people, let alone the rest. But things change quickly and we are focusing on the younger generation in the big cities, many of whom have smartphones and the internet. When they adopt our e-wallets, they will then be the ambassadors and promoters of our services to their friends and families. They will then influence others to join and I am confident that we will grow our business to two billion users by 2025. It will not be easy, but we will try our best to achieve that.

VIJAY SHEKHAR SHARMA, CEO AND FOUNDER OF PAYTM

"He was from a small town; he didn't know English; he didn't know anything about business management or any coding language, and he became the founder of one of the most revolutionary markets in e-commerce history."[44]

Whilst in China with Ant Financial, I met Vijay Shekhar Sharma, the amazing founder of Paytm, one of Ant's partner firms. Inspired by Alipay and Jack Ma, Vijay founded Paytm in 2010 after some years of struggle. In fact, his personal story is truly fascinating and he presented this on stage to an audience of 2,000 Taobao elite merchants who attended the Netrepreneurs conference Alibaba was holding, which I also attended.

Vijay was born in a small town in northern India and excelled at school. A child prodigy, he was top of the class and moved on to college at just fourteen years of age. Unfortunately, his teaching in his hometown had all been in Hindi, so when he joined college as a child prodigy, he soon fell behind due to his lack of language skills and lack of English. Vijay dropped out of college but taught himself English and took up coding. With a few friends, he built a content management system for online services that became incredibly popular in India, making him and his friends a fortune on paper. Misfortune hit Vijay again however when, in 2005, his friends conned him of his fortune and left him penniless. This was the darkest time for the young, aspiring technology professional and, for a few years, Vijay had to sleep on friends' sofas while walking miles to find work and eating nothing. It was during these dark days that he gained focus to reinvent himself through his company, One97, and started to build new capabilities around mobile networks.

---

44 "Inspiring Story of Vijay Shekhar Sharma's Life, Paytm Founder," *Follow Me Around*, 30 August 2016.

In 2010, inspired in part by what he had seen taking place with Alibaba in China, Vijay presented the idea of Paytm, short for Pay through mobile, to the board of One97. They were not impressed. In order to persuade them, Vijay offered 1 per cent of his equity in One97, worth around $1 million, to try out the idea. It succeeded far more than anyone could have dreamed.

Vijay went on to create a website that would allow people to recharge their mobile telephones using prepaid services from the website. It was three years later, after attending Alibaba's annual meeting, that Vijay became inspired by the idea of a Paytm mobile wallet. Vijay often remembers seeing vegetable vendors in Hangzhou using their mobile phones to receive payments from customers using QR codes and thinking that this would work in India. This led him to establish the Paytm wallet in 2013. By the end of 2014, Paytm was being used by 20 million Indians; by July 2015, 100 million; and by February 2017, 200 million people. When I met Vijay in July 2017, the numbers had reached 230 million active users, with the firm aiming to reach over six million merchants.

Vijay, you were inspired by Alipay and Alibaba to create the Paytm wallet when you came to their summit in 2012. How did you take that inspiration and make it a reality?

What we learnt by listening to Jack Ma was that commerce was getting huge online. I knew that this was a big opportunity, as things are turning digital, but I didn't know how big until I heard Jack talking back in 2012. For example, I knew that search and information was a big use case, but I had not thought about how money, payments and shopping would be so big. After all, online commerce had been available through Amazon in the United States for years, but still only accounted for about 10 per cent of all shopping. When I heard Jack talking about the volume of commerce going through his platforms in China and doubling year-on-year, I thought wow. These numbers sounded so incredibly unreal that, if true, we had to build this in India too, as China was at about the same point as India in terms of e-commerce. In particular, I was inspired by the idea that you only had to pick up your mobile phone and get on the internet and that was it. You could start to buy.

I took the idea from there and took it to the board at One97 and said, "Let's build the Alipay and Taobao for India." However, the board was not ready to take that risk, as the company was very focused on B2B and large corporates. Equally, I am a technology guy, not a marketing or consumer guy, so they rejected me on both fronts. I was confident though and offered $1 million as that was the amount we needed to risk, and I personally guaranteed that investment. That's all that was needed to get things started.

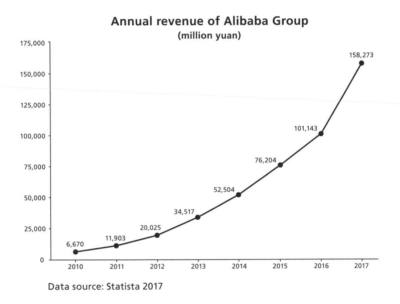

Annual revenue of Alibaba Group
(million yuan)

Data source: Statista 2017

And how did you end up getting Ant Financial and Alibaba as your major investors?

Well, we knew we wanted to launch a payments business and a commerce business. The catch is, which comes first? In China, commerce came first and payments came second. In India, we could see that customer acquisition and retention costs on payments would be easier versus commerce, which was a lot higher. The infrastructure for commerce in India does not exist yet and would involve huge costs to build but, for payments, it is far simpler. In fact, early on, what we found was that if we wanted to expand the payments business, we had to spend money on the commerce business. Similarly, when we wanted to expand the commerce business, we had to spend on the payments business. In a way, we ended up with both, as they were feeding into each other. When I went to raise money, it then became a question of where we were investing: in this or that? In payments or commerce? I responded by asking why we had to choose as the two are complementary. However, investors look at the two businesses in different multiples with different valuations, so that was a challenge. Then, when we met Jack Ma and Alibaba, he was very convinced of what we were doing as he was doing it himself in China. That is why I thought, I need to go to Alibaba when seeking investment.

How does your relationship with Alibaba pan out?
Well, we look at Taobao and Tmall and want to bring those ideas to India. We are taking lessons from China and seeing how to translate them to India. e-commerce in India is still in its early days, and we believe we can learn from how Alibaba has scaled and grown and, similarly, want to bring that to India.

It is interesting that you were able to get started as I understand that it is quite difficult to get things past India's regulator, the Reserve Bank of India (RBI). How did you find the regulatory reaction?
Well, what you find as you go around the world is that no country necessarily wants to be in the position that they have reached, but they have reached that position through the rules and regulations that their predecessors built. In my country, India, they were not proud of their numbers when it came to benchmarking on inclusion for example, and that reflected as a failure of their controls. We found, therefore, that the regulators were actually very open-minded. In particular, we showed them that we were not like a bank back then, but just a wallet, and got a wallet licence on that basis. Looking back now, I think people misunderstood what we could do. They saw us as

a layer over the top of banking, where people could link their bank accounts to our mobile wallet and move money from their bank to the wallet. That's all they saw Paytm as—a convenience play that would sit on top of banking services. There is digital banking and Paytm, and both would be needed. We were a young company, with low margin costs and high levels of customer service. They worried whether we could afford it—the wallet and the low margins—and their main concern was whether we could afford to do this. It was going to cost about $5 million to launch, and the regulators were worried that we would not be able to afford or maintain such investments. I met them in person and showed them we were committed, that we could afford to do it and that it was all about innovation. They then saw us as innovation.

Were they not nervous about an Indian firm growing with Chinese investment, considering the political backdrop between the two countries?
To the extent that we hold our data securely in India and maintain full privacy, there is no concern. As long as we keep our data local and our decisions are made without bias from our overseas partners and investors, then there is no issue. If we are independently controlled and making decisions in the interests of our domestic needs, there is no issue. If we compromise those principles, then there could be an issue, but we would not do that. The bank is 51 per cent owned and domiciled in India, and the board is independent and includes former RBI employees, so I don't think that we will have any issues.

The point is that there is a software company and then there are structured, licensed entities. The licensed entities are totally independent. The software company is where we have influence, control and work with others. The licensed entities are where the government and regulator want the control, and they have it.

Why weren't the Indian banks already doing this?

Banks are not technology firms. Banks buy technology and are technology purchasers, whereas companies like us are technology producers. The reason why banks weren't already doing this is that they would have been looking to buy such a facility from somewhere, rather than having to build it. Someone has to build it first. So, by design and by structure, FinTech is a classic case of if it is successful, the successful guys will already be ahead and if it's not successful, then that is too great a risk for a bank.

Then you have Aadhaar and the KYC stack and the payments stack, UPI.

We had an away day with the NPCI executive team. I asked them to give me a use case for what they built this for, and then we could see what we could do with it. They told me that they had built these services for banks and that these are available for the banks to exploit and use for more financial inclusion, simpler payments and wider services at lower cost. The stacks are there to help banks build services and be more like FinTech companies. It was meant to be a gift for the banks, and yet the banks are not using it.

But it must have been a gift for you then?

Well, as a non-bank, these stacks are a challenge for FinTechs to use, which is why we now have a banking licence.[45] It is like a loaf of bread when you want to make a sandwich. You can buy the loaf, but it is only available to banks to make the sandwich.

Demonetisation probably made a difference to your business too, I guess?

We had 115 million user accounts in October 2016. When demonetisation kicked in in November 2016, we got 45 million new accounts in just sixty

---

45   Paytm received a final licence approval from the Reserve Bank of India for its payments bank on 18 May 2017, which then launched on 23 May.

days. Today, there are 235 million Paytm user accounts that are active (July 2017). And merchant wise, there were 1.5 million merchants at the end of 2016, and we hope to get another five million this year.

And how does it work for the merchants?

Well, they have heard of Paytm but don't know how to use it. Then when they see how simple it is, it gets a viral effect. To begin with, they think that it can only be used to make a payment, and don't understand how to take a payment. They think that they might have to buy some expensive equipment or something but then we show them that they only need to show a QR code to the customer. That's all. Just a QR code that they can have on their stall counter, and they see how easy it is. The user just scans the merchant's QR code when they buy something, and the merchant gets the money sent straight into their account. We could have gone NFC contactless of course, but we chose the QR code as the technology.

Why?

I was in China on a visit and talking to one of the engineers here, an Israeli guy. I asked him, "If there is one thing you can tell me that I should do, what would it be?" To which he replied, "Own the QR code in India." So that was that.

And what is the sort of demographic or geographic spread that you're finding with Paytm users?

Two interesting numbers. We have around 12 to 15 per cent of users aged thirty-five and above, which is really good because not many people experiment with new technology when they get to that age, so we really like that part. The second number is that 60 per cent of the people come from Tier 2 cities and more, not Tier 1. That shows that this is a mass, not a niche, product. In a city like Delhi, 40 per cent of customers who have an internet connection use us.

You've become a verb almost, like "I Paytm'd you".

I didn't know this till recently. We were totally not clued into this. It was one of our customers who was telling me that we Paytm'd. This then became our advert: Paytm me. Doesn't every entrepreneur want to have a verb like this based on their product?

And I believe that your ambition is to bank 500 million Indian citizens by 2020. Is that right?

That's correct. We are targeting primarily the unbanked today however. Our success criteria are based on financial inclusion, and that's a key focus for us. Our success criteria are based on delivering services to people who do not have those services today. Interestingly, we have delivered a payment service to those who were banked also, but they do not get that sort of capability from their bank. We may therefore get a number of banked people, too. People who feel that their bank just does not give them the sort of services they want or need, or are not treated well by their bank, but our primary target is the unbanked. People who don't have deposit accounts. We don't think of our business as banking only either. It is investments, payments, lending, insurance and all aspects of financial delivery. Our intention is always to go into the market that is not served, as the market that is not served is always bigger than the markets currently served.

We will be launching a money market fund, and we also have a gold-based wealth management service. People are used to buying gold in India, and we launched digital gold in April this year and became the largest gold seller across the country. Our aim is to sell 5 tonnes of gold in the year to March 2018. That amount of gold would be worth about 14 billion rupees ($217 million) at current prices. Clients are able to buy and sell even minuscule amounts of gold digitally for as little as 1 rupee ($0.0155). In fact, we will not only allow users to trade in digital gold, but will ship gold coins across much of India for those who want the metal delivered. This is actual physical gold that is stowed away in our vaults when you make a purchase.

We are doing this as it is our way into full wealth management in India for everyone.

You seem very ambitious, what is your long-term ambition?
To create the first $100-billion company to come out of India. That will take around ten years.

So Paytm will be like the Alibaba of India?
I don't think we will be the Alibaba of India. We will be the Paytm of India.

Any final comments before we end this discussion?
Well, one thing I can say is that the new models of payments and financial services are coming from countries outside the West, and the way in which they are developing and experimenting in this country (China) can provide a lot of insight and lessons for other countries. This country should be looked at like a textbook. The issue is that many other countries do not realise this because China speaks Chinese, and they don't see what China is doing for this reason. A lot of overseas firms should view these developments as almost like a laboratory for the future. Instead, they will more than likely wake up to what is happening when Chinese firms start to acquire big names in overseas markets, by which time it will be too late.

CHEN LONG, CHIEF STRATEGIST, ANT FINANCIAL

Can you tell me how you see Ant Financial's direction?

Our company's essence is that we are a technology-driven company that works with partners in an ecosystem as a platform company. The world does not need another bank or financial institution. There are already too many of them. They do not need another one, but they do need a platform company to enable financial connectivity through the internet. The result of this is that we want to provide inclusive financial services everywhere, to every individual on the planet.

We also like to use the word "TechFin". Jack Ma made this differentiation between TechFin and FinTech, and there is a debate about how tech is being applied to finance, something that we are trying to clarify. There is similarly a debate about internet finance and FinTech. Banking people like to see it as internet finance or digital finance. Essentially, they are saying that they are financial institutions using IT to drive costs down through cloud computing and other internet-based systems. We believe this is how the financial world looks at FinTech. It's all about creating more efficiencies to drive costs down.

We are a technology company and look at this very differently, as our debate is where to start things from. There is nothing there to start with, so we have to start from somewhere. That is why we think of this as TechFin, where technology companies are creating financial markets. It is very different to FinTech, which empathises with the Tech. We think FinTech is a very pale word, and does not capture the most exciting part of what technology brings to finance, which is to reconstruct the experience of finance.

We are not talking about technology upgrading finance, but technology creating a completely new thing that has never been experienced before. The chemistry between technology and finance to create a completely new thing. In any successful product we have provided, we always have this chemistry effect, which is awesome to me.

Alipay, for example, is not a payments system. If anyone knows our history, where we were providing an escrow service, it was based on fax machines. It was not a payments system. In the beginning, the technology was poor. People often think we used very good technology to build Alibaba, but it was not like that. Instead, we used new technologies to gradually build a new China, and new commerce builds new opportunities that build a new society that needs new finance. If you look at any finance, for it to have lasting life, it needs new challenges, new commerce and new structures. It is like DNA.

Alipay is like that. In the beginning, it was very basic technology based on fax machines. We had to work with the banks to receive and release the money. People using Alipay had to have a bank account. It was a basic escrow system, using fax to contact the sellers to say that we had got the money so they could send the product, and to contact the buyers to make sure that they had received the goods and were happy with them, so we could release the money to the sellers. The buyer and seller never saw each other and this was a massive transformation of trust in China. It was an example of a new species of finance and commerce, breaking the limits of time and space.

Traditional payments do not work in this new world. You cannot send paper money to buy something a thousand miles away. You cannot swipe a credit card to do that either. These people are trying to buy and sell, but they don't see each other and they don't trust each other. It is important to remember this, that Alipay was created to solve a trust issue. It was not about payment, although payment was part of it, it was all about solving trust or the lack of it. We were using the banking account, the traditional system, to do the payment. We were not doing that.

And this is important to Ant Financial today, as we are all about looking at the chemistry of technology to solve a practical problem with finance. That is how we do things. Any product we create is to provide a better experience to solve a problem that people have using the online services we offer today.

Another product that illustrates the creativity of TechFin, for example, is Ant Forest. Ant Forest makes traditional financial people confused. They wonder why you would want to plant trees through a payments app. This is what I am trying to illustrate, that it is outside the traditional thinking space. They just would not think of doing this. It would not make sense to them. But it is something new that can solve a problem through the combination of the chemistry of new technologies with finance. If you are just trying to upgrade your technology, you would never do this. But if you use the creativity of TechFin, then it makes perfect sense.

We call this Green Finance. It is the integration of digital payment and big data technology, to know your location and other details, to capture and measure your carbon footprint. We have really thought about this and know that we have to motivate people to use it. We can't have people playing just once a month, but all the time. So, we have made it like a game. A competition between you and your friends. There's the measurement part about getting Alipay users to play Ant Forest and then there's the scientific part, working with experts to show the impact this is making on your carbon footprint. You can collect carbon savings yourself, but you can also collect them with your friends and from your friends, creating peer pressure to show who is most active. It is creating social interaction, and that is the psychological part of this. Without this, you might only play once a month but if you know that your friends could steal your energy, then it motivates you to be far more involved every day. It's fun too, especially if you steal your friend's energy! It makes this a high-frequency activity and it is all about making this world Greener. That is the point. Making payments fun through gamification that creates a better planet. It has a real-life purpose and makes that purpose far more enjoyable.

Ant Forest is one of the most successful mobile phone apps ever launched. It took just six months to get over 200 million people playing, and that is one of the fastest rollouts of an app ever in China (*note:* Pokémon Go is not available in China due to safety and security fears). That is a good example of showing imagination that is far more creative than just finance and technology.

In summary, where we come from is that we are a technology company that focuses on reconstructing finance using technology that delivers TechFin. FinTech is not what we do, as that misses the point of reimagining finance. It is just talking about an upgrade, not a reconstruction. Even with this, we do have some financial activities. Sometimes this is because we have to, so yes, we have a banking licence. In China, you sometimes have to have those as an entry into performing certain activities. Ask Jack Ma though, and he would say that we have a banking licence not to provide banking, but to provide the platform for financial inclusivity.

Bearing in mind that you are describing a new financial system, what impact do you think the new system will have on the old one? What impact is Ant Financial having on the large Chinese banks, for example?

Well, I do not think it is disruptive, in the traditional way in which people talk about disruption. Look at the facts. I am not aware of a single financial institution in the world that has gone bankrupt due to a big money outflow caused by technology. Can you name one?

Well, Bear Stearns and Lehman Brothers, but they were not technological but managerial.

Exactly, so the story about technology disrupting banking is a hypothetical point of view. It is just a story. It has not been proven, yet. All the evidence points to traditional financial institutions still holding on to their assets. There is no big outflow. So, I don't think it is disruptive in that sense at all. I then thought about why that is the case and, if you look at the history of innovation and change in financial products and markets, it is very slow because people do not trust change. Trust is a key part of this. For example, ask yourself why you open a bank account but very rarely move that account around between banks. We almost never compare the bank rates. We just open an account and let the money stay there. There are two human psychological elements at work here. First, we are slow to accept changes because trust is important in finance. Second, we are lazy. That is why we become stuck with our bank. That is what I observe about financial innovation in history. Financial institutions, therefore, have no pressing need to change, and they have a lot of capital. Banks can therefore change at a pace that suits them. Some will change faster than others, but it does not really matter. The only thing that is really hitting them is their legacy, which is holding them back. But it is not disruption in the traditional sense, as they have time to change. Banks have to change, but it is not fast change. They have time to change.

In the short term, we will steal a little of their business and make them change. In the beginning, we were complementary. We focused on a blue ocean strategy, dealing with small amounts of money. For example, microloans are complementary. We have provided microloans to over six million SMEs. This must be a record. In the whole of China, there are probably around 70 million individuals who want to set up a company, and so we have covered a good part of that figure. But the average loan size is around ¥40,000 ($6,000). This is complementary, therefore, to bank services, and extends the breadth and depth of reach of finance to be far more inclusive.

At the moment, we are working in different spaces but, in the long run, this will change. In the future, finance will have three important features. First, it will be like water. It will be everywhere and available to everyone. In the future, there will be no separation between finance and use case. They are together and finance will be everywhere in our lives, our consumption, our sales and our supply chain. One feature is that it will be everywhere. The second feature is that finance will be customer-driven, C2B. Think about how it is today. You may have $100 million, and all you know is how much you spend and how much you save. In other words, right now, it is all around function and product. It is not customer-driven. It is designed for a B2C structure, but the future will see that change to C2B.

The third part is that this is an ecosystem. All financial institutions and FinTech companies will work together. It will not be one firm saying that it will do all this and you will do all that. It will be much more of an ecosystem, with everyone working together to surround the customer with all the capabilities they need. These are the important trends. In the short term, we are in different spaces but, in the long term, we will be working together to provide a complete service for a customer-driven ecosystem. The boundaries of the companies and their services will all be blurred in that future.

How does Ant Financial's business fit with governmental views, now that you have become the biggest payments company in the world and a significant platform player?

Companies will become bigger and smaller at the same time. Our planning abilities and organisational abilities allow us to build bigger and bigger companies. Companies like Apple will soon have $1 trillion market cap, and that is all to do with technologies and efficiencies. The question then becomes: what are you and what is your relationship with society when you are this big? I think it will be good for society, because we are seeing more and more platform firms that are supporting hundreds of businesses. That is good for everyone. It is good for businesses, start-ups and society. Someone has to build these platforms. Governments are not going to build them. What you are delivering really is power that is democratised. Governments cannot stop that, as it is happening or maybe has happened, and this is good for society. You have big companies and their power is not in their size, but in their ability to provide society with democratised services. That is obviously good, and you can only keep that platform size for as long as you do not abuse your power. The question then becomes: how are you ensuring that you do not abuse that ability? How can you show people? Obviously, you have to behave, and then you have to work with the government and governance in an ecosystem that is more transparent.

The world is moving into global platforms where the boundary of company and government becomes blurred. In fact, what you are seeing is where platform governance becomes very, very important. You have to work with governments, regulators, consumers and competitors to have new rules that you can sustain.

I guess this gets even more difficult as you go global as, for example, America and India have very different views about a Chinese company being a powerful player in their markets.

Globalisation is very important to us. Of course, that brings a lot of challenges and we have to abide by the rules and customs of the local markets. In fact, we would emphasise, however, that globalisation is different to making your business international. For example, if we were a bank, we would just talk about setting up another office in another country. That is not what we are doing. What we are doing is seeking local partnerships and helping those local partners to become more meaningful. We want to bring our capabilities to the local markets, and being global means being local in our definition. We believe this will be good for the whole world, but countries are separated by politics and local needs, so we just try to respect these differences.

This is why you are investing in Kakao in South Korea, Ascent in Thailand, Paytm in India and so on.

Exactly. You cannot just say that we are a company from China here to open a business. You will fail. Our strategy is to find local partners and to say to people, "This is your company." It is a local entity and we are partners. We can export our technology, our expertise and our know-how, and help the local firm grow. We may be connected, which makes us global in that sense, but this is a connected world of many local companies, not one large entity.

This may be true but I guess that concerns arise about data privacy, for example, and how and what data you have access to and where it is stored. Equally, concerns about how you use my data.

There are several points here. First, the age of data privacy should also be talked about as the age where our data benefits us. There was no credit scoring thirty years ago. In the United States, they use Facebook as part of their lives, and do you want to come off it so you can be private? The point is, you get so much of this for free, and that is the benefit to you. You give your data and you get free services back. Completely free. The benefit is almost incalculable. In China, we now are moving towards a cashless society, with consumers breaking the limits of space and time. It's a new lifestyle that brings a lot of benefits. The issue here is that we don't want to hurt people.

Second, to make this sustainable in a digital age, you do have to have data privacy and data security, however. That demands a new set of consumer rights and rules for privacy and protection. That is a constructive and important dialogue in the digital platform world.

For us, we have it in our interests to have this rule set and to be clear and transparent in how we do this. It is not like we just say we can do it. It is possible. We have rules. Before anyone can use data within Ant Financial, it has to be desensitised. There is a procedure to mark any sensitive data. All confidential information must be removed. It must be encrypted. If it is a large amount of data, it has to go through an internal approval process. These are all basic procedures and rules we have to follow and, in the digital age, you must have those.

This allows us to understand our customers really well, but we don't know you. We don't know who you are. Our machines do. That has to be the case. We know a lot of your habits, but we just don't know who you are. It's the computers and technology making the decisions based upon big data.

Going back to what I was saying earlier, Ant Financial is not just working at this, there is a governance of an ecosystem on our platform that includes governments, regulators and service providers. We are all working together collectively to solve these problems as it is for everyone's benefit to do so. We have to work together to sustain good governance of our platform in order to retain these benefits.

Eric Jing made a statement in January 2017 that there is an aim to develop Ant Financial into a global firm with two billion customers by 2025 using artificial intelligence and blockchain technologies. Can you expand on that statement for me?

It is easy to understand the reason for using artificial intelligence as it is all about using systems to gain insights from big data to improve service, security and efficiency. That part is easy to understand. AI has to be used in everything. Blockchain is an area that we know is important. Blockchain brings us back to trust, and it can deliver trust in the platform. Trust is so important in so many things, especially in finance. If we can use blockchain to enable more trust in the platform, then that is important to us. We have been experimenting and developing some good areas in which to use blockchain. Lots of experiments. We know we will need to change with blockchain, but just have not worked out the final details yet.

Once I coined a word "FinLife". I was trying to argue that FinTech is only the early stage of FinLife. FinTech is talking about technology at any age, not just at the early stage. Where we want to get to is a complete FinLife. This is a more mature stage of our financial lives being powered by technology. The point to emphasise here is that there are so many FinTech companies in Silicon Valley, and 80 per cent of them or more are not being used. The point therefore is not about technology per se, but that people actually use it. You want people to be almost addicted. That is the powerful part of this.

A lot of people worldwide are talking about the exciting power of FinTech and yet China is one of the few countries that has the scale of user base. It's not about persuading people, they just use it. The mindset has changed. That is a fundamental shift. In the United States, they have not made that shift. That is why China has fifty times the volume of mobile payments compared with the United States.

The point here is that a lot of countries and people talk about how exciting this change is, but they are talking about exciting prospects. They are not talking about how people are actually effectively using it because people don't use it. Or a very limited group of people use it. They are just talking about their ideas.

Blockchain is a very good example of this. People say blockchain will change our lives and yes, I think it will change our lives. You don't have to convince me of this. Two years ago, I went to a conference in Singapore and people talked about blockchain and distributed ledger technology. Last year, they were still talking about it. This year, they are still talking about it. The question is: show me what you are doing here? Show me your work. Show me how it is being used. Stop talking about it and show me results.

I often use the example of Ant Financial's experiment with giving to charity using blockchain as a good example of actually doing something.
We did that more than a year ago, so we *are* doing things. We are experimenting and we have ideas, and we know blockchain is good in areas that need transparency and trust, like giving to charities. We have done this. It is a disruptive technology.

What I'm trying to say here though is that people worldwide are experimenting. It's a bit like they talk about blockchain and they talk about FinTech, but what are they actually doing? A lot of people talk about FinTech, but they don't know what they are talking about. They haven't defined it and FinTech is so wide and diverse. They need to clarify their discussion and focus on what they are actually talking about. What do they mean by FinTech? Some such companies are widely used already and have great power, some of them have good prospects and some of them have question marks. People don't distinguish between these companies well, they just call them FinTech. This is important as some of these companies have not got anyone actually using their service, but people talk about them without differentiation.

For me, blockchain is important. It is a very important technology but it is hardly used today, so we cannot talk about it more until it is being used.

In China, you are obviously the biggest player alongside Tencent's WeChat Pay. I guess Tencent must be your biggest competitor and wondered how you see that competition.
Different companies have their different strengths and this is not a zero-sum game. Finance is a very undercovered area in terms of risk and legacy. Risk is easy to see, as SMEs have not been served well and there are millions of them to serve when you can manage the risk with technology. People use their mobile in China but not in the United States, so does that make the U.S. financial system a good one? No. But this is because America's systems are old and ours are new. It makes for different experiences and opportunities.

In the end, there will be many, many players and right now, almost 95 per cent of the financial assets in most countries are captured by the traditional financial institutions, and they are the bigger players. It is not like they are going to die or anything tomorrow. They are a different species, and they will co-exist. It also means that, for Tencent and Ant, we have a lot of market to reach. It is not a zero-sum game.

We are also different companies. We, as a company, deal with money. That is our business. Go to our home page and our task is to help you manage your money, deal with money and have confidence with money. Go to WeChat's home page and you cannot talk about money. You have to go several layers deep into its system before money is relevant. We are different companies with different focuses.

In this sense, we are different companies with different angles and different strengths. We know that social networking is not our greatest strength. For every company, they have a boundary and a different DNA. If we had a very strong social network, we could not be too serious about money. If we want to have too good a social network, we will have problems as people will think we are too light and not serious enough.

Internationally, it is also different. WeChat is just used in China by Chinese people, but Alipay goes beyond the country's boundaries, as we have expanded globally.

I agree with you there, as Ant Financial has already started building global partnerships and Tencent obviously cannot have the same partners, so it would already be weak if they or others tried to copy your strategy. That is why Ant is a major case study in my book. Just to finish our discussion, what is your personal vision for the future Ant Financial over the next ten years?

We know our direction and our key points, as I mentioned at the start. We are a technology-driven platform company that works with partners to create value for inclusive and sustainable financial service for everyone. We see that the future of financial services is so undercovered in so many areas around the world, and we want to create a world with our partners that provides finance everywhere, like water, and is available for all use cases. Not just those limited to B2C providers, but for everything people need. It must be customer centric, and financial institutions and FinTech companies should work together to deliver this through an ecosystem that serves those purposes.

I would also like to add, from our point of view, that we hope the world can understand the benefits that digital technology can bring to every sector, not just finance. Some of the fear of technology is a hypothesis that has no evidence as to why we should fear it. Rather we should embrace it, and we need to share that consensus. The problem is also that not everyone understands FinTech, and what is good or bad FinTech. We have to distinguish between what is good and what is bad. In general, as a principle, the more standard and simple technology in finance is, the better, as it can give less uncertainty. If it is less standard and more complicated, then it is more risky. It will also change at a much slower pace and we would need to be more cautious.

If you look at the progress of technology in finance, payment is a start because payment is the least financial part of finance. It just involves transferring funds from A to B. It is not about storing those funds or investing them. Just moving them. Then there is our money market fund Yu'e Bao, but there is very little uncertainty about that because it is easy to understand. But when you move onto peer-to-peer lending, crowdfunding and wealth management, it has far more uncertainty. This means that these areas will grow slower because they are more complicated.

That's the principles of our business and understanding the boundaries between good and bad FinTech. Otherwise, it is very easy to get confused.

Finally, we need to improve the RegTech area, as regulators do not use technology but understand banks very well. I have talked to many of them and they have very little understanding of this. They don't know what technology and RegTech can do. The same applies to a lot of finance people. They don't know what FinTech is. They think it's having an app, but it's not. The key is understanding what people need and making sure that people use the FinTech.

ABOUT THE AUTHOR

© Chris Skinner

CHRIS SKINNER is known as an independent commentator on the financial markets and FinTech through his blog, the Finanser.com, and as the author of the bestselling books *Digital Bank* and *ValueWeb*. *ValueWeb* describes the impact of FinTech and how mobile and blockchain technologies are changing the face of finance in building an Internet of Value. As a result of the emerging Internet of Value, banks have to become digitalised, and *Digital Bank* provides a comprehensive review and analysis of the battle for digital banking and strategies for companies to compete.

Described by Seth Wheeler, Brookings Guest Scholar and Former Special Assistant to the President for Economic Policy at the White House, as "one of the most authoritative voices on FinTech anywhere", Chris has previously written many books covering everything from European regulations in banking through the credit crisis to the future of banking.

In his day job, Chris is chair of the European networking forum the Financial Services Club and Nordic Finance Innovation, as well as a non-executive director of the FinTech consultancy firm 11:FS. He is also on the advisory boards of various firms including B-Hive, Exscudo, IoV42, Moven, Meniga, Pintail and the Token Fund.

Chris has been voted one of the most influential people in banking by *The Financial Brand* (as well as one of the best blogs); a FinTech Titan by Next Bank; one of the FinTech leaders that you need to follow by *City A.M.*, Deluxe and Jax Finance; one of the top five most influential people on BankInfoSecurity's list of information security leaders; and one of the top forty most influential people in financial technology by the *Wall Street Journal*'s *Financial News*. He has also been voted Game Changer of the Year and Financial Markets Advisor of the Year by *Finance Monthly*, CEO of the Year by *CV Magazine*, FinTech Speaker of the Year by *TMT Global* and has been an advisor to the White House, the World Bank and the World Economic Forum.

Find out more about Chris at https://chrisskinner.global/.